MONUMENTAL WASHINGTON

MONUMENTAL WASHINGTON

THE PLANNING AND DEVELOPMENT OF THE CAPITAL CENTER

BY JOHN W. REPS

PRINCETON UNIVERSITY PRESS PRINCETON, NEW JERSEY 1967

Printed in the United States of America
by The Colonial Press Inc., Clinton, Mass.

TO MY WIFE CONSTANCE PECK REPS

Contents

List of Illustrations

Preface

In 1964, with the unveiling of a detailed and imaginative plan for the comprehensive redevelopment of Pennsylvania Avenue in Washington, D.C., the attention of the nation once again focused on the future form and appearance of the capital city of the United States. As in 1792, when the city's first plan was revealed by President Washington, and 1902, when the Senate Park Commission proposed wholesale improvements and changes for the center of the city, newspapers and professional journals throughout the country gave full coverage in news summaries, editorial comment, and critical analysis. This widespread interest of both lay and professional circles demonstrated anew that, wherever Americans may live, they regard the city of Washington with special concern and deep attraction.

Only the future will tell how successful the current planners of monumental Washington have been in preparing their recommendations and how many of their proposals will be carried out. In these efforts to reshape the capital center, an understanding of similar struggles in the past may be of material assistance. The American philosopher George Santayana once wisely observed, "Those who cannot remember the past are condemned to repeat it." It is one of the purposes of this book to provide an understanding of the many attempts over the years to build a capital city worthy of a great nation and to reach some conclusions about their wisdom and effectiveness.

The lessons to be learned from an inquiry into the development of Washington should, however, have wider application. It may well be that modern city planners elsewhere can find much here that is useful as they continue their tasks of reshaping urban America. But this book is addressed to many others in addition to my fellow professionals. It will, I hope, be of interest to every citizen who is concerned with the future of his own city, as well as that of our capital, and who lends a hand, if only at the voting booth, to assure its well-being. The number of such citizens has steadily increased in recent years as the issues of rapid urbanization have thrust themselves before us. Each new generation of civic leaders has much to learn from the example of Washington, and it is for them as well as professional planners that this book has been written.

The chief theme of this study is the plan prepared for the central portion of Washington in 1901 and the fate of its proposals. It is the story of how a few skilled and dedicated men working together for less than a year at the turn of the century set the pattern for the subsequent development of one of America's major cities. That plan, prepared by the Senate Park Commission, may be regarded as the country's first modern city planning report. The exhibition of its drawings and models in 1902 was doubtless also the first of its kind in America. The report of the Commission became the model for subsequent city planning studies throughout the nation. The roots of modern American city planning are thus to be found in the soil tilled so assiduously by that small group in 1901 and 1902. Their mode of work and the format of their recommendations have changed only in details despite the rise of a profession of urban planners and the development of a host of technical and analytical methods to aid them in their work.

Central Washington as we know it today thus had its basis in a plan prepared almost seventy years ago, reinforcing an earlier form prescribed by the city's original planner, Pierre Charles L'Enfant. This portion of the city possesses a powerful image. It is an image not to everyone's taste; certainly it does not symbolize all of urban America, much of which is cast in quite a different form. Yet it is an image which has a distinctive atmosphere and character, making Washington unique among American cities, all too many of which appear to have been produced on some urban assembly line.

Washington, unlike most of the capitals of the western world, exists almost entirely as a governmental city. Its *raison d'être* is national administration, the buildings for the federal establishment occupy its commanding sites, and the majority of its citizens find employment in the myriad tasks of governing a large and complex nation. The symbolic value of the structures devoted to public uses looms large, unobstructed by the diverse activities which blur the governmental image in such European capitals as London, Paris, or Rome. Washington stands, in a very real sense, as the civic center of America, and the hundreds of thousands of visitors who annually throng to the city bear witness to the special character of its townscape and to the near reverence with which it is regarded by nearly every citizen of the nation.

During the decades between the two world wars professional designers severely criticized the type of planning which had been followed in Washington and attempted elsewhere. The emphasis in civic improvements on the creation of monumental building groups, impressive boulevards, and formal parks drew almost universal condemnation. Several generations of young planners and architects were taught that American urban design as exemplified in Washington represented the opposite extreme of what should be attempted. While some of this criticism was certainly justified, especially as it related to the design of individual buildings, much of it was ill-founded. Fortunately, in recent years critics and designers have begun to appreciate the unique qualities of Washington and that, however inappropriate in other cities, monumental vistas and symmetrical grouping of buildings must be created and maintained in the capital. This does not mean, of course, that individual buildings must be imitations of Greek or Roman temples or Renaissance palaces; rather, it means the discovery of contemporary solutions to the age-old problem of achieving monumentality in an urban setting.

The designers of the Senate Park Commission plan of 1902, in adopting classical models for their proposed buildings, seemed to deny the existence of an emerging new style of architecture. In my view this was unfortunate, although tastes differ on this matter. This decision, however, should not obscure the splendid quality of their plan and the validity of their general concept. The powerful, unified scheme that they proposed—and which has largely been accomplished—has triumphed over the banality and superficiality of many of the individual buildings constituting the central composition of the great Mall and its surrounding structures. What is significant is that the location and proportion of these buildings and monuments are harmonious and consistent and in scale with the city, the site, and the symbolic quality for which the capital was intended.

This book focuses almost exclusively on a limited but important topic—the strategies and tactics employed in creating civic beauty for the seat of national government. It may be argued that, given the nagging social problems which Washington shares with virtually all of our cities, the vast sums spent over the years for buildings, boulevards, monuments, and parks might have been more appropriately employed in such programs as education, social work, and crime prevention. It might also be true that, among the capital projects, less emphasis should have been placed on embellishment of central Washington and more on slum eradication and neighborhood improvements elsewhere in the city.

Only recently has the proper allocation of urban resources between capital improvements and social welfare become a matter of systematic study. Washington would provide a useful example for such analysis, although its help as a guidepost for the future might be surprisingly limited. For as our increasingly affluent society enters a new phase of exploration of the urban environment, it is no longer a question of whether aesthetics, efficiency, or economy is the most important. We can, and should, have them all.

I make these points explicitly at the outset, but without apologies. My attention has been consciously restricted to matters directly affecting urban design in the belief and fear that we may not give this subject adequate attention in our new enthusiasm for solving the vexing social problems of the urban scene.

The plan of 1902 cannot be understood without a knowledge of the city as it then existed, how it was originally planned, and how it developed. The first three chapters of this book deal with the city's establishment and growth from 1791 to 1900 and with a number of proposals advanced from time to time for its improvement. The pace then becomes slower and the probing into details more intensive. Successive chapters take up the way in which the Park Commission set about its task, the plan which it produced, and the immediate results of its recommendations. A later chapter summarizes the major planned changes in the city center from the creation of the Lincoln Memorial to the present. In the final chapter the influence of the Washington plan on city planning elsewhere in the country is briefly reviewed, and an attempt is made to explain how it came about that such a remarkably high proportion of the proposals of 1902 ultimately were carried out. More than one hundred plans, views, and photographs illustrate the planning history of Washington and document the development of the city since its founding.

My earlier work, *The Making of Urban America,* surveyed broadly the history of city planning in the United States. This is the first of what I hope will be a series of more intensive investigations of certain significant aspects of that heritage.

MONUMENTAL WASHINGTON

CHAPTER 1

Washington: The Founding and the Founders

The planning of Washington, D.C., was at once an act of faith, a political maneuver, a symbolic gesture, and a remarkable achievement in city planning. The history of its founding is a fascinating story; almost equally so is the subsequent growth and development of the city into one of the greatest examples of urban design on the continent and, perhaps, in the world. Like no other city in America, its expansion has been inextricably linked to the changes and advances of the national government itself. Moreover, the persons who have been responsible for its founding, its growth, and its embellishment include the greatest of our statesmen and the most skilled among our planners, architects, and artists. Washington stands as a symbol of what we are capable of achieving in shaping our urban environment, although, paradoxically, its physical form is neither typical of most of our cities nor necessarily a desirable model. It is a city whose original plan, ably reinforced and slightly modified a century after its establishment, has served well for nearly two hundred years. It is, in short, a uniquely fascinating city which man has shaped and which in turn has influenced the men who have experienced its uncommon atmosphere and its monumental qualities.

Political uncertainty and controversy shrouded its beginning. Following the long war of independence, the site of the capital city for the new nation became a matter of extended and sometimes bitter discussion in the Continental Congress. Dozens of locations were considered. Some of these were established communities; other sites lay undeveloped. The regional differences between north and south manifested themselves in this matter. The southern states refused to approve a northern location, while the northern states were reluctant to sanction a site in the south.

At one point, in the fall of 1783, the Continental Congress actually approved a plan for two capital cities, one at Georgetown in Virginia and the other at the falls of the Delaware. This bizarre arrangement was repealed in the following year, but not before one wit suggested that a single town on a wheeled platform could be built and moved from one site to the other as the need arose. The statue of General Washington, just authorized by the Congress, was also to be portable so that it could accompany the mobile town!

Other solutions were proposed from time to time, but to no avail. The Constitutional Convention in 1787 succeeded only in formalizing the impasse. Without debate the delegates adopted the following clause in Article I of the proposed constitution, giving Congress the power:

"To exercise exclusive legislation in all cases whatsoever over such district (not exceeding ten miles square) as may, by cession of

1

particular States and the acceptance of Congress, become the seat of Government of the United States, and to exercise like authority over all places purchased by the consent of the Legislature of the State in which the same shall be, for the erection of forts, magazines, arsenals, dry-docks, and other needful buildings."

With the first meeting of the new congress under the constitution in 1789, the debate over the capital's location began anew. Finally, in 1790 a decision was reached—the result of some political vote trading in which Thomas Jefferson played a prominent role. In exchange for their support of Alexander Hamilton's scheme for funding the national debt and the assumption of the prior obligations of the several states by the federal government, southern congressmen were assured of Hamilton's backing of a southern location for the capital. The result was the so-called Residence Act, which was approved by President Washington on July 16, 1790.[1]

The Residence Act did not specify a site. Instead it authorized the President to select a location not more than 10 miles square on the Potomac River "at some place between the mouths of the Eastern Branch and the Connogochegue." The territory thus described, shown on the map in Figure 1, was approximately 80 miles long, the southern end of which began at Alexandria, Virginia, seen near the map's center. The act further provided for presidential appointment of three commissioners who were to arrange for the acquisition of "such quantity of land . . . within the said district, as the President shall deem proper for the use of the United States and according to such plans as the President shall approve . . . provide suitable buildings for the accommodation of Congress and of the President, and for the public offices of the Government of the United States." [2] By December 1800 the commissioners were to have all in readiness for the transfer of the

government to the new location. Until that time, the act specified that the capital would be fixed at Philadelphia.

There seems to be little doubt that the exact site for the capital would be chosen near Georgetown, a few miles north of Alexandria, in preference to any other within the designated area. Indeed, even before Washington put his signature to the act Jefferson was writing almost identical letters to James Monroe and John Randolph referring to the "bill for removing the federal government to Philadelphia for 10. years & then to Georgetown . . ." [3] Washington was, of course, familiar with the location, having surveyed the town plot of nearby Alexandria many years earlier and being a frequent visitor to Georgetown from his estate at Mount Vernon, only a few miles distant.

The President apparently felt an obligation to make at least a show of inspecting the other sites within the 80-mile stretch designated in the act. In October 1790 he rode through the territory, where at each village and hamlet residents presented him with petitions and statements describing the advantages of that location. In November he went to Philadelphia, where Congress was to meet early the following month. There he discussed the matter with Jefferson, who had already been at work on the form of conveyance to be used in securing the necessary land and in implementing the provisions of the Residence Act.[4] Jefferson's advice to the President can be reconstructed from his notes dated November 29, 1790, prepared either to guide his discussion with the President or to record what he had suggested at their meeting.[5]

Jefferson pointed out that while the Residence Act did not

---

[1] Jefferson recorded his conversations with Hamilton and his subsequent success in persuading Virginia Congressmen Alexander White and Richard Bland Lee to support Hamilton's financial measure in his *Anas*. See the text of his "Note on Residence Bill" in Saul K. Padover (ed.), *Thomas Jefferson and the National Capital*, Washington, 1946, pp. 11–12.

[2] An Act for Establishing the Temporary and Permanent Seat of the Government of the United States, July 16, 1790, 1 Stats. 130.

[3] Letters from Jefferson to Monroe and Jefferson to Randolph, New York, July 11, 1790, in Padover, *Jefferson*, p. 19.

[4] Jefferson on September 17, 1790, sent a memorandum to Charles Carroll, the owner of land at the confluence of the Potomac and Anacostia Rivers previously platted as the town of Carrollsburg, suggesting the terms that might be agreed to by proprietors of land needed for the capital. Jefferson sent a copy of this communication to Washington on the same date. The text appears in Padover, *Jefferson*, pp. 29–30. This suggests strongly that the site at the southern end of the 80-mile territory specified in the Residence Act had virtually been selected even before the President's inspection tour.

[5] Jefferson note, "Proceedings to be had under the Residence Act," November 29, 1790, in Padover, *Jefferson*, pp. 30–35.

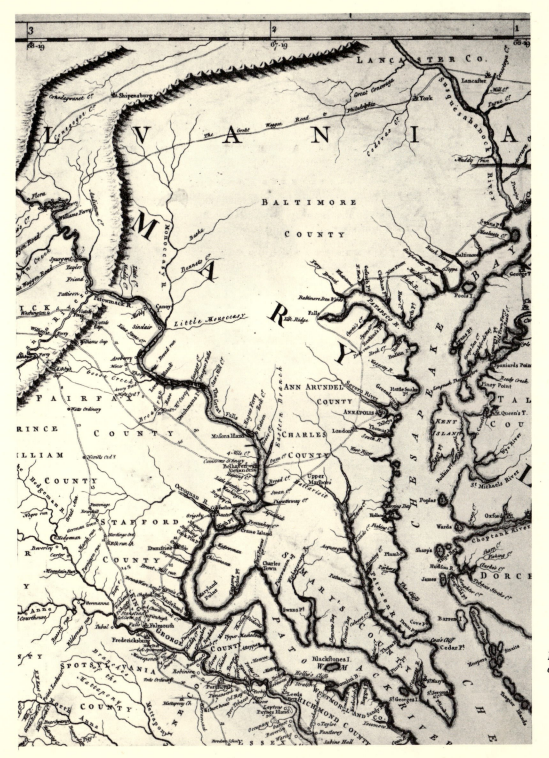

Figure 1. Portion of Map of Virginia
and Maryland: 1755

Figure 2. Sketch by Thomas Jefferson Showing Suggested Land Division in a City Block of the Proposed Capital City: 1790

specify that a new town should be laid out, he had "no doubt it is the wish, & perhaps expectation" of Congress that this should be done. He suggested two possible procedures for the acquisition of the necessary land. One was to purchase the land, or to take it by eminent domain if necessary, at double the present value, "estimated as . . . [it] . . . would have been had there been no thought of bringing the federal seat into their neighborhood." The other was to induce each proprietor to "cede one half his lands to the public, to be sold to raise money." It was a variation of this latter procedure that was subsequently worked out by the President.

Jefferson mentioned that a land area of 1500 acres would be sufficient. He suggested that the streets should "be at right angles as in Philadelphia, & that no street be narrower than 100. feet, with foot-ways of 15. feet. where a street is long & level, it might be 120. feet wide." Jefferson proposed that the blocks, or "squares" as he referred to them, should be "at least 200. yards every way, which will be of about 8. acres each." Lots would be 50 feet wide, but of varying depth. A marginal sketch in his notes, reproduced in Figure 2, indicates his unusual plan of lot division. Lots would front on all four sides of each block and extend to diagonals drawn from the four corners. Corner lots would thus be only 50 feet deep, while interior lots would have progressively greater depth from the corners to the center. His sketch, however, indicates only 8 lots along each street, which would make the blocks 400 feet square, rather than the 600 feet mentioned in the notes.

Sites for various kinds of public activities would be needed. Jefferson mentioned the following: "the federal Capitol, the offices, the President's house & gardens, the town house, Market house,

publick walks, hospital." For the presidential residence he suggested that two blocks should be set aside, with one block each for the Capitol and the market. Nine blocks "consolidated" would be devoted to "public walks."

Jefferson's notes also mention other aspects of the new city. He was even then thinking of such matters as the height of buildings and their location on their sites:

"I doubt much whether the obligation to build the houses at a given distance from the street, contributes to its beauty, it produces a disgusting monotony, all persons make this complaint against Philadelphia, the contrary practice varies the appearance, & is much more convenient to the inhabitants.

"In Paris it is forbidden to build a house beyond a given height, & it is admitted to be a good restriction, it keeps the houses low & convenient, & the streets light and airy, fires are much more managable where houses are low. This however is an object of Legislation."

The notes conclude with a brief description and a second sketch of a little gridiron town at the confluence of the Potomac and its Eastern Branch, now named the Anacostia River, as indicated in Figure 3. The principal frontage of 14 blocks was along the Anacostia, with only four blocks shown on the Potomac. Jefferson observed that "the former will be for persons in commerce, the latter for those connected with the government."

Early in 1791 the President was ready to act. On January 22 he

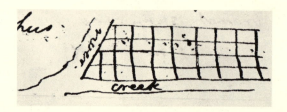

Figure 3. Sketch by Thomas Jefferson of a Plan for a Capital City on the Site of Carrollsburg, District of Columbia: 1790

appointed the three commissioners for which the Residence Act provided: Thomas Johnson, Daniel Carroll, and David Stuart. Two days later he issued a proclamation designating the district in which the capital city was to be located. In sending this proclamation to Congress, Washington requested a minor amendment to the Residence Act extending the southern boundary of the territory to include the town of Alexandria in Virginia and a portion of the south bank of the Anacostia River lying in Maryland. Congress acted promptly and amended the law in this respect.[6]

An accurate survey of the site was essential. For this task Washington secured the services of Andrew Ellicott, an experienced surveyor, who promptly began this work. On February 14 Ellicott was able to report to Jefferson the results of his preliminary surveys. Ellicott was not engaged as the city planner; his responsibility was to run the boundaries of the district and to prepare as quickly as possible certain topographic information.

Early in March a new appointment was made. This was Major Pierre Charles L'Enfant, whose initial duties were clearly specified by Jefferson in a letter probably written in the first week of March 1791:

"You are desired to proceed to Georgetown, where you will find Mr. Ellicot employed in making survey and map of the Federal territory. The special object of asking your aid is to have drawings of the particular grounds most likely to be approved for the site of the federal town and buildings. You will therefore be pleased to begin on the eastern branch, and proceed from then upwards, laying down the hills, valleys, morasses, and waters between that, the Potomac, the Tyber, and the road leading from Georgetown to the eastern branch, and connecting the whole with certain fixed points of the map Mr. Ellicot is preparing. Some idea of the height of the hills above the base on which they stand, would be desirable. For necessary assistance and expenses, be pleased to apply to the Mayor of Georgetown, who is written to on this subject. I will beg

the favor of you to mark to me your progress about twice a week, by letter. . . ."[7]

This letter mentions nothing about the preparation of a plan for the intended city. It seems highly likely, however, that Washington, who evidently had selected L'Enfant, as least hinted that this would be his eventual assignment. The choice of L'Enfant for such a task is clarified by a description of his background and experience. This biographical digression is also essential for an appreciation of the plan which L'Enfant was to produce in the weeks that lay ahead.

L'Enfant's father, Pierre L'Enfant, was a painter of some distinction who was elected a member of the Royal Academy of Painting and Sculpture in 1745, nine years before the birth of his son. For 8 years, beginning in 1758, he was commissioned to aid in the decoration of the building of the Ministry of War at Versailles. Thus, during the years between his fourth and twelfth birthdays the younger L'Enfant lived in Versailles and doubtless became thoroughly familiar with the magnificent gardens of the royal château, which André LeNôtre had designed in 1661. Here he could experience the grand vistas down the *allées* cut boldly through the forest, the *rond points* where two or more of them intersected, and the long axis of the canal extending away from the château. The town itself was a kind of mirror image of the gardens on the other side of the royal residence. Three great avenues, one on axis and the other two symmetrically arranged on angles at either side, provided a formal entrance to the forecourt of the château. Off these avenues, as open spaces in the regular grid of streets, were squares and market places of varying size. Versailles as it existed in 1746 appears in Figure 4. From this combination of grid and diagonal streets and its wealth of formal open spaces both urban and landscaped, L'Enfant may well have acquired at an early age the design vocabulary which he used so fluently in his plan of Washington. *from the design of Versailles*

In 1771 L'Enfant entered the Royal Academy of Painting and Sculpture in Paris, where at that time his father was a teacher. Here

[6] The appointment of the commissioners may be found in William Tindall, *Standard History of the City of Washington*, Knoxville, 1914, pp. 47–48. Tindall also gives the text of the Proclamation, pp. 52–54, and Washington's request for the amendment to the Residence Act, p. 55

[7] Letter from Jefferson to L'Enfant, March 1791 (date omitted), in Padover, *Jefferson,* pp. 42–43.

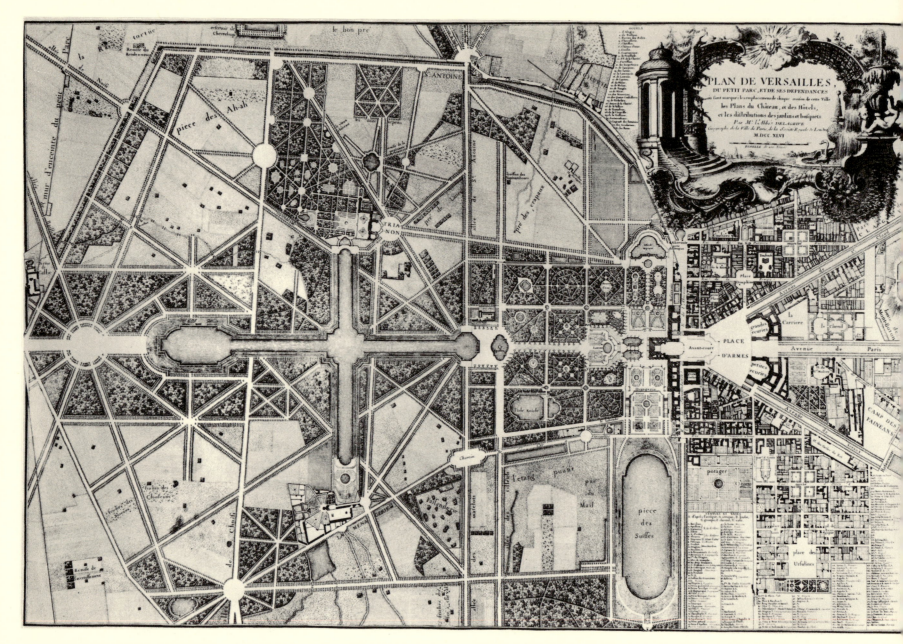

*Figure 4. Plan of the Town, Château, and Gardens of
Versailles, France: 1746*

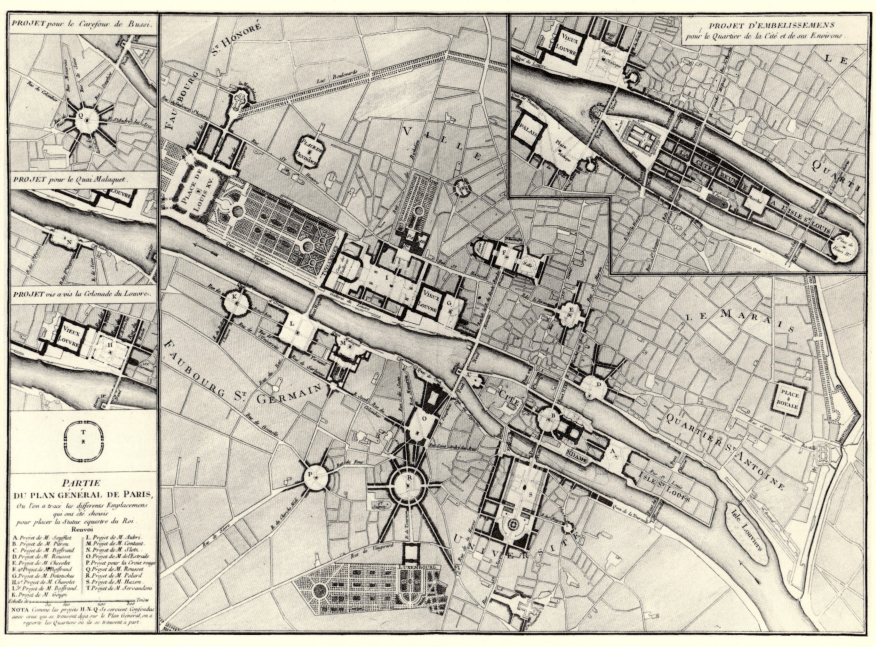

Figure 5. Plan of Paris Showing Proposed Squares and Monuments to
Louis XV: 1765

he saw every day the great formal axis of central Paris based on the Gardens of the Tuileries, also designed by LeNôtre, and the adjoining Place de la Concorde, planned by Gabriel in 1763, from which extended the beginning of the Avenues des Champs Elysées to the west. There is every reason to believe that he had some familiarity as well with other urban or landscape compositions on a similar scale and employing the same design principles. Among these would certainly have been the imposing gardens laid out by LeNôtre at Fontainebleau, St. Cloud, Chantilly, and the earlier Vaux-le-Vicomte. It is not at all improbable that he gained some knowledge of such foreign cities as St. Petersburg and Karlsruhe, and possibly of the baroque plans proposed by Christopher Wren and John Evelyn for rebuilding London after the great fire of 1666.

In Paris there were other examples of civic design. Most imposing were the Champs de Mars, leading from the Seine to the Military Academy, and the gardens of the Invalides, a short distance to the east planned in similar fashion. On a smaller scale, but perhaps also an influence on the young student, were such urban squares as the Place Royale (now the Place des Vosges), the Place Vendôme, and the Place Dauphine. Designs for a number of other squares, each intended as a setting for a monument to Louis XV, had been published in 1765 by Pierre Patte as a record of the submissions in a design competition. This important and beautifully illustrated volume included a map of Paris, reproduced in Figure 5, showing the location and layout of each of these proposed open spaces.[8] While Patte's drawing was not intended as a plan for the wholesale rebuilding of the city, this composite map may have suggested the monumental glories which an entirely new city might achieve. Patte's work was, of course, well known to all artists, and it is almost inconceivable that L'Enfant would not have seen and studied it. The separation of artists and architects, in our day rather pronounced, was not then nearly so distinct. The ease with which L'Enfant was later to establish himself as an architect in New York suggests that this subject

[8] Pierre Patte, *Monuments Érigés en France à la Gloire de Louis XV*, Paris, 1765.

had not been overlooked in his artistic training and that his predilections lay in this field.

L'Enfant joined a number of his countrymen in volunteering for service on the side of the colonists in the American Revolution. He received a commission as a lieutenant in the French colonial forces, a subterfuge to protect him and his companions should their ship be intercepted by the British on the way to America, since they could then claim they were bound for the French possessions in the West Indies. He apparently arrived in Portsmouth, New Hampshire, in April 1777 and joined the colonial forces shortly thereafter as a volunteer, not yet having received a commission in the American army.

L'Enfant's artistic talents were employed by Baron von Steuben, who was then preparing his famous manual, *Regulations, Order and Discipline for the Army of the United States*. L'Enfant completed eight drawings for this work in 1779, and on Steuben's recommendation was commissioned a Captain in the Corps of Engineers. Later, in May 1783, Congress promoted him to a brevet Major of Engineers. It is this title that has led so many writers to identify him mistakenly as an engineer by training and experience. In fact, his assignment to the engineering corps was rather arbitrary and in no way reflected his background.

At Valley Forge in the winter of 1777–1778 L'Enfant met George Washington, possibly first when he was commissioned by Lafayette to draw the General's portrait. Evidently the two got along well, and there is a record of correspondence between them indicating great cordiality. Following the war L'Enfant was asked to design the medal for the Society of the Cincinnati, of which Washington was elected President-General. When L'Enfant indicated he wished to return to France for a visit in the winter of 1783–1784, Washington commissioned him to take with him letters conferring membership in the society on a number of distinguished French officers and to arrange for the striking of the medals in Paris. At an early date, therefore, Washington knew of and relied on the artistic talents of the man upon whom he would eventually call to prepare the design of the nation's capital.

While L'Enfant's visit to Paris was brief and much of his time was involved in organizing the Society of the Cincinnati in France, he must have taken the opportunity to refresh his knowledge of that city and to look at its most recent developments. Foremost of these, and then still under construction, was the quadrangle of buildings enclosing the gardens of the Palais-Royale. This was designed with an arcaded walkway at the ground floor level. When L'Enfant later recommended that the major street extending eastward from the Capitol in Washington be built in this manner with shops on the ground floor, he may have been thinking of this project or the still earlier treatment of the buildings surrounding the Place Royale in Paris.

On his return to America, L'Enfant began the practice of architecture in New York. In 1786 he was commissioned to design the east window of St. Paul's Chapel, and in 1788 he prepared the design for a temporary domed structure to shelter the dignitaries attending a great pageant sponsored by the Federalists in New York to help secure the ratification of the constitution. He also designed or worked on remodeling a number of mansions in the New York area. His most important public commission was the remodeling of the New York city hall in 1788 and 1789 as the first capitol of the United States and the site of President Washington's inauguration. For this work the City Council awarded him the freedom of the city and granted him ten acres of land, a gift which he declined.

By 1789, therefore, L'Enfant had achieved considerable renown as a versatile designer. His friendship with Washington had deepened, and it was thus not entirely presumptious of him to write the President on September 11, 1789, suggesting his employment in the design of a new capital city which had been provided for in the recently adopted constitution.

"The late determination of Congress to lay the Foundation of a city which is to become the Capital of this vast Empire, offer so great an occasion of acquiring reputation, to whoever may be appointed to conduct the execution of the business, that Your Excellency will not be surprised that my Ambition and the desire I have of becoming a usefull citizen should lead me to wish a share in the undertaking.

"No nation perhaps had ever before the opportunity offerd them of deliberately deciding on the spot where their Capital city should be fixed, or of combining every necessary consideration in the choice of situation—and altho' the means now within the power of the country are not such as to pursue the design to any great extant it will be obvious that the plan should be drawn on such a scale as to leave room for that aggrandisement & embellishment which the increase of the wealth of the Nation will permit it to pursue at any period however remote—viewing the matter in this light I am fully sensible of the extant of the undertaking and under the hope of the continuation of the indulgence you have hitherto honored me with I now presume to sollicit the favor of being Employed in this Business." [9]

While Washington's reply to this communication has not been recorded, he undoubtedly must have remembered it when the time came to select a designer for the new city. It seems likely also that the two men may have discussed this possibility between 1789 and 1792, when the location of the capital was being debated in Congress. L'Enfant's eventual appointment for this important task may not have been inevitable, but he certainly possessed qualifications and knowledge about such matters unsurpassed by anyone in the country at a time when city planners were unknown and architects of experience were extremely scarce.

It was apparently at Washington's suggestion that L'Enfant was first assigned to work along the Anacostia or Eastern Branch section of the new federal district. The President clearly favored a site close to Georgetown, but he had to consider the cost of land acquisition. He reasoned that if L'Enfant were seen at work some distance from that existing town, land owners nearer to Georgetown would be willing to sell at somewhat reduced prices. Through trusted friends in Georgetown he secretly began negotiations to buy

[9] Letter from L'Enfant to Washington, New York, September 11, 1789, as quoted in H. Paul Caemmerer, *The Life of Pierre Charles L'Enfant,* Washington, 1950, pp. 127–29. The letter continues with a suggestion that more attention be given to fortifying the seacoast of the country and expressing his wish to be appointed "Engineer to the United States" in charge of this work and related projects for the improvement of the nation. Caemmerer's book is a valuable source, and I have relied on it for much of my information about L'Enfant's life and background.

as much land as possible before revealing the exact location of the city within the district.[10] He hoped by this method to avoid paying exorbitant prices for land inflated by the speculative interest then beginning to be felt in the vicinity. Underlying this plan was the assumption, probably shared by everyone, that the new city would be relatively small and might be located in any one of several sites within the 100-square-mile district.

Two of these sites, however, stood out above all others. One embraced the existing platted town of Carrollsburg at the confluence of the two branches of the Potomac. This was the site already considered by Jefferson as a possibility. The other was on the Potomac between the mouth of Rock Creek, which formed the eastern boundary of Georgetown, and Goose or Tiber Creek to the south and east. Here was another small settlement, Hamburg, which, like Carrollsburg, was largely a paper town with only a very few scattered structures. The balance of the area that eventually was to make up the new city was held by a dozen or so proprietors in tracts of substantial size. Figure 6 shows the location of Georgetown, Hamburg, Carrollsburg, and the estates of the proprietors of other lands in the district.

L'Enfant submitted to Jefferson some of his preliminary impressions of the site in letters written from Georgetown on March 10 and 11.[11] Fog and rain hampered his movements, but his first comments were cautiously enthusiastic. Perhaps Jefferson feared that his presence in the vicinity of Carrollsburg would unduly increase the flurry of speculation, for on March 17 he requested L'Enfant to begin surveys between Rock Creek and Tiber Creek and to prepare maps of his work for the President to inspect on his projected visit to Georgetown the end of March. A postscript to Jefferson's letter indicates the strategy that was being followed: "It is the desire that the public mind should be in equilibrio between these two places till the President arrives, and we shall be obliged to you to endeavor to poise their expectations."[12]

Jefferson's attention also shifted to the Hamburg site. Sometime toward the end of March, probably before the President arrived in Georgetown on March 28, Jefferson prepared a sketch plan for the new city for the site lying on the Tiber.[13] This plan is of great importance because of its source and because of its possible influence on L'Enfant.

Jefferson's plan, reproduced in Figure 7, incorporated some of the features he had earlier advocated for the Carrollsburg site. The town appears as a checkerboard of square blocks, 11 blocks east and west and 3 blocks deep. A note on the plan states that each block was to be 600 feet square and laid off in lots 60 feet wide. The space normally occupied by three blocks would be used for the President's house and gardens, with an equal area set aside for the Capitol. Connecting these two focal points Jefferson showed a strip of land 8 blocks long and 1 block wide along the Tiber for "public walks." Although the distance between the Capitol and the President's house was much less than L'Enfant was eventually to provide in his plan, the spatial relationship is similar, and his "public walks" may be regarded as the genesis of L'Enfant's great mall.

Two notes on the map clearly indicate that Jefferson anticipated a town of substantial size but favored an original settlement of compact dimensions. The blocks shown by closely spaced dots were "to be sold in the first instance." The other dots surrounding this area of initial development show the points of intersection of future gridiron streets. The total area amounted to about 2,000 acres, comparable to the size of Philadelphia. Jefferson has some-

[10] The text of Washington's letter to Benjamin Stoddert and Will Deakins, Jr., on February 3, 1791, asking them to purchase land as if for their own use appears in Tindall, *Washington*, pp. 62–63. The following should also be consulted: Allen C. Clark, "Origins of the Federal City," Columbia Historical Society *Records*, xxx–xxxvi (1935), pp. 1–97.

[11] Letters from L'Enfant to Jefferson, March 10, 1791, and March 11, 1791, in Padover, *Jefferson,* pp. 44–45, 45–47.

[12] Letter from Jefferson to L'Enfant, March 17, 1791, in Padover, *Jefferson*, p. 51.

[13] The plan itself is undated. It may have accompanied Jefferson's draft of a presidential proclamation designating the Hamburg location as the site for public buildings, which bears the date of March 30. This date, however, may be incorrect, or there may have been an earlier draft. Washington referred to the draft in a letter written from Mount Vernon on March 31, so it must have been in his hands some days earlier. Probably the Jefferson plan and the draft proclamation were both given to the President before he left Philadelphia for Georgetown, where he arrived early in the morning of March 28.

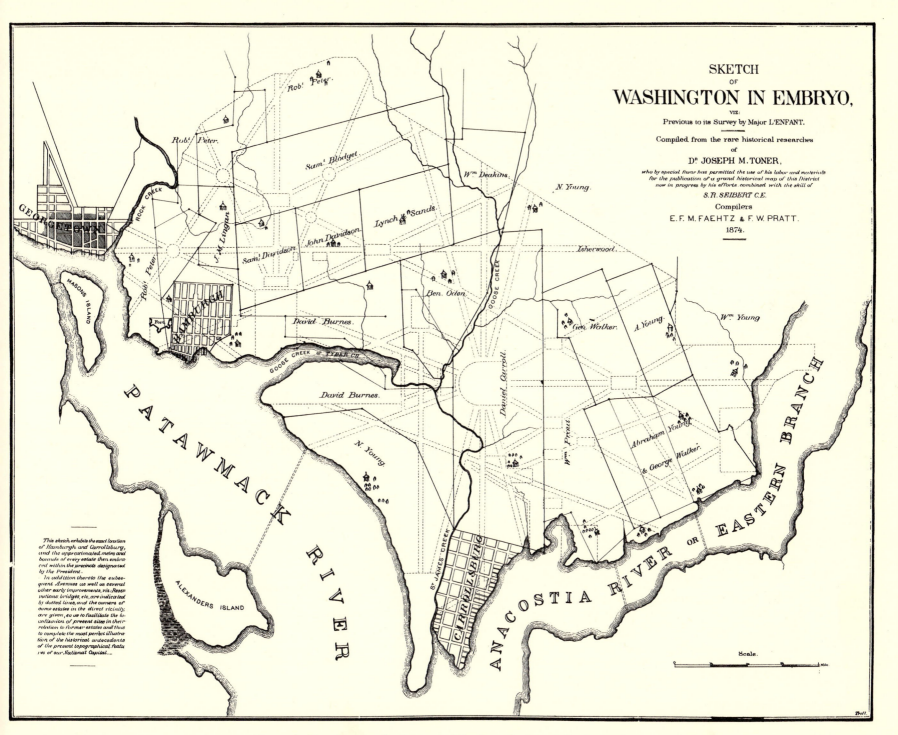

Figure 6. Map Showing the Division of Land on the Site of the National
Capital: 1791

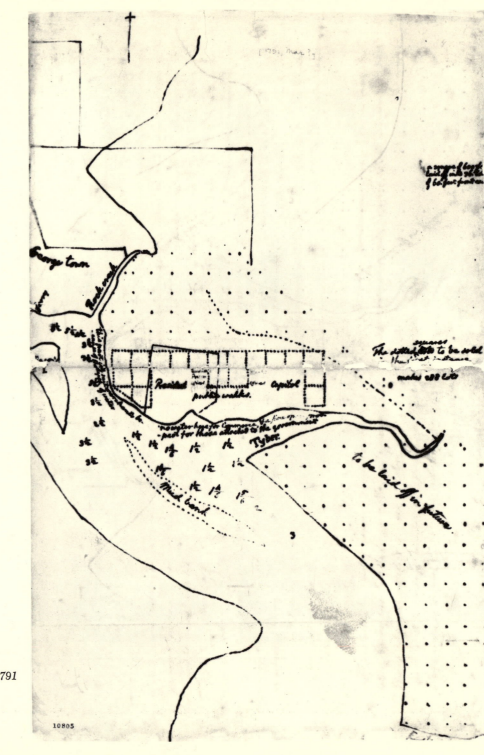

Figure 7. *Thomas Jefferson's Plan for Washington: 1791*

times been described as the advocate of a mere village for the new capital city, but this drawing and its marginal notes clearly refute this charge. Moreover, Jefferson's plan was prepared on the assumption that only this amount of land could be acquired on reasonable terms. Had he known of the arrangement that Washington was about to conclude with the proprietors of land in the district his proposed plan might have been even more generous.

President Washington, wishing to make a final decision on the exact site of the city and the terms of land acquisition, rode to Georgetown to confer with his agents and the owners of land in the district. On the evening of March 28 he met with Ellicott and L'Enfant to go over their surveys and to discuss with them the advantages of various locations for the principal buildings. The next morning he and his advisers went out to inspect the land, but a thick fog prevented him from gaining much information of value.

At six in the evening of March 29 the President met with the two principal groups of landowners, those in the vicinity of Georgetown and their rivals from Carrollsburg. Washington's diary records what took place.

"I represented that the contention in which they seemed to be engaged, did not in my opinion comport either with the public interest or that of their own; that while each party was aiming to obtain the public buildings, they might by placing the matter on a contracted scale, defeat the measure altogether . . . that neither the offer from George-Town or Carrollsburgh separately, was adequate to the end of insuring the object. That both together did not comprehend more ground nor would afford greater means than was required for the Federal City; and that, instead of contending which of the two should have it they had better, by combining more offers make a common cause of it. . . ." [14]

In view of later developments it seems likely that it was L'Enfant who had convinced the President that the plan for the city should embrace the entire district or a very large part of it, and that even the area shown in the Jefferson plan would not be sufficient. This view was to prevail, and it was doubtless Washington's prestige and great powers of persuasion that brought it about.

Sometime later that evening or during the following day, the two groups of proprietors reached agreement on the terms suggested by the President, for on March 30 Washington met again with this now united group and received from it a signed statement specifying the manner in which land would be acquired and laid out for the city and the compensation they would receive. Washington, obviously elated by the success of his mission, wrote to Jefferson the next day summarizing the conditions:

"The terms . . . are That all the land from Rock-creek along the river to the eastern-branch and so upwards to or above the ferry including a breadth of about a mile and a half, the whole containing from three to five thousand acres, is ceded to the public, on condition that, when the whole shall be surveyed and laid off as a city, (which Major L'Enfant is now directed to do) the present Proprietors shall retain every other lot, and for such part of the land as may be taken for public use . . . they shall be allowed at the rate of Twenty five pounds per acre. . . . No compensation is to be made for the ground that may be occupied as streets or alleys." [15]

The President had reason for satisfaction, for on this visit he had settled the land question, vastly enlarged the area available for the new city, and had entrusted the planning of the city to L'Enfant, his old acquaintance, in whose skill he had full confidence. The preliminaries had thus been disposed of. The President could turn his attention to other matters. Ours, consequently, can now be devoted to L'Enfant's activities and the plan he was to produce.

L'Enfant may have at first been engaged only to identify favorable sites for the chief public buildings, but he could not confine himself so narrowly. Inevitably and understandably his mind was stimulated to consider certain aspects of the city plan that would be needed to knit together these sites into a great composition. We

[14] Washington diary entry for March 29, 1791, as quoted in Tindall, *Washington*, pp. 75–76.

[15] Letter from Washington to Jefferson, March 31, 1791, in Padover, *Jefferson*, p. 54. The full text of the agreement may be found in H. Paul Caemmerer, *Washington: The National Capital*, Washington, 1932, pp. 19–21; and in Tindall, *Washington*, pp. 76–78.

have written evidence of this. One of the surviving L'Enfant documents is entitled "Note relative to the ground lying on the eastern branch of the river Potomac and being intended to parallel the several positions proposed within the limits between the branch and Georgetown for the seat of the Federal City." While this is undated, it seems virtually certain that it was submitted by L'Enfant to the President on his arrival in Georgetown on March 29. Written in L'Enfant's imperfect English, the note analyzed the site generally, pointed out the commanding position of Jenkin's Hill, discussed the desirable location for bridges and docks, and included observations on the streams and terrain. Anticipating his later more specific proposals, L'Enfant even described a great avenue leading from Georgetown to a bridge on the Anacostia as ". . . a direct and large avenue . . . with a middle way paved for heavy carriages and a walk on each side planted with double rows of trees . . . a street laid out on a dimension proportioned to the greatness which . . . the Capital of a powerful Empire ought to manifest." [16]

There is also in this note a foreshadowing of L'Enfant's later recommendations for a development policy based on several nodes of settlement, rather than one of grouping all or most buildings in a compact single center. He believed that more rapid growth would occur under his system as each node was enlarged by subsequent building development along principal avenues connecting them. In this his ideas varied from those of Jefferson. Nor was this his only disagreement with the author of the earlier plan for the new city. In his note to the President, L'Enfant included a vigorous condemnation of the checkerboard or gridiron plan, stating:

". . . it is not the regular assemblage of houses laid out in squares and forming streets all parallel and uniform that . . . is so necessary, for such a plan could only do on a level plain and where no surrounding object being interesting it becomes indifferent which way the opening of streets may be directed.

"But on any other ground, a plan of this sort must be defective, and it never would answer for any of the spots proposed for the

Federal City, and on that held here as the most eligible it would absolutely annihilate every of the advantages enumerated and . . . along injure the success of the undertaking.

"Such regular plans indeed, however answerable they may appear upon paper or seducing as they may be on the first aspect to the eyes of some people must even when applyed upon the ground the best calculated to admit of it become at last tiresome and insipid and it never could be in its origin but a mean continuance of some cool imagination wanting a sense of the real grand and truly beautiful only to be met with where nature contributes with art and diversifies the objects." [17]

Jefferson doubtless had an opportunity to read this document and realized how different were his ideas from those of L'Enfant. In writing L'Enfant on April 10, however, he stated: "I am happy that the President has left the planning of the Town in such good hands, and have no doubt it will be done to general satisfaction." [18]

As he began the task of designing the new city, L'Enfant felt the need to examine the plans of certain European cities. Turning to Jefferson for assistance, he explained his requirements:

"I would be very much obliged to you . . . if you could procure for me whatever map may fall within your reach—of any of the differents grand city now Existing such as—for example—as london —madry—paris—Amsterdam—naples—venice—geno—florence

---

[16] Undated note by L'Enfant, the text of which appears in Elizabeth S. Kite, *L'Enfant and Washington*, Baltimore, 1929, pp. 43–48.

[17] *ibid*. It is doubtful if this almost violent denunciation of the gridiron plan was provoked by L'Enfant's examination of Jefferson's sketch. Washington sent the sketch to L'Enfant with a letter dated April 4, explaining that Jefferson had prepared it on the assumption that the Carrollsburg lands would not be available. The letter included this statement: "Although I do not conceive that you will derive any material advantage from an examination of the enclosed papers, yet, as they have been drawn under different circumstances, and by different persons, they may be compared with your own ideas of a proper plan for the Federal City, under the prospect which now presents itself." The letter refers to two plans, only one of which was Jefferson's. This other plan has never come to light. Letter from Washington to L'Enfant, April 4, 1791, in Caemmerer, *L'Enfant*, p. 144.

[18] Letter from Jefferson to L'Enfant, April 10, 1791, in Padover, *Jefferson*, p. 59. In this letter Jefferson mentioned that he had submitted his own ideas to the President on the city plan and relied on Washington to transmit to L'Enfant "such of mine as he approved," adding, "I avoid interfering with what he may have expressed to you."

. . . for, notwithstanding, I would reprobate the Idea of Imitating and that contrary of Having this Intention it is my wish and shall be my endeavor to delinate on a new and original way the plan the contrivance of which the President has left to me without any restriction soever—yet the contemplation of what exists of well improved situation iven the parallel of these with deffective ones, may serve to suggest a variety of new Ideas and is necessary to refine and strengthen the Judgment particularly in the present instance when having to unit the useful with the comodious and agreeable viewing these will be offering means of comparing [and] enable me the better to determine with a certainty the propriety of a local [locale] which offer an Extensive field for combinations." [19]

Jefferson responded to this request, sending L'Enfant on April 10 his maps of the following cities: Frankfurt, Karlsruhe, Amsterdam, Strasbourg, Paris, Orleans, Bordeau, Lyons, Montpelier, Marseilles, Turin, and Milan.[20] These plans, "on large and accurate scales," may have been the source of some of L'Enfant's subsequent proposals, although they are not mentioned by him in any later communication. Only that of Karlsruhe showed the use of a symmetrical radial street pattern, and it is doubtful if the others provided much in the way of inspiration for any of the details of the plan of Washington.

L'Enfant worked with great speed. By the beginning of the third week in April he could discuss with a visitor some of his proposals for "Quays, bridges, etc., magnificent public walks, and other projects. . . ."[21] During April, May, and the early part of June L'Enfant prepared the first draft of his plan for the capital city. This plan, together with a long memorandum dated June 22, 1791, describing its features and its methods of preparation, he submitted to the President either at Mount Vernon, where he stayed from June 13–26, or at Georgetown, which he reached early

on June 27. Washington visited Georgetown to settle some new differences that had arisen between the proprietors and the commissioners over the extent of the area to be acquired for the city. He also took this occasion to visit the site with L'Enfant and Ellicott and to make a final determination of the location of the public buildings.

When the proprietors had finally agreed to the exact terms of the deeds they were to execute, Washington, as his diary records,

". . . called the Several Subscribers together and made known to them the spots on which I meant to place the buildings for the P: and Executive departments of the government—and for the Legislater of Dº. A Plan was also laid before them of the City in order to convey to them general ideas of the City—but they were told that some deviations from it would take place—particularly in the diagonal streets or avenues, which would not be so numerous; and in the removal of the President's house more westerly for the advantage of higher ground. They were also told that a Town house, or exchange wd be placed on some convenient ground between the spots designed for the public buildings before mentioned, and it was with much pleasure that a general approbation of the measure seemed to pervade the whole." [22]

The plan referred to has unfortunately been lost, and we can only surmise that it was similar to the final L'Enfant plan which was completed shortly after the middle of August, although showing additional avenues and with the President's residence located somewhat east of its present site.[23] It is likely, too, that many of the details of the later and final scheme had not then been worked out. L'Enfant's accompanying memorandum explaining the plan, and

---

[19] Letter from L'Enfant to Jefferson, April 4, 1791, in Kite, *L'Enfant and Washington*, p. 42.

[20] Letter from Jefferson to L'Enfant, April 10, 1791, in Padover, *Jefferson*, p. 59.

[21] *Journal of William Loughton Smith (1790–1791)*, April 22, 1791, Massachusetts Historical Society *Proceedings,* LI, Boston, 1918, pp. 60–62.

[22] Washington Diary, June 29, 1791, as quoted in Tindall, *Washington*, p. 101.

[23] William T. Partridge has attempted a reconstruction of the "lost" avenues from L'Enfant's description of this draft plan and from his design submitted to the President in August. See his "L'Enfant's Methods and Features of his Plan for the Federal City," National Capital Park and Planning Commission, *Reports and Plans, Washington Region,* Supplementary Technical Data to Accompany Annual Report, Washington, 1930, pp. 21–33. Partridge's study is an excellent analysis of L'Enfant's planning methods, and his drawings illustrating the components of the plan of the city are of great value.

his methods of working indicate what he hoped to achieve. After an introduction apologizing for the small scale of the plan and its lack of detail, the memorandum describes the basis for the street system, a combination of the gridiron pattern on which was superimposed a great design of radial boulevards connecting directly the sites for the principal buildings:

"Having determined some principal points to which I wished to make the other subordinate, I made the distribution regular with every street at right angles, North and South, east and west, and afterwards opened some in different directions, as avenues to and from every principal place, wishing thereby not merely to contract [contrast] with the general regularity, nor to afford a greater variety of seats [sites] with pleasant prospects, which will be obtained from the advantageous ground over which these avenues are chiefly directed, but principally to connect each part of the city, if I may so express it, by making the real distance less from place to place, by giving to them reciprocity of sight and by making them thus seemingly connected, promote a rapid settlement over the whole extent, rendering those even of the most remote parts an addition to the principal, which without the help of these, were any such settlement attempted, it would be languid, and lost in the extent, and become detrimental to the establishment." [24]

L'Enfant proposed that the avenues be broad, with roadways 80 feet wide, an additional 30 feet on each side "for a walk under a double row of trees," and with another 10-foot strip on each side separating the trees and the building lots. He described the chief avenue extending diagonally across the city from a crossing of the Anacostia to Georgetown, the present Pennsylvania Avenue. Along its extent he located the principal buildings, the "Presidential palace" and the "Federal House." The presidential residence and its "garden park and other improvements" were to stand on high ground toward the western edge of the city facing the Tiber and overlooking a broad stretch of the Potomac. The Capitol was to be located on Jenkin's Hill, a feature of the district which had first caught the designer's attention. Here was a spot which, in

[24] L'Enfant memorandum, in Kite, *L'Enfant and Washington*, p. 53.

16

L'Enfant's words, "stands really as a pedestal waiting for a superstructure." No other location, he said "could bear a competition with this."

Other features of the proposed plan were reviewed, including the "public walks" connecting the presidential grounds with the Capitol; an equestrian statue on the banks of the Potomac where the axes of the Capitol and presidential house intersected; and buildings for the executive branch of government close to the residence of the President. While these proposals were eventually to be realized, one of L'Enfant's recommendations was unfortunately never carried out. He proposed to channel the waters of the Tiber and lead them under the Capitol, ". . . letting the Tiber return to its proper channel by a fall, which issuing from under the base of the Congress building, may there form a cascade of forty feet high, or more than one hundred wide, which would produce the most happy effect in rolling down to fill up the canal and discharge itself in the Potomac. . . ."

In this memorandum L'Enfant described in considerable detail his proposed development policy designed to encourage rapid growth of the city. He suggested that construction ". . . should be begun at various points equi-distant as possible from the center; not merely because settlements of this sort are likely to diffuse an equality of advantages over the whole territory allotted, and consequently to reflect benefit from an increase of the value of property, but because each of these settlements by a natural jealousy will most tend to stimulate establishment on each of the opposed extremes. . . ." The city would quickly take form, he thought, as the nodes of settlement became joined.

An important feature of L'Enfant's plan to promote this policy was a canal to connect the Potomac and the Anacostia. He suggested confining the banks of the Tiber for the western section of the canal which would run along the north side of the public walks. It would then turn south where the grand cascade from the Capitol entered and continue to the Anacostia. At its mouth on the Potomac and along its banks the canal, L'Enfant felt, would stimulate initial development of mercantile activities and lead to additional residential growth nearby.

The memorandum emphasized the relationship of the three great features of modern central Washington: the White House, the Mall, and the Capitol:

"I placed the three grand Departments of State contiguous to the principle Palace and on the way leading to the Congressional House the gardens of the one together with the park and other improvement on the dependency are connected with the publique walk and avenue to the Congress house in a manner as most [must] form a whole as grand as it will be agreeable and convenient to the whole city which form [from] The distribution of the local [locale] will have an early access to this place of general resort and all along side of which may be placed play houses, room of assembly, accademies and all such sort of places as may be attractive to the learned and afford diversion to the idle." [25]

It is obvious that at this time the basic plan of the city had already been determined in considerable detail. During the next six weeks this plan was revised and additional features added. Some of the diagonal avenues were eliminated, and L'Enfant gave further thought to the policies that should be adopted in promoting the city's rapid development. On August 19 L'Enfant dispatched another report to the President. Accompanying this was an outline plan of the city, appearing in Figure 8, showing the principal streets in single dotted lines as well as a number of open spaces. This was intended to show the President the progress that had been made in surveying the chief features of the city as then planned. A portion of the report is of special interest because it refers to the great central composition of the city and because it mentions for the first time a site for the "Judiciary Court," a feature that unaccountably was not specifically designated on L'Enfant's later and final plan.

[25] L'Enfant memorandum, June 22, 1791, in Columbia Historical Society *Records,* Washington, 1899, II, pp. 32–37.

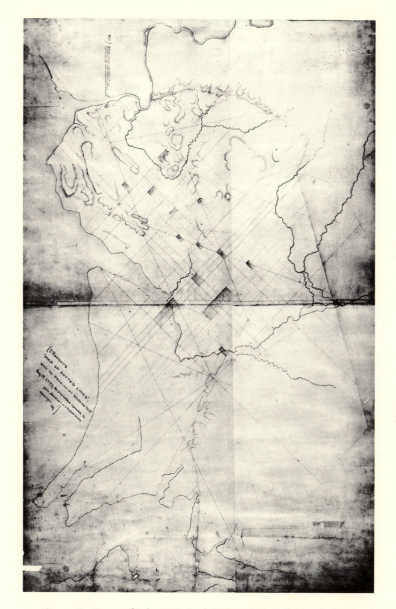

Figure 8. Pierre Charles L'Enfant's "Map of Dotted Lines": 1791

"The grand avenu connecting both the palace and the Federal House will be most magnificent and most convenient, the streets running west of the upper square of the Federal House and which terminate in an easy slope on the canal through the tiber which it will overlook for the space of about two mile will be beautifull above what may be imagined—those other streets parallel to that canal, those crossing over it and which are as many avenues to the grand walk from the water cascade under the Federal House to the President park and dependinly extending to the bank of the Potowmack, and also the several squares or area such as are intended for the Judiciary Court—the national bank—the grand church—the play house—market and exchange—all through will offer a variety of situation unparalled in point of beauties—suitable to every purpose and in every point convenient. . . ." [26]

L'Enfant expanded on his proposed strategy to promote speedy growth of the city by the development of nodes of settlement at several points. This time he pointed out also that it would be unwise to put up for immediate sale lots in the new but unimproved town. He suggested instead that the government borrow large sums to be used for public improvements, using the public share of the platted lots as security. The construction of the canal and other public works would enhance the value of the lots, which could be disposed of slowly at much higher prices than if sold immediately.

This policy, of course, ran directly counter to that of Washington, Jefferson, Madison, and others in the government who were under considerable pressure to show immediate results. At this time many persons were skeptical of the wisdom of trying to create a new capital city, while interests in Philadelphia and New York continued to work for the retention of the seat of government in the north. Indeed, Washington and Jefferson had already promised that land sales would begin shortly, and to retreat on this now would merely provide new ammunition for the enemies of the Potomac site. It seems doubtful anyway that the strategy would have worked as L'Enfant thought. Half of the lots in the new city would revert to the original proprietors as soon as the plan was completed, and private sales from this source would surely have supplied any conceivable demand.[27]

Some days later in August L'Enfant journeyed to Philadelphia, where he presented his final revised plan to the President. This drawing has survived, although it has become almost illegible. An exact copy made in 1887 from the imperfect manuscript is the form in which we know the plan today and is the one shown in Figure 9. On one entire side of the plan and a portion of the other L'Enfant provided a detailed description of its features and a legend locating the principal buildings, open spaces, monuments, and fountains. Here are most of the main elements of the modern city, modified slightly from L'Enfant's earlier drawings and with additional details which he had worked out since his earlier reports to the President.

Among these additions were 15 squares, each one intended to be embellished by one of the states of the union with "Statues, Columns, Obelisks, or any other ornament." This feature followed his proposal for nodal growth, since he expected each state to make "improvements around the Square to be completed in a limited time," and these little settlements "round those Squares must soon become connected." These squares were also intended as visual focal points, for, as the designer stated, "The situation of these Squares is such that they are the most advantageously and reciprocally seen from each other, and as equally distributed over the whole City district, and connected by spacious Avenues round the grand Federal Improvements and as continguous to them, and at the same time as equally distant from each other, as circumstances would admit."

L'Enfant's explanations emphasized his concern to create a city

[26] Letter from L'Enfant to Washington, August 19, 1791, the text of which appears in the Columbia Historical Society *Records,* II, pp. 38–48.

[27] L'Enfant's proposals for delaying land sales were discussed by Washington and Jefferson and later, on September 8 and 9, considered by the commissioners in the presence of Jefferson and James Madison. They were rejected as undesirable. See Tindall, *Washington,* pp. 120–21 and Jefferson's "Notes on Commissioners' Meeting," September 8, 1791, in Padover, *Jefferson,* pp. 70–73. Jefferson records also a number of other important decisions: The prohibition of wooden houses; limitation of building height to 35 feet and the requirement that buildings fronting on the principal avenues be built to that height; prohibition of projecting "stoups and projections of every kind into the streets"; the naming "of streets alphabetically one way and numerically the other"; and the naming of the town the City of Washington in the Territory of Columbia.

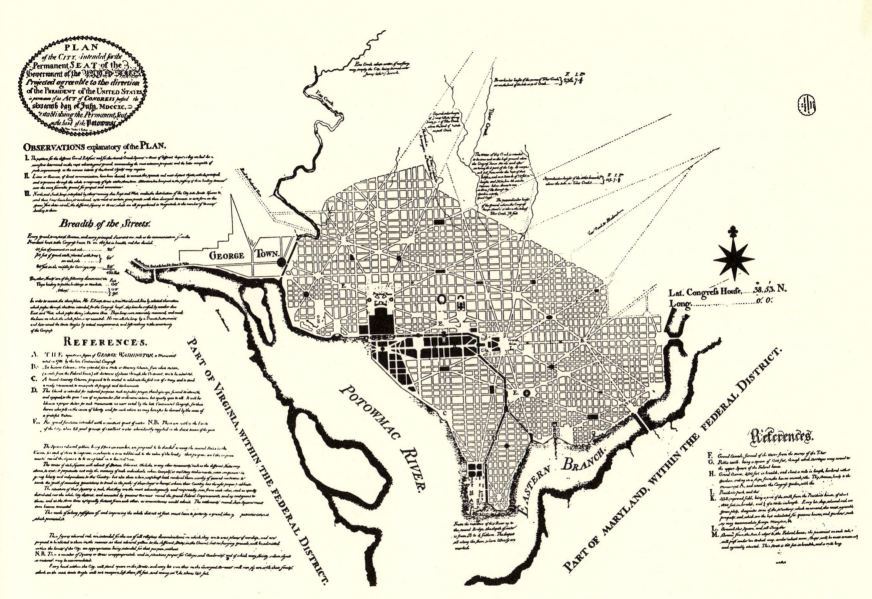

Figure 9. *Plan for Washington by Pierre Charles L'Enfant: 1791*

of beauty and magnificence. "Five grand fountains intended with a constant spout of water" appear at intervals on the plan marked with the letter "E." He described also three important monuments: An equestrian statue of Washington at the intersection of the Capitol and President's house axes; a "Naval itinerary Column," marked "C" on the plan, on an open space facing the Potomac; and "An historic Column also intended for a mile or itinerary Column, from whose station, (a mile from the Federal house) all distances of places through the Continent are to be calculated," at what is the modern Lincoln Park.

The square marked "D" on the plan, occupied by the old Patent Office Building and now the location of the National Portrait Gallery, was to be set aside for a "Church . . . intended for national purposes, such as public prayer, thanksgivings, funeral orations, &c. and assigned to the special use of no particular Sect or denomination. . . ." Other church sites were provided, colored in red on the original drawing but whose location cannot now be determined because of the faded condition of the manuscript. Several of the squares and open spaces not specifically designated were to be reserved "for Colleges and Academies" and for societies "whose object is national."

The design incorporated, of course, the sites located earlier for the Capitol and the President's dwelling. L'Enfant's plan did not specifically designate a site for the Supreme Court. The modern Judiciary Square, three blocks east and south of the proposed church, was, however, given that title almost from the beginning. The L'Enfant drawing shows a large open space at this location. It seems likely, although it is by no means certain, that he intended this for the "Judiciary Court," as he called it in his earlier memorandum to the President.[28]

Nor does the plan locate the "Town house" which the President had promised to the proprietors at the meeting when L'Enfant's first plan was shown to them. It is possible that L'Enfant intended this to be placed on the large square south and slightly east of the Capitol facing one of the five great fountains. Nearby, on the Anacostia, the plans show two canal indentations, each labeled "Canal to the market."

The plan shows a group of buildings at the point of land originally occupied by Carrollsburg, between one of the two branches of the Tiber Canal and the Potomac, now the site of Fort McNair and the National War College. From the elaborate design of the harbor enclosures shown off Greenleaf Point and the proximity to the proposed Naval Column, we might assume that L'Enfant intended this as the Navy headquarters, although this, too, is mere conjecture. Three undesignated open spaces appear along the Anacostia at the eastern boundary of the city. Two of these were perhaps intended as monumental entrances to the capital from the bridges to the eastern shore, uses which they now serve at the head of the East Capitol Street Bridge and the John Phillip Sousa Bridge. The middle and largest was shifted somewhat to the north. Ellicott's version of the L'Enfant plan shows this on its present site as occupied by a major building rivaling in size the Capitol itself. This is the location of the present District of Columbia General Hospital, and it is possible that L'Enfant envisaged this use for the site shown on his plan.[29]

Linking all of these spaces was the combination radial and gridiron street system which L'Enfant had conceived almost from the beginning as the unifying element of his great city. The reasons for this pattern, earlier explained to the President at greater length, are summarized in the legend on the map:

"Lines or Avenues of direct communication have been devised to connect the separate and most distant objects with the principal and to preserve through the whole a reciprocity of sight at the same time. Attention has been paid to the passing of those leading Avenues over the most favorable ground for prospect and convenience.

[28] On the plan of the city prepared by James R. Dermott in 1797 or 1798 this area is labeled "Judiciary Square." The importance of this site cannot be appreciated from a mere examination of the plan. It is on a pronounced rise in the terrain, the highest point near Pennsylvania Avenue from the Capitol to the White House. Leading from it to the southwest is Indiana Avenue, directly on axis with the proposed location of the statue of Washington. To the south, 4th Street now extends to Fort McNair at the mouth of the Anacostia, although in the L'Enfant plan 4th Street ended somewhat short of that important location.

[29] The Dermott plan of the city labels this space "jail and other buildings." The plan of Washington drawn by Robert King in 1800 shows this area as the "marine hospital."

"North and South lines, intersected by others running due East and West, make the distribution of the City into Streets, Squares &c. and those lines have been so combined as to meet at certain given points with those divergent Avenues, so as to form on the spaces first determined, the different Squares or Areas, which are all proportional in Magnitude to the number of Avenues leading to them "

The main avenues were to be 160 feet wide, divided as L'Enfant had earlier proposed to the President. Streets "leading to public buildings or markets" were to be 130 feet in width, while the remaining streets were to be 90 and 110 feet wide.

For the center of this elaborate composition I'Enfant provided a major link between the Capitol and the President's house. He described this as a "Grand Avenue, 400 feet in breadth, and about a mile in length, bordered with gardens, ending in a slope from the houses on each side. This Avenue leads to the Monument A, and connects the Congress Garden with the President's park and the Well improved field, being a part of the walk from the President's house of about 1800 feet in breadth and ¾ of a mile in length." The original drawing indicated buildings in red bordering this "field," now the Washington Mall. These sites, according to the designer, were "the best calculated for spacious houses and gardens, such as may accommodate foreign Ministers, &c."

Finally, L'Enfant suggested the location of the principal shops and the manner in which these buildings should be designed. What is now East Capitol Street, leading to the east front of the Capitol, was to be developed with arcaded sidewalks, "under whose cover Shops will be most conveniently and agreeably situated." In his earlier memorandum L'Enfant had also suggested that commercial development should take place along "the streets from the grand avenue to the palace [President's house] and towards the canal."

Here truly, if not "a plan wholly new," was an urban composition unique at least to America both in scale and in concept. All the baroque design motifs of European planning developed over the years in the old world suddenly and splendidly found application on this virgin site for the capital of the newest of the world's nations. It was a supreme irony that the plan forms originally conceived to magnify the glories of despotic kings and emperors came to be applied as a national symbol of a country whose philosophical basis was so firmly rooted in democratic equality.

And yet, inappropriate as this design may have been as a reflection of the constitution of the new government, it must have appealed to the aspirations of its leaders for national grandeur. Even the sophisticated Jefferson, who can hardly have failed to appreciate the anomaly of the L'Enfant plan, apparently never objected to the design. Perhaps he, Washington, and the others to whom this task had been entrusted showed, by their acceptance of the plan, their ultimate faith in the nation's ability to rival Europe in power and architectural glory. Certainly it was an act of faith in the future to adopt this plan so obviously beyond the resources that could immediately be mustered for its completion. Their vision, and that of L'Enfant, took decades to be vindicated. That long view has prevailed, and in that fact there is a most important lesson for those who today contend with the vexing problems of city rebuilding.

In preparing this plan L'Enfant drew on many sources. His familiarity with many of the great renaissance and baroque compositions of Europe has already been examined, and there can be little doubt that his general inspiration must have come from such monumental developments as Versailles. Yet the plan of Washington was no mechanical imitation of any European model. L'Enfant was a child of his age who had early learned the design vocabulary of his elders. It was a language that came easily to him, and he spoke it with conviction and eloquence in this graphic statement that is his monument.

Our concern focuses mainly on the central portion of this plan— the noble triangle formed by the Capitol, the White House, and the Washington Monument, linked by the Mall and Pennsylvania Avenue. In his treatment of these spaces L'Enfant doubtless borrowed ideas from his European background. The pairs of radial boulevards extending from all four sides of the Capitol square and from three sides of the space set aside for the presidential mansion had by the late eighteenth century become a commonplace device for enchancing the setting of important buildings or monuments.

There were, however, a few American sources on which L'Enfant might have drawn, expanding their almost domestic scale to the monumental proportions he deemed appropriate for a great capital city. Jefferson's concept of the "public walks" connecting the executive and legislative branches of the government may well have influenced the designer. So, too, may the plans for the two most elegant capitals of the colonial period: Williamsburg and Annapolis. At Williamsburg there is a relationship between the Capitol and Governor's Palace almost identical to that L'Enfant created at Washington. Annapolis exhibited a little baroque plan of radial streets connecting two circular open spaces used as sites for church and Capitol.[30]

Yet nowhere in the world had a city been planned on this scale and employing these design elements. Nor were the devices of civic design blindly applied simply because they were fashionable. L'Enfant's description of his methods clearly reveals his concern first with locating the most commanding spots for the principal uses and buildings, not in finding places for them later after an abstract street pattern had been imposed on the site. His concern with topography was paramount; only later did he seek to introduce a formal rhythm by the regular placement of subsidiary streets.[31]

The plan, of course, was not without flaws. Most serious is the distance from the President's house to the Capitol—a separation so great that the reciprocal relationship is almost lost. His failure to make better use of the Potomac frontage was also a major shortcoming. And, as has been most frequently remarked, the combination of radial and grid streets created scores of awkwardly shaped parcels and remnants of land difficult to utilize and creating visual disorder. Yet, with full realization of these faults, one must still conclude that this was a great city plan conceived in an in-

credibly short time by one of the most remarkably talented persons of his era.

What L'Enfant might have achieved had he been able to refine and revise this masterpiece in the rough will never be known. His difficult temperament and excessive zeal soon led to his removal from any further responsibility for the city's planning and development. Three separate acts of procrastination, impetuousness, or insubordination were involved. The first was L'Enfant's delay in arranging for a printed plan of the city to be displayed at the first land sales on October 17. The second was his hasty removal of the house of Daniel Carroll of Duddington, one of the proprietors, who had constructed it in the bed of one of L'Enfant's mapped but unimproved streets. The third was his adamant refusal to submit, at Washington's direction, to the authority of the commissioners.[32]

Ellicott was directed to supervise the printing of the city map. He had to rely on the information in his possession, for L'Enfant stubbornly refused to surrender his own drawings. The official plan, reproduced in Figure 10, finally appeared in October 1792, engraved in Philadelphia by Thackara and Vallance, although a slightly earlier and smaller version was also produced in Boston by Samuel Hill. They are virtually identical, and both show changes from the L'Enfant drawing. Some of these changes were made under Jefferson's directions, some were doubtless caused by Ellicott's lack of complete information, and Ellicott himself may have altered the original design.

The Ellicott version of L'Enfant's plan, however, did not differ in any material way from the original. The most obvious changes were the straightening of Massachusetts Avenue, the omission of a few short stretches of certain of the minor diagonals, and the addition of one or two others. One feature which was supressed and which justifiably angered L'Enfant was the designer's name. Only Ellicott's appears in the abbreviated references and observations printed along the sides of the plan.

Ellicott's map is valuable for our purposes because it shows in

[30] For plans and an extended description and analysis of Williamsburg and Annapolis see my *The Making of Urban America,* Princeton, 1965, pp. 103–14, and sources cited therein.

[31] The most perceptive analysis and criticism of the L'Enfant plan is by Elbert Peets. See his essay on Washington in *The American Vitruvius,* New York, 1922, compiled by Peets and Werner Hegemann, and his "L'Enfant's Washington," *Town Planning Review,* xv, pp. 155–64. See also Partridge, "L'Enfant's Methods."

[32] For these and related events see Caemmerer, *L'Enfant,* pp. 169–215. Washington's irritation and dismay at L'Enfant's actions is set forth in his long letter to the commissioners dated November 20, 1791, the complete text of which appears in Tindall, *Washington,* pp. 125–29.

Figure 10. Plan of Washington by Andrew Ellicott: 1792

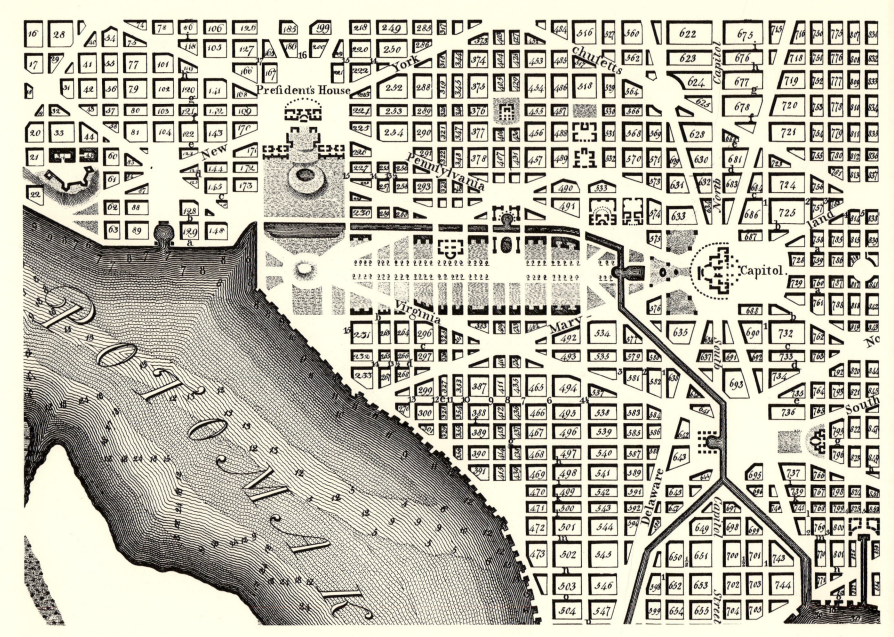

Figure 11. Central Portion of the Ellicott Plan of Washington: 1792

heavy lines the outline plans of a number of major buildings. Quite likely these were based on preliminary designs prepared by L'Enfant, which he had completed at least as early as February 1792.[33] Most of these were for the sites already discussed. Several others appear, however, and can be seen on the central portion of the map reproduced in Figure 11. Two of these are shown facing Pennsylvania Avenue, flanking its intersection with 3rd Street. Another is located on the north side of the Tiber Canal directly south and on the axis of the national church. South of this building on what is now the Mall the plan shows what appears to be an oval pool with two narrow buildings or colonnades enclosing this space, beyond which an open space connects with the "Grand Avenue" running down the center of the Mall. The intended use of these buildings can only be a matter of conjecture. It is possible that the building or building complex north of the canal, into which projects an extension of the canal, was designed as the market for that section of the city.

The Mall itself is shown in greater detail than on the surviving

L'Enfant manuscript drawing. The "Grand Avenue" appears lined with trees as the formal drive L'Enfant intended. Along its outer edges are two lines of buildings, perhaps the foreign ministries proposed here by the designer. One much larger and obviously monumental building is drawn on the north side of the Mall between 10th and 12th Streets. This may well have been the "play house" or theater mentioned by L'Enfant in one of his reports to the President. The presidential residence stands in the middle of a large open space from which radiate four major and two minor diagonal boulevards. South of the mansion on either side of a park strip are two other major structures. Doubtless these were meant for the executive offices. Their location was obviously determined by the desire to keep open the vistas to the President's residence down the major diagonal boulevards and the less important grid streets terminating at the open space in which it was located.

Such was the history of the plan for the national capital and the men who were responsible for its preparation. It is doubtful that any one of them felt full satisfaction with the results—but at least the great undertaking was launched. Now, with the outline of the city at last determined, work could proceed with turning this paper vision into reality.

[33] See letter from Washington to Jefferson, February 22, 1792, in Padover, *Jefferson*, pp. 29–33: "The Plans of the buildings ought to come forward immediately for consideration. I think Mr. Walker said yesterday he (L'Enfant) had been shewing the different views of them to Mr. Trumbul."

CHAPTER 2

Washington after L'Enfant

L'Enfant's vision of a great capital on the banks of the Potomac to rival the most glorious cities of the past or present far outran the resources of the infant nation. Indeed, for a time, it seemed doubtful if the administration could even fulfill the minimum conditions of the Residence Act and "provide suitable buildings for the accommodation of Congress and of the President and for the public offices of the United States" by the end of 1800.

Demands on the new government were large, and money was scarce. The commissioners of the District counted on sales of lots in the new city to finance a substantial part of building construction and street improvements. In this expectation they were to be sadly disappointed. L'Enfant's procrastination in arranging for a printed plan of the city showing the location of the various blocks containing lots to be sold at the auction on October 17, 1791, resulted in the sale of only 35 lots and proceeds of little more than $2,000.[1] Even the final printing of Ellicott's plan did not lead to greater success with the second lot auction a year later.

The commissioners, finding this source of funds a failure, attempted without success to borrow money for the construction of the Capitol and the President's house. Finally, in desperation they agreed to a proposal by James Greenleaf, Robert Morris, and James Nicholson. This syndicate was permitted to purchase 3,000 lots at a favorable price in exchange for a loan of $2,200 each month until the public buildings were completed. Greenleaf, Morris, and Nicholson agreed to construct 10 houses each year for 7 years, but the speculators overextended themselves, and bank-ruptcy put an end to this arrangement in 1797.[2] Public sales of lots during this period brought in some additional cash because of the speculative interest that developed, but other sources had to be found.

The state of Virginia had donated $120,000 and Maryland $72,000 for improvements in the capital city, but these funds proved insufficient.[3] Attempts to borrow money abroad failed. President Washington turned to Maryland for additional help. On December 7, 1796, he sent a forceful, almost desperate, plea to Governor J. H. Stone asking for a loan of $150,000.[4] The General Asembly approved a loan of $100,000, but took the precaution of conditioning it on the pledge of the personal credit of the commissioners as well as that of the federal government.

Slowly work progressed on the difficult task of creating a city from a wilderness, but for a number of years it was difficult to tell one from the other. Thomas Twining, who visited the city in April 1796 after reading some of the glowing descriptions of it distributed by land speculators, tells of entering a wooded area through which a trail had been cut by removing the upper parts of the trees.

"After some time this indistinct way assumed more the appearance of a regular avenue, the trees here having been cut down in a straight line. Although no habitation of any kind was visible, I

---

[1] Constance McLaughlin Green, *Washington: Village and Capital, 1800–1878*, Princeton, 1962, p. 14.

[2] *ibid.*, p. 15.

[3] Joseph B. Varnum, *The Seat of Government of the United States*, New York, 1848, p. 28.

[4] Letter from Washington to Stone, December 7, 1796, the text of which appears in Varnum, *ibid.*, pp. 28–29.

had no doubt but I was now riding along one of the streets of the metropolitan city. I continued in this spacious avenue for half a mile, and then came out upon a large spot, cleared of wood, in the centre of which I saw two buildings on an extensive scale. . . ."[5]

The two buildings were the Capitol, then being constructed, and a nearby tavern. Twining mentions that from this spot he could see "avenues" similar to the one he had traveled piercing the woods in several directions. He remarked on his surprise at seeing the city in such a "sylvan state," since he had been deceived by promotional pamphlets and posters into believing that the city was well advanced.

Later that year Francis Baily, an Englishman whose descriptions of other eastern cities were both accurate and detailed, recorded his impressions of the capital city.

"The private buildings go on but slowly. There are about twenty or thirty houses built near the Point, as well as a few in south Capitol Street and about a hundred others scattered over in other places: in all I suppose about two hundred: and these constitute the great city of Washington. The truth is, that not much more than one-half the city is *cleared:*—the rest is *in woods;* and most of the streets which are laid out are cut through these woods, and have a much more pleasing effect now than I think they will have when they shall be built; for *now* they appear like broad avenues in a park, bounded on each side by thick woods; and there being so many of them, and proceeding in so many various directions, they have a certain wild, yet uniform and regular appearance, which they will lose when confined on each side by brick walls."[6]

Work on the public buildings had commenced with the completion of the city plan. Late in 1792 the commissioners revealed plans for a competition to select designers for the Capitol and the President's mansion. The design submitted by Dr. William Thornton was eventually chosen for the Capitol, the cornerstone of which was laid on September 18, 1793. Only the old north wing

of the present building was completed by 1800. A mile away down the swampy hollows of Pennsylvania Avenue work was also proceeding on the presidential residence. This is shown in Figure 12 as it existed in 1820 after rebuilding following its partial destruction by fire set by the British during the War of 1812. James Hoban, who had won the prize for its design, also assisted the less experienced Thornton in supervising construction of the Capitol. Between these two principal buildings and elsewhere in the city only a few other structures, mostly residences, were under way. Not only was there considerable skepticism about the actual removal of the seat of government from Philadelphia to the new city, which tended to discourage private building, but the regulations that had been adopted by the commissioners in October 1791 made construction somewhat more expensive than in other cities.[7] Although these were suspended by the President in June 1796, their effect in the early years of city development inhibited growth and private investment, especially by speculators who aimed at quick profits.[8]

As the year 1800 approached, the date appointed for the movement of the seat of government from Philadelphia, the commissioners redoubled their efforts to ready the city and the public buildings. They reported that all would be ready by summer, an estimate that proved more optimistic than accurate. In June the executive offices moved to the new city, and in November Congress sat for the first time in the Capitol. President Adams and the members of the Senate and the House of Representatives exchanged congratulations, while Washington society looked on. But in truth the city scarcely deserved the name, nor were the public accommodations completed. Mrs. Adams moved into a presidential residence still partly unplastered and with most of the rooms unfurnished. The East Room, designed for ceremonial occasions, became for a time the place where the family washing was hung. A

[5] Thomas Twining, *Travels in America 100 Years Ago*, New York, 1894, p. 100.
[6] Francis Baily, *Journal of a Tour in Unsettled Parts of North America in 1796 & 1797*, London, 1856, pp. 127–28.

[7] The building regulations adopted by the commissioners and promulgated by the President are quoted in William Tindall, *Standard History of The City of Washington*, Knoxville, 1914, pp. 122–23.
[8] Originally the regulations were suspended from 1796 until 1800. Jefferson, in 1801, ordered a further 9-month extension of this period. See "Declaration Suspending Building Regulations," March 11, 1801, in Saul Padover, *Thomas Jefferson and the National Capital*, Washington, 1946, pp. 196–97.

Figure 12. View of the North Front of the White House: 1820

view of Georgetown and Washington in 1801, reproduced in Figure 13, shows that the "sylvan state" of the capital as Twining had found it five years earlier had scarcely been altered.

Members of Congress grumbled over the primitive state of the city and its lack of accommodations. Representative John Cotton Smith of Connecticut found the place little to his liking and penned his observations in these words:

"One wing of the Capitol only had been erected, which, with the President's house, a mile distant from it, both constructed with white sandstone, were shining objects in dismal contrast with the scene around them. Instead of recognizing the avenues and streets portrayed on the plan of the city, not one was visible, unless we except a road with two buildings on each side of it, called the New Jersey avenue. The Pennsylvania [avenue] . . . was then nearly the whole distance a deep morass, covered with alder bushes. . . ."[9]

Smith described a row of six houses between the President's house and Georgetown, two other groups of two or three dwellings, and a number of isolated houses, the intervening spaces "being covered with shrub oak bushes on the higher grounds, and on the marshy soil either trees or some sort of shrubbery." He commented as well on the muddy and unimproved streets and on the sidewalk built of chips from scraps of the stone used in the Capitol which cut the shoes of those who chanced to walk on its surface. Yet Smith felt strongly that the site chosen for the city held great promise and that President Washington's action in selecting this location "affords a striking exhibition of the discernment, wisdom, and forecast which characterized that illustrious man." And, Smith continued, during his six years in Congress he always opposed the frequent attempts by northern members of Congress to move the seat of government to some more prosperous and developed community.

Improvements in the city came slowly. One of Jefferson's principal contributions was the planting of rows of poplars along Pennsylvania Avenue, which, as the view in 1834 reproduced in Figure 14 shows, served to confine and direct views along this great diagonal boulevard connecting the Capitol with the residence of the President.[10] Certainly the scattered and isolated buildings facing this intended monumental and ceremonial route provided little in the way of grand civic design as envisaged by L'Enfant.

The Washington Canal, which L'Enfant's plan showed as replacing Tiber Creek and running along the north edge of the Mall and then southward to the Anacostia River, received early attention. Benjamin Henry Latrobe, the talented English architect and engineer who had come to America in 1796, took office in 1803 as Surveyor of Public Buildings. His plan in 1804 for the canal and locks at the mouth of the Tiber appears in Figure 15, one of the many proposals advanced for the improvement of the city by this versatile designer.[11] A private company obtained a congressional charter for the canal's construction, but it was not started until 1810, opening five years later. Although the canal was supposed to bring commercial prosperity to the city, its value for shipping turned out to be largely an illusion, and its stagnant waters served chiefly as a handy dumping place for trash and garbage. It was thus not only a menace to health but a source of noxious odors that stifled development along its banks except for woodyards, local industries of various types, and other unsightly uses. The Center Market, authorized by the City Council in 1802 on a site between 7th and 9th Streets north of the Canal, added still further to the confusion, odor, noise, and filth that was to characterize this part of the city until well into the next century.

The most impressive sights of the new city were, of course, the Capitol and the White House and its related buildings for the executive departments. By 1814 the first section of the Capitol, designed by Thornton, had been joined by a covered walkway to a similar structure some distance to the south constructed under

[10] Jefferson's directions on where the trees should be planted appear in a letter from him to Thomas Munroe, March 21, 1803, in Padover, *Thomas Jefferson,* pp. 300–01. Padover also reproduces Jefferson's sketch supplementing the directions.

[11] Latrobe's work in connection with the canal is described in Talbot Hamlin's valuable study, *Benjamin Henry Latrobe,* New York, 1955, pp. 351–54.

[9] Description of Washington in 1800 by John Cotton Smith, as quoted in John B. Ellis, *The Sights and Secrets of the National Capital,* New York, 1869, p. 42.

Figure 13. View of Georgetown and Washington, Looking Southeast: 1801

Figure 14. View of Pennsylvania Avenue to the White House from the Capitol: 1834

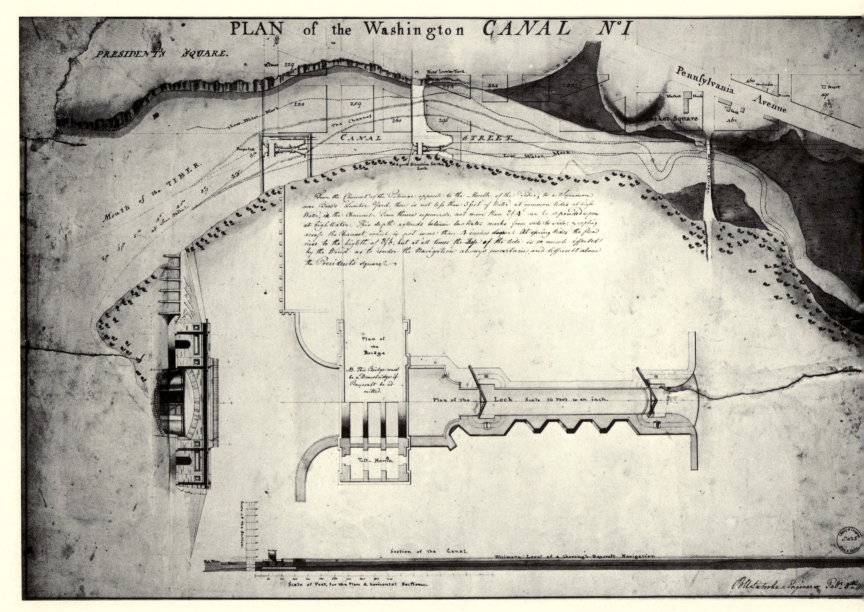

Figure 15. Plan of the Proposed Tiber Canal and Locks by Benjamin Henry Latrobe: 1804

Figure 16. View of the West Front of the Capitol: ca. 1837

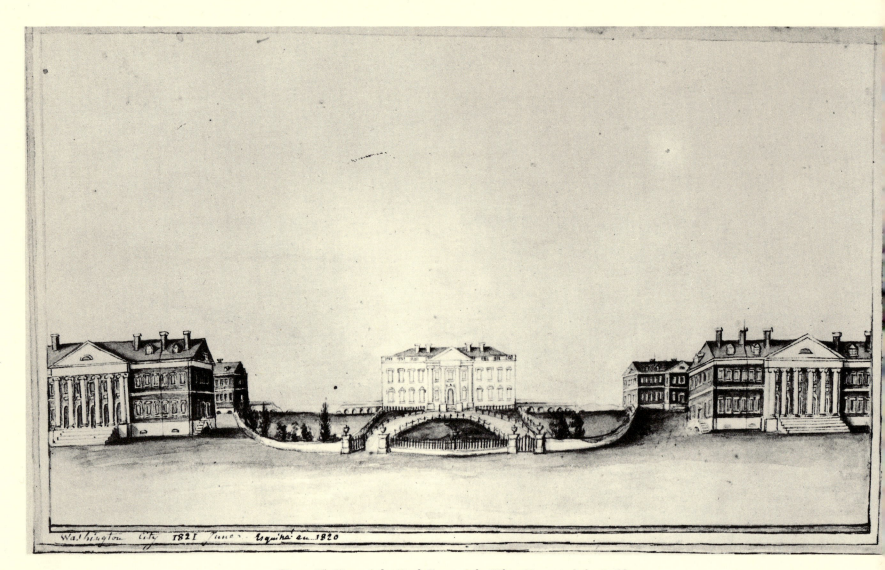

Washington City 1821 June Esquiña eu 1820

Figure 17. View of the North Front of the White House and the Buildings
of the State, Treasury, War, and Navy Department: 1821

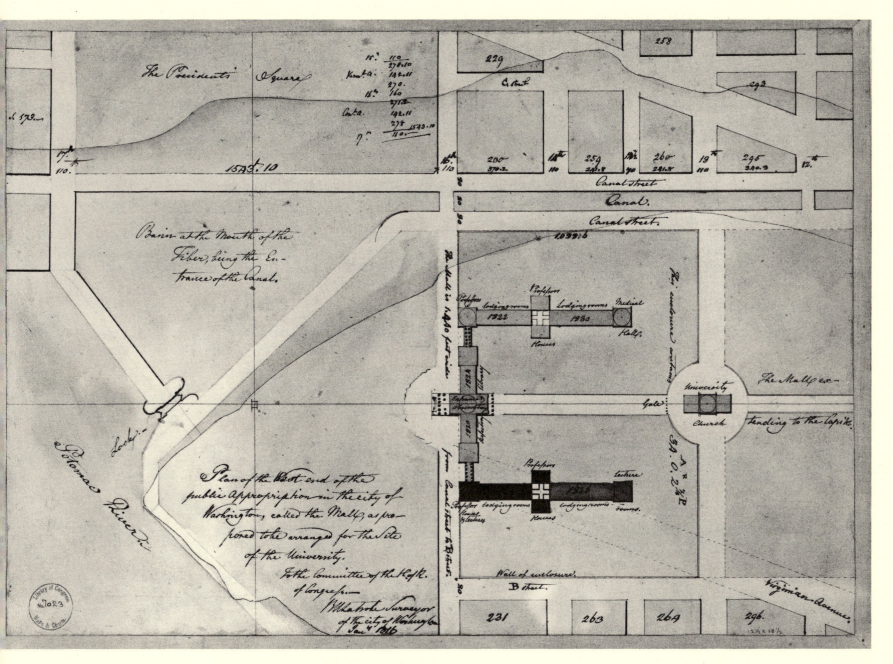

Figure 18. Plan of the Proposed National University by Benjamin Henry Latrobe: 1816

Latrobe's supervision. The space between the two wings was soon filled with a much more massive building designed by Charles Bulfinch connecting the House and Senate structures. By 1837, the approximate date of the view reproduced in Figure 16, the building had assumed monumental proportions with its great west portico projecting toward the Mall and with its copper-sheathed wooden dome glistening in the sun.

At the other end of Pennsylvania Avenue additional buildings occupied the White House grounds. The view in Figure 17, sketched in 1821, shows the north front of the White House. To the east stood two pleasant red brick buildings in Federal Style. The most northerly was occupied by the Department of State, the other by the Treasury. On the right can be seen two almost identical structures. These were the buildings for the War and Navy Departments. The State and War Department buildings, facing that portion of Pennsylvania Avenue which runs east-west north of the White House, were embellished with Ionic porticos and classical pediments in an architectural echo of the White House. The total effect must have been charming.

The Mall, that intended great unifying element for the city, lay virtually unoccupied, although it nearly became the site of major activity in 1816. In that year Latrobe found himself engaged in a project for a national university, an institution which had been considered almost from the founding of the city.[12] Madison, in his message to Congress on December 5, 1810, recommended

the creation of a university, and he repeated this suggestion in his last year of office. Apparently Latrobe's plan of 1816, however, was the first serious study of the form and location for this project. His drawing, dated January 1816, is reproduced in Figure 18 which shows the complex of buildings he proposed for a site near the western end of the Mall directly on the Capitol axis and not far from the proposed site for a memorial to President Washington due south of the White House.

The university was to occupy a walled enclosure extending from 13th to 15th Streets and from B Street southwest (now Independence Avenue) to the Tiber Canal on the north. At the eastern entrance Latrobe proposed a university church standing in the center of a circular space marking the intersection of 13th Street and a boulevard down the center of the Mall. Beyond a gate this boulevard was to continue to the central building, an observatory, with the library and refectory occupying its north and south wings. Colonnaded passageways led beyond to corner structures to be used for professors' houses. Extending at right angles to the east were ranges of connected buildings at either end of the main building. In the center of each, Latrobe showed additional residences for professors flanked on either side by student lodgings. At the end of the projecting wings were to be the medical hall and lecture rooms.

The remarkable similarity of this design to that of the University of Virginia, founded in 1817 by Thomas Jefferson and designed by him, is at once apparent. To what extent Jefferson may have contributed to Latrobe's scheme of a year earlier or may have borrowed from it for his own university plan is not clear. We do know that Latrobe, at Jefferson's request, submitted a number of suggestions for improving the former president's design for the University of Virginia. One of Latrobe's proposals, modified by Jefferson, resulted in the Rotunda, the magnificant central structure that unified the parallel rows of lecture rooms, student dwellings, and professors' houses at the Charlottesville site—an almost exact duplicate of the Latrobe plan for the university on the Washington Mall.[13]

[12] Latrobe himself recounts the interest of President Washington in the founding of a university in the capital. In 1796 Latrobe met Washington at Mount Vernon. During one conversation "The subject was chiefly the establishment of the University at the federal city. He mentioned the offer he had made of giving to it all the interests he had in the city on condition that it should go on in a given time, and complained that, though magnificent offers had been made by many speculators for the same purpose, there seemed to be no inclination to carry them into reality. He spoke as if he felt a little hurt upon the subject." Benjamin Henry Latrobe, *Journal of Latrobe,* New York, 1905, pp. 61–62. According to Green, "President Washington had set aside nineteen acres of land in the city for a national university and had willed his shares in the Potomac Company for its support, but Congress delayed action until the stock was worthless and then, under pressure from extreme states' rights advocates, concluded that the Constitution forbade an appropriation for such a purpose." Green, *Washington,* p. 42.

[13] For Latrobe's contribution to Jefferson's design, see Hamlin, *Latrobe,* pp. 468–70. The founding of the University of Virginia and Jefferson's role

But the long-delayed creation of the national university was once again deferred, and the Latrobe plan was soon forgotten. It was just as well, for splendid as was his concept for what Jefferson was later to term an "academic village," the project would have

in its planning is treated in John S. Patten, *Jefferson, Cabell and the University of Virginia,* New York, 1906. For reproductions of the early Jefferson manuscript plans and views of the proposed university, see William A. Lambeth and Warren Manning, *Thomas Jefferson as an Architect and a Designer of Landscapes,* Boston, 1913; and I. T. Frary, *Thomas Jefferson Architect and Builder,* Richmond, 1931.

made impossible the later, and greater, development of the Mall and its related monuments.

Aside from the Capitol and the White House and its associated buildings, the only other public structure of any consequence in the central part of the city was the City Hall, begun in 1820 on a design prepared by George Hadfield. This occupied the public reservation which came to be known as Judiciary Square. On L'Enfant's plan this appeared as an elongated space, opening to the Mall along what was clearly intended as a minor cross-axis

Figure 19. View of the City Hall, from the South: ca. 1866

following the present line of 4th Street. The building, a view of which is shown in Figure 19, featured a low dome, similar to that of the old Capitol, the entrance was a Greek pediment supported by six columns, and at each end were two projecting porches. Following what later seemed to be a Washington tradition, the building was not completed until 1850, although part of it was occupied earlier by the city government, and the eastern wing was used by the circuit and criminal courts of the United States. The building today, minus its dome, is an impressive structure on an imposing site and a tribute to the skill of its designer.

Somewhat outside the central city, on the banks of the Anacostia between 2nd and 11th Streets southeast lay the Navy Yard, established in 1799. This quickly developed into an important installation, as can be seen in Figure 20, a view of the city in 1834 from the south bank of the Anacostia. Covered drydock facilities appear in the foreground, and other portions of the yard can be seen. Beyond, atop Jenkins Hill, looms the Capitol; the White House can be seen left of center; and at the far left appears the Arsenal, erected at the confluence of the Anacostia and the Potomac, now the site of Fort McNair.

A somewhat less romanticized view of the city in 1838 is reproduced in Figure 21. This is from the west side of the Potomac looking from the Custis-Lee mansion northeast to the mouth of the Tiber Canal, the then desolate Mall, and the White House with its open gardens stretching down to the water near the present site of the Washington Monument. The view indicates that, despite four decades of efforts at municipal improvements, the capital city amounted to little more than an overgrown village spread loosely over its enormous site and dotted here and there with large but unrelated public buildings.

The scattered dwellings, the unbuilt-on public reservations, the streets that were muddy or dusty depending on the weather, the weedgrown Mall, all contrasted markedly with the grandiose plan and the great area of the city. Visitors from home and abroad alike seldom failed to mock the pretensions of future grandeur held out by the supporters of the city and its imported plan. The setback to urban growth and public improvements brought about by the burning of the President's house, the Capitol, and the build-

ings occupied by the Treasury, State, War, and Navy Departments by British troops in 1814, strengthened such observations.

Visitors from the British Isles seemed to take particular delight in criticizing the capital city of their former colony. On his visit in 1804 the Irish poet Thomas Moore was inspired to write the following satirical lines:

In fancy now beneath the twilight gloom,
Come, let me lead thee o'er this "second Rome,"
Where tribunes rule, where dusky Davi bow,
And what was Goose Creek once is Tiber now.
This embryo capital, where Fancy sees
Squares in morasses, obelisks in trees;
Which second sighted seers e'en now adorn
With shrines unbuilt and heroes yet unborn,
Though now but woods and J——n they see
Where streets should run and sages *ought* to be.[14]

Morris Birkbeck, who visited Washington in 1817 while in America to establish a colony in Illinois, scornfully commented on the marble carvings brought from Italy to adorn the Capitol, and doubtless with the French L'Enfant also in mind, as showing "how *un*-American is the whole plan." [15] In the same year a Scot observer, John M. Duncan, dourly observed:

"To lay out the plan of a city . . . is one thing, and to build it is another; of all the regularity and system which the engraved plan exhibits, scarcely a trace is discernible upon the ground. Instead of beginning this gigantic undertaking in a central spot, and gradually extending the buildings from a common focus, they appear to have commenced at once in twenty or thirty different places, without the slightest regard to concentration or the comforts of good neighborhood; and a stranger looking round him for Washington, sees two houses here, and six there, and a dozen yonder, scattered in straggling groups over the greater part of three or four square miles. Hitherto the city does not contain above fourteen thousand

[14] Thomas Moore, "To Thomas Hume, Esq., M.D. from the City of Washington," *Poetical Works,* New York, 1868, p. 178.
[15] Morris Birkbeck, *Notes on a Journey in America from the Coast of Virginia to the Territory of Illinois,* London, 1818, p. 29.

Figure 20. View of Washington from the South Bank of the Anacostia River: 1834

VIEW OF THE CITY OF WASHINGTON,

THE METROPOLIS OF THE UNITED STATES OF AMERICA.

TAKEN FROM ARLINGTON HOUSE, THE RESIDENCE OF GEORGE WASHINGTON P. CUSTIS ESQ.

Figure 21. View of Washington from the West Bank of the Potomac: 1838

inhabitants, but these have taken root in so many different places, that the public crier . . . is obliged to make the circuit on horse-back." [16]

Humorous names for the city and its features were legion. The minister from Portugal, the Abbé Corrêa da Serra, apparently originated the title of Washington as "The City of Magnificent Distances." Pennsylvania Avenue was referred to as "the great Serbonian Bog," the Capitol as "the palace in the wilderness." Georgetown, it was said, was "a city of houses without streets," and Washington "a city of streets without houses." [17]

Strangely enough, Mrs. Frances Trollope, who found little else in America to the liking of her refined senses, perceived the underlying merit of building a great city on a preconceived plan when she stopped in Washington in 1830:

"I was delighted with the whole aspect of Washington. . . . It has been laughed at by foreigners, and even by natives, because the original plan of the city was upon an enormous scale, and but a very small part of it has been as yet executed. But I confess I see nothing in the least degree ridiculous about it; the original design, which was as beautiful as it was extensive, has been in no way departed from, and all that has been done has been done well. . . . To a person who has been travelling much through the country, and marked the immense quantities of new manufactories, new canals, new rail-roads, new towns, and new cities, which are springing, as it were, from the earth in every part of it, the appearance of the metropolis rising gradually into life and splendour, is a spectacle of high historic interest." [18]

In contrast to Mrs. Trollope's admiration for the city stand Charles Dickens' scathing remarks written after his tour of America in 1842. He recalled Corrêa de Serra's earlier appellation for the city, observing that Washington "might with greater propriety be termed the City of Magnificent Intentions." He noted "Spacious avenues, that begin in nothing, and lead nowhere; streets, mile-long, that only want houses, roads and inhabitants; public buildings that need but a public to be complete; and ornaments of great thoroughfares, which only lack great thoroughfares to ornament. . . ." [19]

Although Dickens admired the Capitol and its imposing site, his over-all impression of the city was devastatingly uncomplimentary:

"Take the worst parts of the City Road and Pentonville, or the straggling outskirts of Paris. . . . Burn the whole down, build it up again in wood and plaster; widen it a little . . . ; put green blinds outside all the private houses, with a red curtain and a white one in every window; plough up all the roads; plant a great deal of coarse turf in every place where it ought *not* to be; erect three handsome buildings in stone and marble, anywhere, but the more entirely out of everybody's way the better; call one the Post Office, one the Patent Office, and one the Treasury; make its scorching hot in the morning, and freezing cold in the afternoon, with an occasional tornado of wind and dust; leave a brick-field without the bricks in all central places where a street may naturally be expected; and that's Washington.

"Such as it is, it is likely to remain." [20]

Although primitive conditions as described (and exaggerated) by these observers existed in many of the other young cities of America, the situation in Washington, which was undeniably bad, was aggravated by the system of local government in the District and the failure of Congress to provide adequate funds for general municipal improvements. Instead of establishing a unified governmental body for the District of Columbia, Congress allowed the existing cities of Georgetown and Alexandria to continue, incorporated a new city of Washington, and established a county government for that portion of the District outside the boundaries of the three incorporated cities. In 1800 the population in Washington City numbered only slightly more than 3,000, while Georgetown

[16] John M. Duncan, *Travels Through Part of the United States and Canada in 1818 and 1819,* Glasgow, 1823, p. 254.
[17] H. Paul Caemmerer, *Washington the National Capital,* Washington, 1932, p. 41.
[18] Frances Trollope, *Domestic Manners of the Americans,* London, 1832, p. 176.

[19] Charles Dickens, *American Notes,* London, 1842, p. 97.
[20] *ibid.,* pp. 96–97.

41

had about the same number and Alexandria could boast nearly 5,000. Not until 1840 did the population of the City of Washington, then 23,364, amount to more than half of the District's population of 43,712.[21] The burden of providing for most of the new streets and such utility services as could be arranged thus fell on the taxpayers of only a portion of the residents in the federal district. Later, as will be seen, a consolidation of local governments was carried out, thus permitting a unified tax base. By that time, however, one-third of the District had been retroceded to Virginia by congressional action in 1846, thus removing from governmental jurisdiction that portion of the original district which lay west of the Potomac.

Difficulties facing the infant City of Washington increased. While the value of federal lands and buildings mounted as construction of governmental structures proceeded, no taxes could be levied on this property to help pay for local projects and services. Congress, pressed for funds to provide for the needs of an entire nation, persistently slighted the requests for assistance that were continually laid before it by city authorities. This niggardly attitude, which prevailed for decades, resulted in the miserable conditions that Dickens and other visitors found so repugnant.[22] Doubtless this parsimonious treatment by Congress found favor with those who hoped that the seat of government would be moved to another location. This feeling was shared by many if not most of the senators and representatives from northern states.

By mid-century, despite these difficulties, the capital city had begun to take shape. On Jenkins Hill the two wings of the Capitol, united at first only by a wooden passageway, had finally been joined by a central structure designed by Etienne Hallet. As modified and extended by Latrobe and Bulfinch the central element was topped by a low wooden dome sheathed in copper.

In 1851 President Millard Fillmore laid the cornerstone for a

[21] Census figures taken from Green, *Washington,* p. 21.

[22] The case for federal assistance to the city was forcefully summarized by Joseph Varnum in 1848 in his *Seat of Government,* pp. 28–37. Varnum argued that proceeds from the sale of government lots should be devoted to municipal improvements and that payments in lieu of taxes on federal property should be made. According to his calculations, the federal government "owed" the city in 1848 the sum of $1,800,000.

vast expansion of the Capitol following designs prepared by Thomas U. Walter. This new plan provided for two large wings at right angles to and on either side of the existing building. These were to provide new chambers for the House and Senate, together with offices and ancilliary facilities. A new and much larger dome of cast iron was also projected to replace the old one of copper-covered wood. The House wing was occupied in 1857, that of the Senate two years later; the dome was not to be completed until after the Civil War.

The view of Washington in 1852, appearing in Figure 22, shows the Capitol as it was soon to be. In the distance are several other new or projected buildings. Uncomfortably near the center of the Mall and somewhat more than halfway from the Capitol to the Potomac can be seen the Smithsonian Institution, begun in 1847. In 1826 James Smithson, an Englishman who had never visited the United States, left his fortune to the government of that nation for an institution devoted to further research and the diffusion of knowledge. It took Congress twenty years to decide to accept the bequest and to provide a site, but at last the cornerstone was laid for a building to house a museum, library, and research facilities. James Renwick prepared the plans for the structure, a romantic red brick building with towers and turrets in the Norman or Lombard style, an unlikely design indeed for a major building on such a highly visible site in a city where neo-classic motifs had been utilized so consistently.

Much nearer the Capitol and encroaching equally on the Mall—although not visible in the view of 1852—lay the Botanic Garden, authorized by Congress for a site at the foot of Capitol Hill and almost directly in front of the Capitol's west front. Here were to stand the greenhouses containing specimens of plants brought back from all over the world by the expedition commanded by Lt. Charles Wilkes. The choice of the site may have appeared reasonable to members of Congress in the middle of the nineteenth century when the Mall was little more than a vast meadow, but it proved to be one of the many unfortunate decisions taken by that body which half a century later was to make immensely more difficult the revitalization of L'Enfant's plan for the Mall.

North of the Mall and the Washington Canal and south of

Figure 22. View of Washington from the Capitol Northwest to the White House: 1852

Figure 23. View of the Robert Mills Design of 1836 for the Washington Monument

Pennsylvania Avenue, the view reveals a hodge-podge of buildings and vacant lots that already had become something of a slum and was destined to deteriorate further when the city became a place of refuge for escaped and freed slaves during and after the Civil War. The expansion of Center Market over the years added to the surrounding blight.

By 1867 this section of the city would become disgracefully overcrowded. Then known as "Murder Bay," the area was described by the head of the Metropolitan Police in a report to the Common Council in these words:

"Here crime, filth and poverty seem to vie with each other in a career of degradation and death. . . . Whole families are crowded into mere apologies for shanties, which are without light or ventilation . . . . Their rooms are usually not more than six or eight feet square, and not a window or even an opening (except a door) for the admission of light. Some of the rooms are entirely surrounded by other rooms, so that no light at all reaches where persons spend their nights and days. In a space about fifty yards square I found about a hundred families composed of about three to five persons each living in shanties one story in height except in a few instances where tenements are actually built on top of others. . . ."[23]

Far in the distance near the marshes of the Potomac River on a slight rise in the ground the projected monument to President Washington can be seen. Work on the great obelisk began in 1848 following a design prepared by Robert Mills, illustrated in Figure 23. Funds for its construction had been raised by public subscription, the only congressional action being the granting of the site. Owing to unsatisfactory subsurface conditions at the intersection of the White House and Capitol axes, where L'Enfant intended the memorial to be placed, its location had to be shifted some 370 feet east of the White House axis and 123 feet south of the Capitol axis—a deviation from the original city plan that was to cause great problems at a later date. The shaft was 156 feet

[23] W. W. Moore, "Contraband Suffrage," *Journal of the 64th Council of Washington*, June 6, 1867, as quoted in James H. Whyte, *The Uncivil War*, New York, 1958, p. 32.

high in 1854 when lack of funds halted construction until 1879, when the project came under direct federal jurisdiction. The Mills design called for an elaborate base, never to be carried out although for many years artists depicting the federal capital included it in their drawings.

North of the monument, across the Tiber Canal, the White House faced a most unimpressive landscape. While some effort to improve the immediate surroundings had been made, the public reservation lying south of E Street was nothing but an untidy patch of meadow sloping down to the tidal marshes of the Potomac. The romantic view of the south front of the White House shown in Figure 24 bears little resemblance to reality.

Far more imposing was the new Treasury building, designed by Robert Mills in 1836, which extended along 15th Street from Pennsylvania Avenue to G Street. This great structure with its long colonnaded façade appears in Figure 25. Its original size was later extended to the west to assume the form it has today. But even from the beginning its southern end blocked completely the reciprocal view between the White House and Capitol—one of the fundamental features of the city's plan.[24] According to tradition it was President Andrew Jackson, impatient with the delays in constructing a replacement for the old building which had burned in 1833, who finally made the decision about its site. Jackson is properly revered for his statecraft, but he had little appreciation for architecture or city planning, and his ill-informed action must rank as one of the city's great misfortunes.

Seven blocks east of the Treasury on the site designated by

L'Enfant for the national church, another massive public building began to take shape in 1837. This was the Patent Office, designed by William P. Elliott, who produced a restrained Greek Revival structure of great power and dignity. Although not fully completed until 31 years after the laying of its cornerstone, a portion of the Patent Office was occupied as early as 1840. This fine building as it appeared just before the Civil War is shown in Figure 26. Now the National Portrait Gallery, the old Patent Office building provides a fine vista up 8th Street from the more elaborate National Archives building, which it faces three blocks south on Pennsylvania Avenue.

The other major building in central Washington of this period was the General Post Office, later the General Land Office. The site was a poor one, a small block immediately south of the east wing of the Patent Office. Robert Mills' design in 1830 was impressive enough, as the view in Figure 27 demonstrates. Corinthian columns and pilasters extending two floors above a rusticated ground story supported an entablature and parapet, and the use of white marble made this building doubly imposing. But development of private buildings around this node of federal activity soon so hemmed in the structure that only with difficulty could an observer appreciate the architect's achievements. A location facing one of the numerous public reservations or terminating a street vista would have been far more appropriate for this noble edifice, which is currently occupied by the Tariff Commission.

Other federal buildings were erected in the years before the Civil War, although they were located at the edges of the city and thus did not contribute to the realization of the great central composition that L'Enfant had intended. Southwest of the White House on the banks of the Potomac stood the Naval Observatory, which opened in 1844. This site appeared on the L'Enfant plan as a major reservation, although he did not designate its specific use. At the old site of Carrollsburg a penitentiary joined the Arsenal at the mouth of the Anacostia. Northeasterly up that river at the eastern end of the city could be found the Marine Hospital and Poor House, now the site of the District of Columbia General Hospital. Immediately to the south lay the Congressional Cemetery. Of this, one Senator in 1877 referring to the grim, conical-

[24] Varnum, in his review of the problems and prospects of the capital city in 1848, commented on the location of the Treasury as follows: "The treasury building . . . is so badly situated as to ruin its appearance, and entirely exclude from view the President's house, and to obstruct the distant and beautiful prospect from the East room of that edifice, through the line of F street. The building, although nearly four hundred feet in length, will scarcely be visible except from the street immediately before it; and the three finest porticoes will front upon the President's kitchen garden. . . . It is now past remedy. . . . We mention it here for the purpose of expressing the hope that the many works of this kind, hereafter to be erected in Washington, and the objects of the fine arts with which it is constantly proposed to embellish them, will not escape the notice of our academies of design, and men of taste in other cities." Varnum, *Seat of Government*, pp. 26–27.

Figure 24. View of the White House from the Potomac River: ca. 1827

Figure 25. View of the Treasury Building: ca. 1867

Figure 26. View of the Patent Office: ca. 1860

Figure 27. View of the Post Office: ca. 1869

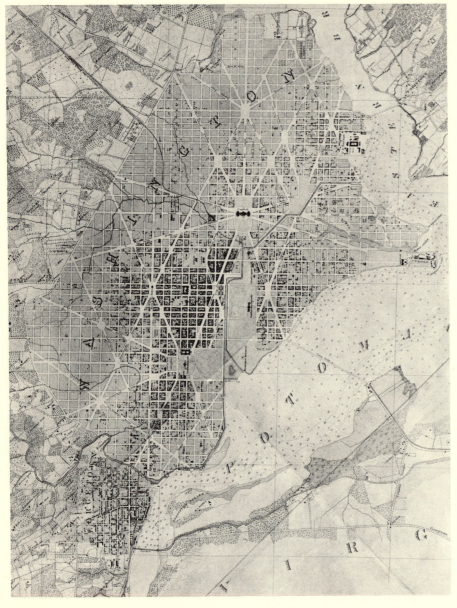

Figure 28. Portion of Topographical Map of the District of Columbia: 1861

topped square monuments remarked that "they added a new terror to death." [25]

By the end of the 1850's some of the scattered areas of development had begun to coalesce. The urban pattern in 1861 appears in great detail on Boschke's topographic map of that year, a portion of which is reproduced in Figure 28. If the city still lacked the monumental quality that Washington, Jefferson, and L'Enfant anticipated, at least the opportunities for its eventual development on these lines had not been basically impaired. The Mall, true enough, was a "mere cow pasture," as Joseph Varnum observed, and the Botanic Garden greenhouses and the Smithsonian Institution had been carelessly located, but no fatal errors had as yet been made. It remained to be seen if the latent opportunities would be seized by those responsible for guiding the growth of the city in the last decades of the century.

One final pre-Civil War effort to improve the city remains to be described. This involved a major attempt to give form and meaning to the Mall, which L'Enfant had envisaged as a great avenue lined by noble buildings at the outer edges of both of its sides. In 1850 President Fillmore retained Andrew Jackson Downing, the prominent landscape gardener, to design the White House grounds and the vast extent of land stretching westwards from the Capitol. Downing was an ardent disciple of the romantic school of landscape design. As editor of *The Horticulturist,* the leading journal of the field, he became quite influential. In its pages he had earlier expressed his unbounded admiration for the curvilinear and "naturalistic" designs for such rural cemeteries as Mount Auburn in Cambridge, and Greenwood in Brooklyn. He pointed to these cemeteries as models for urban parks and argued for the acquisition of land for such purposes.[26] In Washington Downing

[25] Senator George F. Hoar of Massachusetts, as quoted in U.S. Federal Writers' Project, *Washington: City and Capital,* Washington, 1937, p. 614.
[26] The design of these rural cemeteries and the part they played in the 19th-century American park movement are illustrated and described in my *The Making of Urban America,* Princeton, 1965, pp. 325–31. Most of Downing's editorials in *The Horticulturist* dealing with cemeteries and the need for parks can be found in A. J. Downing, *Rural Essays,* New York, 1853.

saw his great opportunity, since here lay a largely vacant site in the very center of the city.

Downing's own practical experience in landscape design had been almost entirely confined to isolated estates in the Hudson River Valley. He was scarcely prepared to cope with the problems of landscape treatment appropriate for an essentially baroque city. Moreover, the fashion of landscape design dictated romantic treatment of all open space, no matter how formal and symmetrical might be the placement of nearby buildings. The *jardin anglais* was the fad; Washington must conform. Indeed, in the first paragraph of Downing's report to the President he stated as one of his objectives "to give an example of the natural style of Landscape Gardening which may have an influence on the general taste of the Country." [27]

For "The President's Park or Parade," the grounds south of the White House, Downing proposed a large open space for military reviews surrounded by a circular carriage drive. Anticipating by more than a century a feature of the recent plan for Pennsylvania Avenue, he proposed a monumental entrance to the grounds of the White House at the end of Pennsylvania Avenue. This was to be a triumphal arch of marble, beyond which two carriage roads would lead to the parade grounds and a third to the White House as the private entrance for the President. Downing's manuscript report includes a small sketch of this architectural element. The location of these features may be seen in the lower right-hand portion of his plan, which is reproduced in Figure 29.

Downing suggested that a suspension bridge should be constructed across the Tiber Canal leading from the White House grounds to what he termed the Monument Park. A small sketch of this structure also appears in his report. This portion of the Mall he proposed "to plant . . . wholly with *American* trees, of large growth, disposed in open groups, so as to alow [sic] of fine vistas of the Potomac river." [28]

East of the Monument Park, in an area of some 16 acres, Downing planned an Evergreen Garden in the form of a series of concentric elliptical paths combined with several diagonals. In it would be found all varieties of evergreen trees, native and foreign, hardy in the Washington climate. Adjoining this section of the Mall in Downing's plan lay the Smithsonian Park or Pleasure Grounds, consisting of "an arrangement of choice trees in the natural style. The plots near the Institution would be thickly planted with the rarest trees and shrubs, to give greater seclusion and beauty to its immediate precincts." [29]

Adjacent to the Smithsonian grounds was to be a Fountain Park, with a fountain and pond as its chief feature. Downing suggested that the canal should be diverted from its present location to provide additional space. He may have known of L'Enfant's earlier proposal for a grand cascade to tumble from the base of the Capitol and enter the canal at this point, and adapted this more formal recommendation to his own naturalistic plan.

Finally, at the very foot of Capitol Hill, where the Botanic Garden had already been established, Downing proposed a new landscape treatment of "hardy plants." At the eastern end of the Botanic Garden, "opposite the middle gate of the Capitol Grounds," would be an exit gateway to the system of interrelated parks, which, in Downing's words,

". . . would afford some of the most beautifully varied carriage-drives in the world. These drives would be hard gravel roads 40 feet wide and . . . would cover an extent of between 4 and 5 miles in circuit. The foot paths, 12 to 20 feet wide, would give additional interest by showing the grounds more in detail.

"The pleasing natural undulations of surface, where they occur, I propose to retain, instead of expending money in reducing them to a level. The surface of the Parks, generally, should be kept in grass or lawn. . . ." [30]

Downing's report concluded with an eloquent statement on the national value of the Washington parks:

[27] A. J. Downing, *Explanatory Notes to Accompany the Plan for Improving the Public Grounds at Washington,* March 3, 1851. Manuscript in National Archives, Record Group No. 42, LR, Vol. 32, No. 1358½. I am indebted to Mr. John N. Pearce of the Smithsonian Institution for calling my attention to this document.
[28] *ibid.*
[29] *ibid.*
[30] *ibid.*

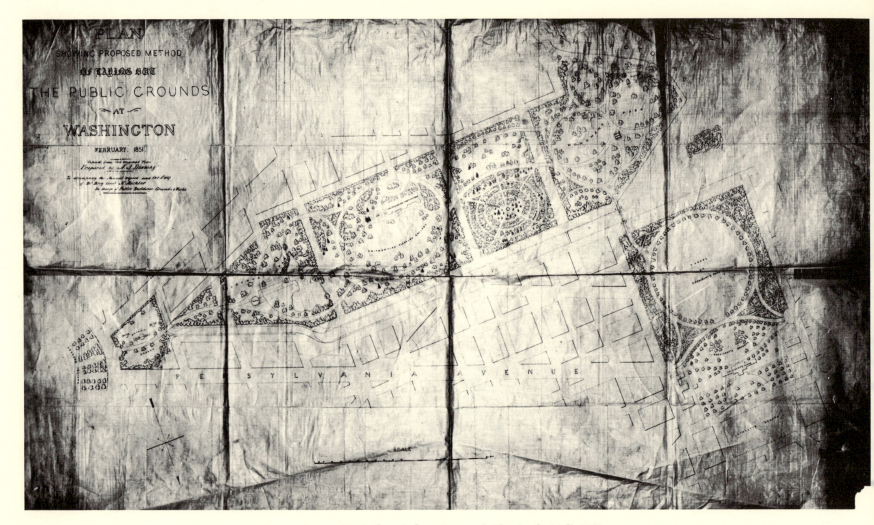

Figure 29. Andrew Jackson Downing's Plan for the Mall: 1851

"A national Park like this, laid out and planted in a thorough manner, would exercise as much influence on the public taste as Mount Auburn Cemetery near Boston, has done. Though only twenty years have elapsed since that spot was laid out, the lesson there taught has been so largely influential that at the present moment the United States, while they have no public parks, are acknowledged to possess the finest rural cemeteries in the world. The Public Grounds at Washington, treated in the manner I have here suggested, would undoubtedly become a Public School of Instruction in everything that relates to the tasteful arrangement of parks and grounds, and the growth and culture of trees, while they would serve, more than anything else that could be devised, to embellish and give interest to the Capital. The straight lines and broad Avenues of the streets of Washington would be pleasantly relieved and contrasted by the beauty of curved lines and natural groups of trees in the various parks. By its numerous public buildings and broad avenues, Washington will one day command the attention of every stranger, and if its un-improved public grounds are tastefully improved they will form the most perfect background or setting to the City, concealing many of its defects and heightening all its beauties." [31]

Downing's plan for the Mall, if viewed without consideration to its location in the city, its relation to existing public buildings, and its essential function of providing direct visual ties with the major elements of the urban scene, was not without merit. The sinuous, undulating lines of the drives and walks exhibit the highest craft of this facile designer. But the scheme was grossly inappropriate for this unique site and indicated Downing's complete misunderstanding of the imperatives so clearly dictated by the L'Enfant plan. Only a portion of a revised version of this plan was ever carried out, and this was to make more difficult the task of later planners in establishing a design more suitable to the surroundings and one which would compliment rather than subjugate the buildings which faced this great central open space.[32]

Improvements to the city and the federal buildings came to a virtual halt during the Civil War. All of the energies of Congress and the Executive focused on the preservation of the union through military victory. With peace came new problems and new requirements. Needed city improvements which had been deferred had to be provided, and the assertion of federal powers during the war were never fully relinquished. The steady growth of federal bureaucracy in the latter years of the century attested to the assumption of new functions by the national government. The necessities of war production speeded the industrial revolution in America, and the transition from a rural and agricultural society to one based on industry and commerce received a powerful stimulus. Inevitably the functions of central government multiplied.

Moreover, Washington became the mecca for the new freedmen, liberated from southern serfdom. The Negro population of Washington, which had numbered roughly one-quarter of its total during the period from 1800 to 1850, jumped to almost one-third by 1870. Substantial numbers of white immigrants from Europe, who began to flood the country after the war, were also attracted to Washington. The white population in 1850 had been 40,000; in 1870 the figure stood at 109,000. The Negro population for the same years increased from 10,000 to 35,000.

Two views of the city in 1869 and 1871 serve as valuable documents illustrating the increasingly urban character of the city. The earlier, reproduced in Figure 30, shows in considerable detail the White House and related buildings. To the left appears Lafayette Square, by that time an urbane residential neighborhood of fine character. To the right the unfinished stub of the Washington Monument stands rather forlornly in the unkempt fields at the west end of the Mall. The portion of the city stretching toward the Capitol to the east is punctuated by a dozen or more major church spires and towers.

The view from the Capitol in 1871, shown in Figure 31, reveals the new cast-iron dome of that structure in all its glory. Just to its left one can see the greenhouses of the Botanic Gardens, with the

---

[31] *ibid.*
[32] A view of the city drawn in 1852 shows what the Mall and the White House grounds would have like looked had the Downing plan been

followed. See *Washington, D.C. with Projected Improvements,* drawn by B. F. Smith, published by Smith and Jenkins, New York, 1852. A copy is in the Division of Prints and Photographs, Library of Congress.

The Corcoran Art Building.   Franklin School.   War Department.   Treasury Department.   Patent Office.   Post Office.   Winder Building.   Navy Department.   Smithsonian Institute.   Agricultural Bureau.   General Grant's Head-Quarters.   Washington Monument.
White House.   Navy Yard.

WASHINGTON CITY, D.C.—SKETCHED BY THEO. R. DAVIS.—[SEE PAGE 170.]

*Figure 30. View of Washington, Looking East from the White House to the
Capitol: 1869*

Figure 31. View of Washington, Looking from the Capitol Northwest to the White House: 1871

Smithsonian beyond. To the right, above the north wing of the Capitol, the gleaming buildings of the old City Hall, the Patent Office, and the General Land Office face southwards toward the residential quarter north of Pennsylvania Avenue. A detailed and accurate map of the city in 1870, which can be examined in connection with these two views, is reproduced in Figure 32. Several of the features shown on this drawing will be referred to later.

If Washington at last seemed to be taking on the character of a city, serious deficiencies still remained. Dr. William Tindall, who served as a Washington city official for many years during this era, recalls the face the community presented in those days:

"Nearly all of the streets were dirt roadways. Where these were improved they were rudely covered with gravel, from which, in dry weather, clouds of dust arose with the breezes or from the passing vehicles, and many of the streets were almost impassable in times of heavy rains. The few that were improved with a more durable surface . . . were paved with the roughest sort of cobble or other irregularly shaped stones, destructive alike to the vehicles which traveled upon them, and to the nerves of those by whom those vehicles were occupied." [33]

Tindall describes Tiber creek, the Washington Canal, Slash Run, and other water courses as little more than open sewers. Disposal of garbage and the keeping of domestic animals led to conditions almost medieval.

"The facilities for the collection and disposal of garbage and other refuse were in keeping with the other primitive features of municipal control. Garbage was fed to hogs in hog pens in almost every part of the city. Many cowsheds also lent their influence to pollute the air. Chickens and geese, and cows and other cattle roamed at large in many localities. One of my friends, upon his return from church one Sunday morning, found a 400 pound hog asleep in his front vestibule. Scavenger service offended both sense and sentiment, and the most noisome kinds of offal and refuse were dumped daily on the surface of the commons in the southwest part of the city, in the vicinity of O Street and the Canal." [34]

Into this urban wilderness in 1871 stepped an extraordinary individual in the person of Alexander Robey Shepherd. During a remarkably brief but enormously productive period he was to bring about a transformation in the appearance of the city of Washington and to complete vast improvements in its street, utility, and sanitary facilities. In his role as an American Haussmann he was to earn the same kind of hatred and eventual disfavor that was the lot of the energetic and ruthless Prefect of the Seine, who had recently completed the renovation of the French capital under Napoleon III. It was under Shepherd's leadership that Washington suddenly emerged as a modern city from its dusty background as an overgrown, sleepy southern village.

Shepherd was an aggressive young businessman, active in construction and land speculation, who had interested himself in the reform of local government in the District. He was one of an increasing number of Washingtonians demanding a unified government for the entire District as one solution to the difficulties of financing necessary local improvements. He may also have been motivated, as others surely were, by the fear that the growing Negro population in the city, which suddenly found itself enfranchised, would gain control of the city government. In addition he was spurred by a recent renewal of the old movement to change the seat of government to some other city. Joseph Medill, publisher of the Chicago *Tribune,* and Horace Greeley, with his advocacy of the west, were among national figures who championed such a step. [35]

---

[33] William Tindall, "A Sketch of Alexander Robey Shepherd," Columbia Historical Society, *Records,* XIV, Washington, 1911, p. 55.

[34] *ibid.,* p. 56.

[35] Albert Richardson, a shrewd observer of the national scene, felt certain in 1867 that the capital would be moved: "I fancy . . . it will not be many generations, before the National Capital will be removed beyond the Mississippi River. For a time, the jealousy of the rival cities of St. Louis, Chicago, and Cincinnati may defer the change, and the fact that we have already expended twenty-five millions in public buildings may make our thrifty tax-payers hold out a vigorous opposition; but, for all that, it is sure to come one day." Albert Richardson, "Our National Capital in the Summer of 1867," *Garnered Sheaves from the Writings of Albert D. Richardson,* Hartford, 1871, p. 159.

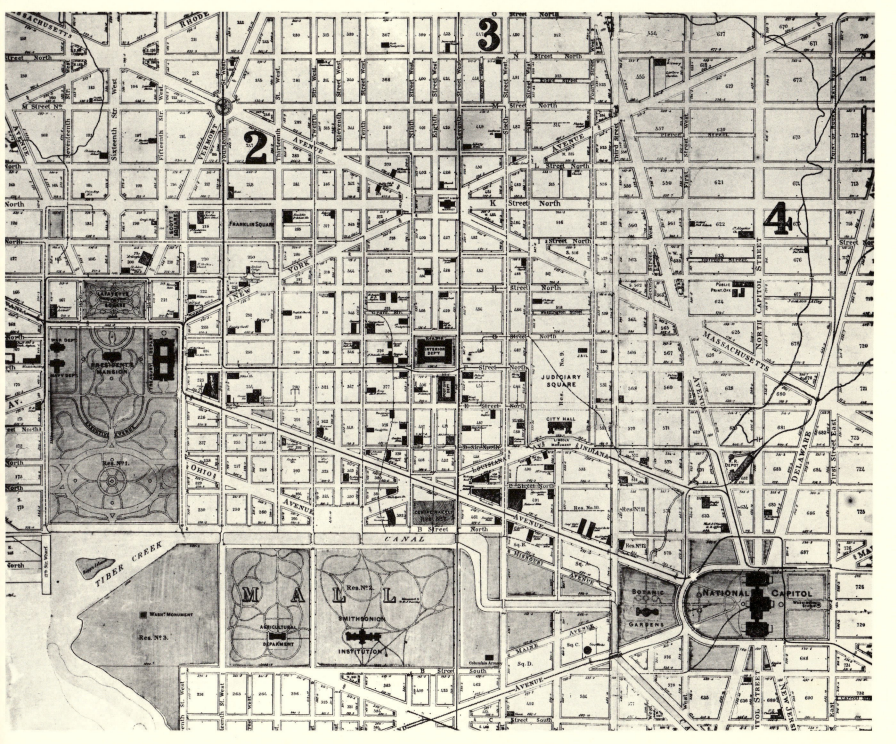

Figure 32. Portion of Plan of Washington: 1870

Congress was persuaded early in 1871 to approve a new form of government for Washington. Under this plan a territorial system of administration was proclaimed covering the entire District. The law provided for a governor, a council of eleven members to be appointed by the President and confirmed by the Senate, an elected house of delegates of twenty-two members, and a five-man Board of Public Works appointed by the President, of which the Governor of the territory would be a member.[36]

Shepherd was only 37, but he had already served as a member of the Washington Common Council for three years, being elected its President in 1862, and he had been elected to membership of the Board of Aldermen in 1870. He seemed to be universally admired as a young man with both ambition and ability. Moreover, he had become friendly with President Grant. It was only natural that he should be appointed to the Board of Public Works and hardly surprising that at its first meeting in May 1871 he would be selected as Vice-President of the Board. Henry D. Cooke, Governor of the District, served as President of the Board *ex officio;* real authority for its activities, however, rested with Shepherd. The territorial plan of government placed almost unfettered authority in the hands of the Board of Public Works, and Shepherd determined that this power should be utilized swiftly and dramatically in a vast public improvement program that would change the face of Washington.

In June the Board revealed a comprehensive plan of street and utility improvements. There can be little doubt that the plan was Shepherd's inspiration. The proposal called for expenditures of $6,250,000, $4,000,000 of which was to be raised by a bond issue and the balance collected through assessments on benefited private property. No such public works program on this scale had even been contemplated before, and neither the elected officials nor the citizens of the District quite grasped its implications. Neither, perhaps, did Shepherd, who for all of his experience in speculative land development and small construction projects, lacked experience in administering a program of this magnitude.

Moreover, the Board of Public Works resolved to carry out the contemplated improvements in the shortest possible time.

Soon the District found itself invaded by grading and construction crews. The Board established standard unit cost figures for various types of construction and awarded contracts for different projects to anyone who agreed to the terms. This saved the time that would ordinarily be spent in taking competitive bids and eliminated the need for careful engineering plans. It also proved a wasteful procedure which added unnecessarily to the cost of the projects and provided a basis for charges of favoritism and corruption which substantial property owners of the city were quick to bring.

The program included the establishment of new grades on many miles of streets and avenues. Little attention had been paid to this in the past; the street lines shown on L'Enfant's plan had simply been hacked through the woods, leaving most of the natural hills and depressions. Adequate storm and sanitary sewage drainage required more uniform street slopes, and extensive cut and fill operations were soon undertaken. The results may have been satisfactory from an engineering standpoint, but for many Washingtonians they proved an unmitigated curse. The former chief clerk of the Board recalled many years later some of the hardships faced by property owners:

"It was not pleasant for a man who owned a house to find his street cut all the way from five to twenty feet down, and his dwelling left up in the air, as it were. On the other hand, the man who owned a house upon a street which was filled for several feet found himself way below the grade, so that possibly he could have stepped from his second-story window to the pavement." [37]

Excavations for sewers, construction of curbs, sidewalks, and streets, the planting of trees, and the building of new bridges and culverts took place all over the city. When Congress returned to Washington late in 1871 its members must have been astounded at the changed appearance of the city. It was inevitable that the

[36] The background of this law is described in Whyte, *Uncivil War,* pp. 90–113; and Green, *Washington,* pp. 313–38.

[37] Franklin T. Howe, "The Board of Public Works," Columbia Historical Society *Records,* III, Washington, 1900, p. 267.

inconveniences and the hardships caused by this vast program should ignite the hostility of many. The Washington *Patriot* gave voice to these complaints:

"Three quarters of the streets are torn up and will not permit of travel. Mudholes and mantraps, dangerous alike by day and by night, swarm in all directions as thick as the leaves of Vallombrose, a putrid stench comes from all sections of the city, offensive to the sense and dangerous to the public health. . . . The streets have been converted into workshops, for on many of the most travelled mammoth saw mills and tar-boiling establishments are to be seen in prominent conspicuousness." [38]

In January 1872 a group of property owners presented a petition to Congress demanding an investigation of the Board. Lengthy hearings were held by the House Committee for the District of Columbia, and, although the committee had some reservations about the legality and wisdom of many of the Board's activities, the majority report concluded that the Board had not overstepped its authority.[39]

For two more years the Board prosecuted its work. In its zeal it far exceeded the original cost estimate. Even with appropriations from the federal government for improvements affecting public buildings and grounds, which a reluctant Congress was at last persuaded to make, the expenses of the District mounted to nearly four times the original figure of $4,000,000. Total costs of the program have never been determined accurately, so chaotic were the records of the Board, but one source indicates that it was at least $26,000,000 and may have been as high as $30,000,000.[40]

The program was unquestionably extravagant, and the amount of the bonds issued to finance it far exceeded the legal limit established by Congress. But the improvements were badly needed and make an impressive list. Street grading operations involved 3,340,-

000 cubic yards of earth. One hundred and nineteen miles of streets were paved in Georgetown and Washington, and 38 miles of improved gravel roads were provided elsewhere in the District. One hundred and fifty-four miles of curbs were installed, and 207 miles of sidewalks were laid.

Sanitary improvements were of an equal magnitude. In the Tiber Creek area 3½ miles of trunk sewers provided badly needed drainage for what had become the most unsanitary area of the District. The old canal was converted to a trunk sewer and filled. Over 7 miles of boundary line interceptors and trunk sewers were built. Draining into these major lines were 60 miles of street mains and an equal length of lateral house connections.[41] The Board also extended water mains to portions of the city hitherto unserved, and many miles of street trees and grass verges were planted. Figure 33 shows the extensive sewer improvements constructed in 1872 and 1873, a public works program probably unprecedented in any American city.

The depression of 1873 and the inability of the Board to finance its operations because of the tight money situation brought its operations to a standstill. It was also faced with mounting public opposition, which this time was successful in its representations to Congress. New hearings were scheduled by a joint committee of the House and Senate, and the results proved unfavorable to Shepherd, who by this time had been appointed Governor of the territory. Although no charges of his personal dishonesty were proved, citizens of the District and Congress alike had had enough of his informal and free-wheeling financial transactions and his almost dictatorial powers.[42]

The congressional committee recommended that the territorial form of government be abolished, and Congress thereupon established a temporary form with administrative power in the hands of three commissioners appointed by the President. Although

[38] Washington *Patriot,* December 4 and 18, 1871, as quoted in Whyte, *Uncivil War,* p. 128.

[39] Report of the House of Representatives Committee for the District of Columbia, May 13, 1872, *Affairs in the District of Columbia,* House Report 72, 43rd Congress, 2nd Session, Washington, 1872.

[40] Tindall, "Sketch of Shepherd," p. 58.

[41] Howe, "Board of Public Works," pp. 265–67.

[42] The hearings and deliberations of the joint committee in 1874 are reported in some 3,000 pages of text. See Joint Select Committee of Congress Appointed to Inquire into the Affairs of the Government of the District of Columbia, *Report,* June 16, 1874, Senate Report No. 453, 43rd Congress, 1st Session, Parts I, II, and III, Washington, 1874.

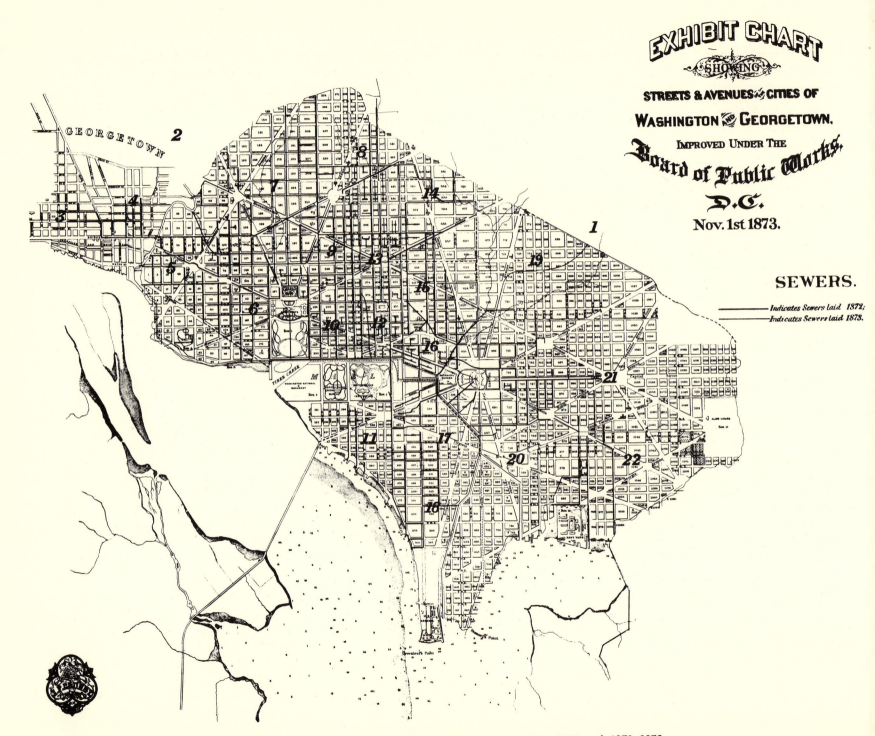

Figure 33. Plan of Washington, Showing Sewers Constructed in 1872 and 1873: 1873

President Grant promptly nominated Shepherd for one of these positions, his appointment was not confirmed. Shepherd spent most of his later life in Mexico engaging in mining operations. But he was not to be entirely forgotten. A new generation of Washingtonians recalled his services in making a modern city and honored him in 1887 at a public demonstration. Later, in 1909 his statue was erected in front of the District of Columbia building on Pennsylvania Avenue from funds raised by public subscription.[43]

The Shepherd era witnessed not only municipal public works but action by the national government in improving some of the squares and reservations that dotted the street pattern of the city. General O. E. Babcock of the Army Corps of Engineers then occupied the dual position of private secretary to President Grant and Officer in Charge of Public Buildings and Grounds. Babcock put under way a program of grading, fencing, and planting the miscellaneous open spaces as work proceeded with street improvements under Shepherd's direction.

The government also undertook a major building project at this time—a huge structure illustrated in Figure 34 to house the State, War, and Navy Departments directly west of the White House and replacing the two older and smaller buildings on that site. This vast pile, vaguely French Renaissance in inspiration, was the creature of A. B. Mullet, Supervising Architect of the Treasury. Presumably many persons agreed with Grant, who, returning from a world tour, was said to observe "that the sight of it climaxed all the curious edifices he had seen in the course of his travels," although Henry Adams called it "Mr. Mullet's architectual infant asylum." [44] Sixty years later there were to be plans for extensive remodeling of its exterior to make it resemble the Treasury building, but these were abandoned, and today it stands virtually as completed in 1888.

An even larger building in the same pompous style was begun in 1886 from designs prepared by John L. Smithmeyer and Paul J. Pelz. This was the Library of Congress, facing the southeastern corner of the Capitol grounds. Two major blunders were commit-

ted in carrying out this project. The first was the decision to close a portion of Pennsylvania Avenue leading southeasterly from the Capitol and to consolidate into one block the land bounded by East Capitol Street and B, 1st, and 2nd Streets, S.E. This cut off one of the major vistas of the Capitol, one which L'Enfant had regarded as extremely important, since Pennsylvania Avenue in his plan led to the bridge crossing the Anacostia River. The second error appeared in the design of the building itself. The designers provided a large dome on top of an already high building, thus conflicting with the great dome of the Capitol. In addition, when the Capitol and the Library are viewed from the west the rival dome appears to cap the House wing and destroys the noble symmetry of that older and grander building.

The placement and massing of the Library of Congress indicated that Congress and the Executive paid little or no heed to the L'Enfant plan. Earlier, in 1868, Congress provided a new building for the Bureau of Agriculture on the south side of the Mall west of the Smithsonian Institution and equally near its center line, as can be seen in Figure 21. The grounds in front of the building, shown in Figure 35, were laid out in formal style, contrasting strongly with the informal treatment in front of the Smithsonian and elsewhere on the Mall. This additional building, almost on the revised axis of the Capitol and the Washington Monument threatened to continue a dangerous precedent which would have made virtually impossible the eventual replanning and unified treatment of these public grounds.

Between the Smithsonian and the Capitol other buildings appeared to join the greenhouses. These and other features of Washington can be seen on the slightly inaccurate but generally revealing view of the city in 1882 reproduced in Figure 36. The elaborate and rather grotesque brick National Museum, now the Arts and Industries Building of the Smithsonian, was located immediately east of the Smithsonian in 1880. Fortunately it was set back from the north line of the Smithsonian and the Agriculture Building and did not intrude on the Mall, although the view incorrectly depicts these two earlier buildings well south of their actual location. Two smaller structures to the east also can be

---

[43] This period of Washington's development deserves full-length treatment. A biography of Shepherd would also be a useful contribution.

[44] U. S. Federal Writers' Project, *Washington,* p. 843.

Figure 34. View from the South of the State, War, and Navy Building: ca. 1888

Figure 35. View of Bureau of Agriculture Building and Its Grounds: ca. 1870

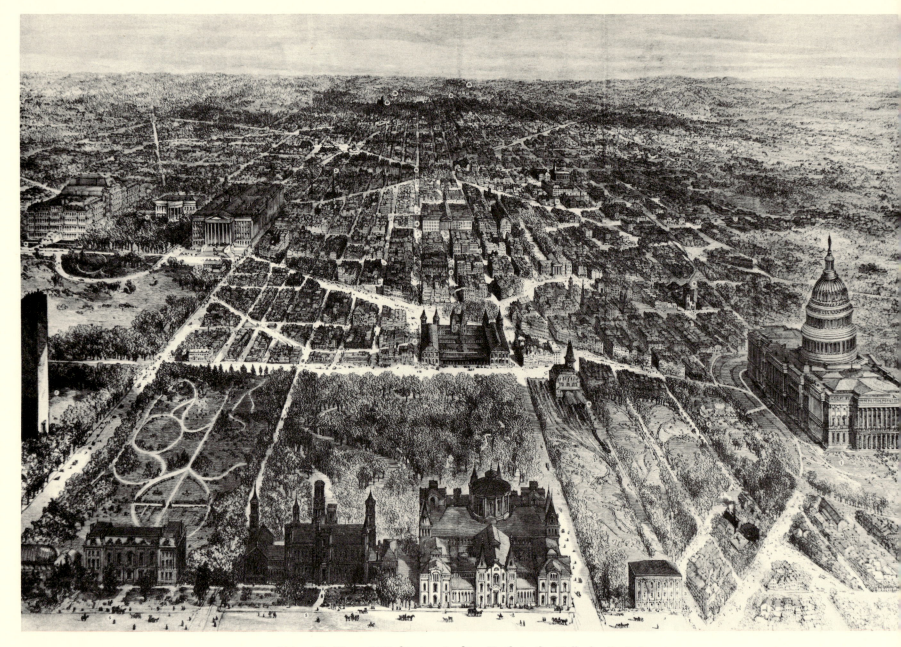

Figure 36. View of Washington, Looking North to the Mall, the Capitol, and the White House: 1882

Figure 37. View of Railroad Tracks at the Foot of Capitol Hill: ca. 1866

seen housing the Army Medical Museum and the Fish Commission.

The Botanical Garden greenhouse, the Smithsonian, and the Agriculture building all infringed to some extent on the Mall. At least these activities had to do with government programs of one kind or another and were thus not wholly inappropriate to the area. This was decidedly not true of another development on the Mall permitted by the Congress—the station of the Baltimore and Potomac (later the Pennsylvania) Railroad, to be seen on Figure 36 at the foot of Capitol Hill.

There were two railroad stations in Washington. The Baltimore and Ohio line terminated at its station at New Jersey Avenue and C Street, which can also be seen north of the Capitol in the view of 1882. This had first opened as early as 1852, and from its sooty precincts trains chuffed back and forth from Baltimore. An attempt was then made to provide connections between Washington and the south. The Alexandria and Washington Railroad, with support from business interests in the city, gained access to the city in 1854 across the Long Bridge over the Potomac. Tracks were actually laid along 1st Street at the very foot of Capitol Hill leading across Pennsylvania Avenue to the B. & O. station. The view in 1866 which appears in Figure 37 reveals the depressing effect this "improvement" must have had on the Capitol. Eventually these tracks were removed, but the fact that they had been permitted at all indicates the depth to which taste and judgment had sunk and the slight regard for the proper treatment of public boulevards and open spaces.

It was thus not altogether surprising that Congress, in 1872, granted to the Baltimore and Potomac a right of way from the south across the Mall itself on 6th Street and generously turned over the southwest corner of 6th Street and what is now Constitution Avenue for its station site. From the southern entrance to the city across Long Bridge, the railroad tracks ran up Maryland Avenue to 6th Street and then north across the Mall to the terminal. The ticket offices and waiting rooms of the railroad were housed in a massive brick building fronting on Constitution Avenue that defies description, while the train shed stretched to the south blocking almost half of the width of the Mall. The de-

plorable effect can be seen clearly in Figure 36. This monumental congressional folly led to endless complications when the time came to replan central Washington—difficulties that were overcome only through the public spirit of the man who then had captured financial control of the railroad.

Brick buildings appeared to predominate in the last quarter of the nineteenth century. At the north end of Judiciary Square in 1883 General M. C. Meigs of the U.S. Army designed the Pension Office. Fifteen million bricks went into this fascinating structure, which vaguely resembles an Italian Renaissance palace. Inside is an enormous court, lighted by a glass roof, the scene of many early inaugural balls. The site was not ill-chosen and made of Judiciary Square an imposing little composition, although there was little functional or architectural relationship between its buildings.

If Congress had been guilty of bad judgment in its cavalier treatment of the Mall, it demonstrated considerable foresight in the final development of central Washington of concern to this study prior to 1900. Following an investigation by a Senate committee in 1881, Congress appropriated the first funds for the improvement of navigation on the Potomac and the reclamation of the tidal flats and marshes west and south of the Washington Monument.

This project involved dredging the river channel and dumping the dredgings so as to fill the marsh area to a level several feet above high tide and flood level. The work proceeded over many years, but by the end of the century it had been substantially completed. An enormous area—more than 600 acres in extent—was reclaimed by this operation. Two separate tracts of land were created, shown on the pictorial map of the city in 1892 reproduced in Figure 38, although not with complete accuracy. To the south, stretching approximately two miles long and parallel with the old shoreline of the Potomac River, the engineers created a new island, known as East Potomac Park. Between the island and the District shore lay the newly deepened Washington Channel, to provide access to wharves and docks. To the north the fill area extended nearly a mile westward from the old water line which had reached almost to the foot of the Washington Monument. This area, West Potomac Park, also contained a narrow peninsula

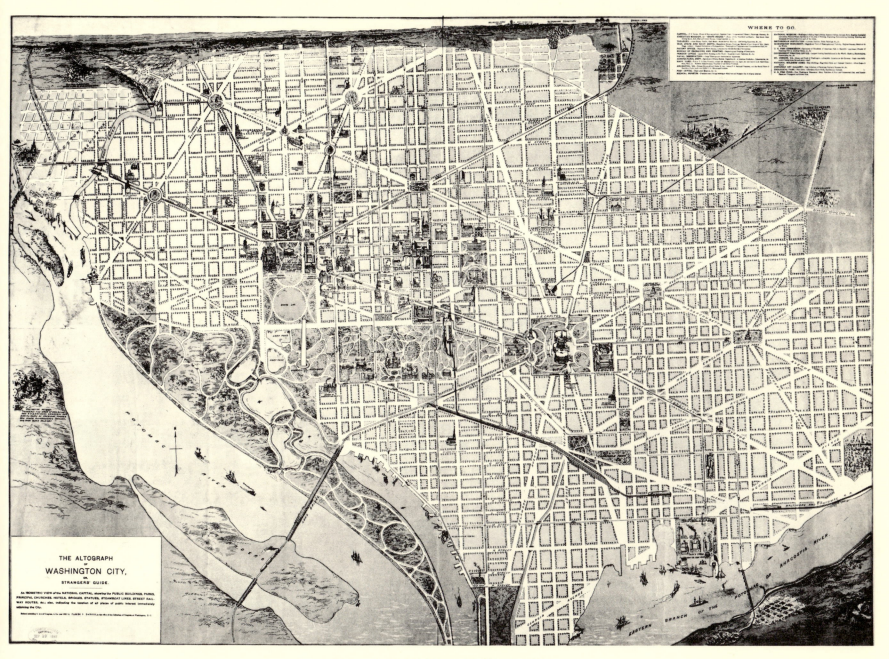

Figure 38. Pictorial Map of Washington: 1892

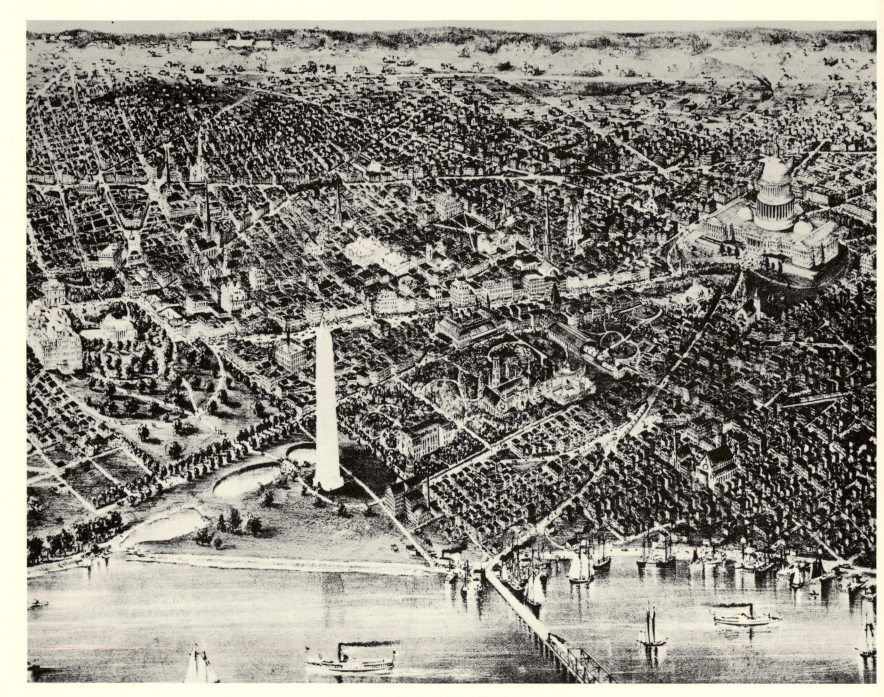

Figure 39. Portion of View of Washington: 1892

stretching southeasterly almost to the tip of the island. In between these two reclaimed tracts the engineers found it necessary to create a tidal basin. Automatic gates allowed water to enter the basin at high tide through an opening to the Potomac. In order to flush the Washington Channel and keep it free of refuse, the gates between the basin and the channel opened at low tide to release the waters of the basin.[45]

Here, then, was central Washington near the turn of the century as Currier and Ives had depicted it in Figure 39 a few years earlier. Mistakes in development had occurred, but there had also been much progress. Most important, the errors, glaring as they might seem, were of minor consequence when compared to the great opportunities that presented themselves. One hundred years had passed since President Adams had led the national government to its new home. Now the city lay on the threshold of a new era.

[45] Some of the engineering details of this project are discussed in "Improvement of Potomac Flats, Washington," *Scientific American,* LXV, No. 12 (September 19, 1891), pp. 180–81, with a view of the dredging operations on p. 175. See also Tindall, *Washington,* pp. 478–80; and Charles Moore, "Notes on the Parks and their Connections," in Senate Committee on the District of Columbia, *Park Improvement Papers,* Washington, 1902, pp. 91–92.

CHAPTER 3

Centennial Plans: Prelude to Progress

With the approach of 1900, the date marking the centennial of the city of Washington as the seat of national government, many persons advanced proposals for physical improvements to help commemorate this important occasion. Certainly the most elaborate and in some ways the most intriguing were those put forward by Franklin W. Smith. Smith, a native of Boston, was a manufacturer of naval hardware, an amateur historian, a would-be architect, a student of classical civilizations, and the proprietor of two commercial museums—one in Saratoga Springs, New York, constructed as a full-scale model of a Pompeian villa; the other, the Halls of the Ancients in Washington, opened in 1898 to display models of Egyptian, Roman, and Assyrian architectural features in full size. Smith had also helped found the Republican party in Massachusetts and thus knew and enjoyed political support from a number of influential members of Congress.

As early as 1890, with the noted James Renwick as his architect, Smith proposed the creation in Washington of a gigantic National Gallery of History and Art. The area of the site proposed equalled the Mall. Its location was to be north of B Street (now Constitution Avenue) to F Street and extending westward from the White House grounds to the Potomac River. The great civilizations of the past were here to be on display in separate galleries and courts within which paintings, dioramas, pieces of sculpture, and artifacts could be seen against the backdrop of buildings representing all known styles of architecture. A broad promenade through the center of this complex would lead to an American acropolis on the banks of the Potomac, where a memorial temple would contain material relating to the past presidents of the United States.

Smith also proposed a series of projects along the north side of the Mall closely related to his contemplated national gallery. He suggested condemning a broad strip of land from the Capitol all the way to the Potomac and from the Mall to one or two blocks north of Pennsylvania Avenue and F Street. The plan accompanying his report, reproduced in Figure 40, indicates the extent of this proposal as well as other features of his project. Both sides of Pennsylvania Avenue were to be replanned. Some buildings were to be constructed by the national government for its own use and the remaining sites sold for private development under strict architectural controls. The trees along the avenue were to be removed; Smith proposed as a substitute colonnades 20 feet in width as a protected promenade.

Two other avenues were to be incorporated in the plan, diverging from the Capitol grounds to terminate at a new national monument or a new executive mansion directly south of the White House. As a further improvement Smith suggested that the railroad station on the Mall be relocated on its south side.

Ten years later Smith elaborated on his proposal and added two new plans. One showed an additional street, Centennial Avenue, running directly west from the Capitol, past the Washington Monument, and across the Potomac on a new bridge. A third plan, shown in Figure 41, converted this straight boulevard to a serpentine avenue through the center of the Mall to a square or

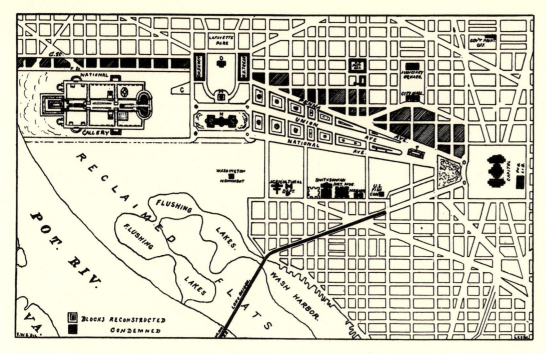

Figure 40. *Plan for Central Washington by Franklin W. Smith: 1890*

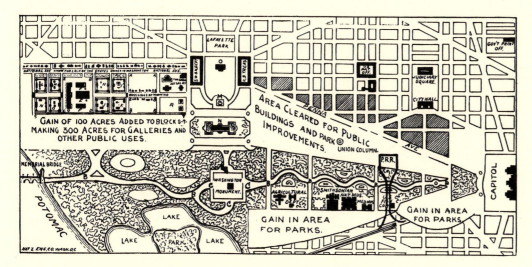

Figure 41. *Plan for Central Washington by Franklin W. Smith: 1900*

plaza around the Washington Monument and then on to a Memorial Bridge spanning the Potomac. This same drawing also shows a series of individual buildings north of his proposed National Gallery. These were intended as permanent exhibitions to be built and maintained by each state in the union. Smith's second report, a profusely illustrated document of almost 200 pages, was taken seriously enough by the Senate of the United States to be published as a Senate Document in 1900.[1]

Smith's plan, although certainly not without merit, must have seemed far too grandiose to be carried out. Its realization would have required wholesale condemnation of the most valuable property in the city. Although Smith could point to the favorable financial results of Hausmann's similar projects in Paris, his plan gained little backing from those in positions of real power.

The events that were eventually to culminate in an official comprehensive plan for the central portion of the city began in 1898. In October of that year a group of distinguished citizens of the District of Columbia met to discuss plans for celebrating the centennial of Washington as the nation's capital. A committee of nine was selected to review suggestions and to meet with President McKinley. The President agreed to include a reference to the centennial in his message to Congress. That document contained several paragraphs on the subject, concluding with these words:

"A movement lately inaugurated by the citizens to have the anniversary celebrated with fitting ceremonies, including, perhaps, the establishment of a permanent memorial to mark so historical an occasion, and to give it a more legal recognition, has met with general favor on the part of the public.

"I recommend to Congress the granting of an appropriation for this purpose and the appointment of a committee from its respective bodies. It might also be advisable to authorize the President to appoint a committee from the country at large, which,

acting with the Congressional and District of Columbia committees, can complete plans for an appropriate national celebration."[2]

The presidential recommendation that some kind of building or memorial be erected to mark the occasion followed the suggestion of the citizens' committee. The committee had mentioned in its report to the President the desirability of "A memorial hall, a bridge connecting the District of Columbia with the sacred ground of Arlington, or some other permanent structure. . . ."[3]

This feature of the President's recommendation, well received in principle, apparently encountered difficulties when specific projects were considered. Initial congressional action provided only for the formation of a committee to be appointed by the President to prepare plans for the centennial celebration. The sum of $10,000 was appropriated to meet committee expenses. The committee was authorized to act in cooperation with any similar committee of the Congress and with the committee from the District of Columbia.

The first meeting of the joint committees took place on February 21, 1900, although separate meetings of the three groups had been held previously. At its morning session the joint committee considered a report of the citizens' committee of the District, which had been the most active of the three groups. That report included a number of recommendations including the following:

"That the laying of the corner stone of an appropriate, substantial, and permanent memorial structure be made a feature of the celebration, and that Congress be urged to provide for such a memorial. In the judgment of this committee, a bridge across the Potomac River to the Arlington National Cemetery, now the property of the United States, would be the most fitting and appreciated. . . ."[4]

The report pointed out that preliminary surveys and plans for this project already existed, and that it would be possible to in-

[1] Franklin W. Smith, *National Galleries of History and Art. The Aggrandizement of Washington,* Washington, 1900. Smith's earlier report appeared under the title, *Design & Prospectus for the National Gallery of History & Art,* Washington, 1891. For a more detailed treatment of Smith and his proposals see Curtis Dahl, "Mr. Smith's American Acropolis," *American Heritage,* VII, No. 4 (June 1956), pp. 38–43, 104–05.

[2] William V. Cox (comp.), *Celebration of the One Hundredth Anniversary of the Establishment of the Seat of Government in the District of Columbia,* Washington, 1901, p. 197.

[3] For the text of the committee report to the President on November 14, 1898, see Cox, *Celebration,* pp. 20–21.

[4] The text of the report is in *ibid.,* pp. 33–35.

clude the laying of a cornerstone during the celebration. Many other projects had been considered, the report stated, listing them as follows:

"The erection of a municipal building for Washington City; a memorial arch at the head of Sixteenth street; a series of statues of American worthies; a new Executive Mansion; the reclamation of the flats of Anacostia River, the eastern branch of the Potomac; the enlarging of the Capitol grounds by the condemnation of adjacent squares; the elimination of Florida avenue as the northern boundary of the city of Washington; the policy of erecting all future Government buildings on the south side of Pennsylvania avenue, and the purchase of the ground for that purpose; a new building for the Supreme Court of the United States, to be erected on a site corresponding to that of the Congressional Library building; the retrocession of the whole or a part of the territory of the State of Virginia originally embraced in the ten-mile square forming the District of Columbia." [5]

A committee of five was then appointed to review the report of the citizens' committee and to bring in its recommendations at the afternoon session. Senator James McMillan, Chairman of the Senate Committee on the District of Columbia, served as chairman of this group, which recommended that the celebration be held in December 1900, that commemorative exercises also should be arranged by the Congress to mark the first session of that body in the city, and that the occasion should include orations, a parade, and an evening reception. The group also proposed that the White House be enlarged and that a great boulevard to be known as "Centennial avenue" be constructed from the Capitol through the Mall to the Potomac River. In supporting this suggestion Senator McMillan had this to say:

"Everyone recognizes that the Executive Mansion is not adequate for the purposes for which it is used. It was built a great many years ago; it is not in good order—in fact, the foundations of the building have had to be supported from time to time, and it is not fit either as an office or a residence for the President of the United States. The committee . . . came to the conclusion that it would be wise to recommend that an enlargement of the Executive Mansion should be made, not to interfere with the architectural beauty of the present structure." [6]

Then, turning to a subject which McMillan had doubtless already considered, he continued:

"It is suggested, at the same time, that an avenue might be opened through the Mall from the grounds of the Capitol to the Potomac River, where the proposed memorial bridge might be built at some future time, making that avenue a boulevard, with trees on either side, and possibly a riding path. This avenue would be known as "Centennial avenue," and would be probably three miles in length. Strange to say, upon looking at the maps which the committee had before it, it was seen that the original plan of Washington, as prepared by Major L'Enfant, provided for just such an avenue, public buildings to be erected on either side of the same." [7]

These recommendations stimulated considerable discussion. Governor John Lind of Minnesota felt that the proposals for an enlarged White House and the Mall boulevard were matters belonging properly to the Congress. Governor G. W. Atkinson of West Virginia stated his belief that an entirely new executive mansion was needed. In the end, the report was adopted, amended only by the addition of a new presidential residence as an alternative to the proposal to reconstruct the existing one. [8]

Senator McMillan lost no time in using his influence to push the project of a boulevard through the Mall. Within five days of the meeting just described he was exhibiting a drawing showing his ideas for such a development. The Senator acted with more

[5] *ibid.*, pp. 34–35.

[6] The report of the committee of five and Senator McMillan's remarks are in *ibid.*, pp. 36–37.

[7] *ibid.*, p. 37.

[8] Press reaction to this proposal was not entirely favorable. An editorial entitled "Centennial Avenue" in the Washington *Evening Star* for February 22, 1900, cautiously supported the project only if the buildings south of Pennsylvania Avenue were cleared and the entire area replanned. On the following day the same paper advocated giving first attention to Pennsylvania Avenue, although it also supported the Mall avenue as a worthwhile project.

haste than wisdom, however, for his plan was certainly ill-conceived. McMillan was a skilled legislator and an adroit politician, but his understanding of civic design left much to be desired if his proposal of February 26, 1900, is any evidence.

McMillan simply drew two parallel lines, 200 feet apart from a point on 1st Street directly west of the Capitol dome to the eastern end of the proposed Potomac bridge, then contemplated as a continuation of New York Avenue, which ran southwesterly from the White House. The alignment of his boulevard thus lay diagonally across the northern half of the Mall as it then existed. An illustration of this scheme, together with a long description of the project and an interview with Senator McMillan appeared in the Washington *Post*. One virtue of the scheme, McMillan pointed out, was that only a small amount of private land would need to be acquired.[9]

The Senator's attention was called to the aesthetic shortcomings of his plan, and he quickly came to realize that professional advice was needed for such an important project. On May 14 he introduced an amendment in the Senate to the sundry civil appropriation bill authorizing studies of both the White House modernization plan and the "centennial avenue" scheme. His amendment provided:

"That the President of the United States is hereby authorized to appoint an architect, a landscape architect, and a sculptor, each of conspicuous ability in his profession, to be associated with the Chief of Engineers of the United States Army, to make an examination and to report to Congress on the first Monday in December, nineteen hundred, plans for the enlargement of the Executive Mansion; for the treatment of that section of the District of Columbia situated south of Pennsylvania avenue and north of B street SW., and for a suitable connection between the Potomac and the Zoological parks."[10]

While the Senate approved the amendment as offered, there was evidently objection in the House. As finally approved on June 20, 1900, after a conference committee had reconciled the differences, the McMillan concept of a team of professionals, "each of conspicuous ability in his profession," was abandoned. Instead, the final bill appropriated $6,000 for the preparation of plans for enlarging the White House, and the Chief of Engineers was directed to make a study of the Mall area and a connection between the Potomac and Zoological Parks. The Chief of Engineers was authorized to "employ a landscape architect of conspicuous ability in his profession."[11]

It is quite possible that this change came about through the action of Representative Joseph Cannon of Illinois, a member of the conference committee, an indefatigable opponent of spending public funds on anything connected with art or architecture, and a powerful member of the House of Representatives. Within a few years he was to become the most influential and feared opponent of those who were to attempt the replanning of Washington. As Speaker of the House during 1903–1911, he was in a position to wield the substantial legislative weight of that office in his efforts to frustrate those concerned with making Washington a more attractive city.[12]

The change in McMillan's proposed legislation placed responsibility for preparing the plans in the hands of the Office of Public Buildings and Grounds of the Army Engineers, which, since 1867, had exercised jurisdiction over the federal lands shown in Figure 42. Only the Capitol grounds, the Library of Congress site, and the portion of the Mall occupied by the Department of Agriculture lay under the control of other federal agencies. In 1900 the chief of this office was Colonel Theodore A. Bingham. Bingham, a graduate of West Point in 1879, had served in various posts as an engineer and had also been posted in Berlin and Rome as a military attaché. He was apparently ambitious, impulsive, and rather impressed with his own knowledge. Like many engineers he also

[9] The Washington *Post,* February 26, 1900. The *Post's* rival, the *Evening Star,* vigorously attacked McMillan's proposal as "violating the sanctity of the parks" and as a "mere street" that would be "straight, uncompromising, ugly." The Washington *Evening Star,* March 3, 1900. Other editorials on March 5, March 6, and May 3 continued the attack.

[10] The text of this amendment, passed by the Senate on May 29, 1900, appears in Cox, *Celebration,* pp. 200–01.

[11] *Plans for Treatment of that Portion of the District of Columbia South of Pennsylvania Avenue and North of B Street SW., and for Connection Between Potomac and Zoological Parks,* Washington, 1900.

[12] For a brief summary of Cannon's activities see Glenn Brown, *Memories,* Washington, 1931, pp. 96–102.

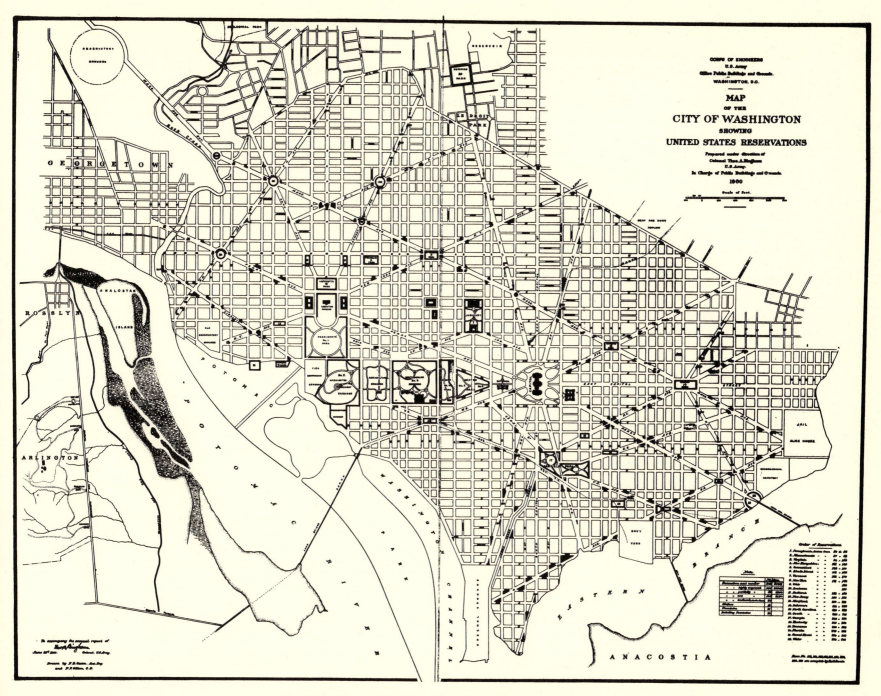

Figure 42. Plan of Washington Showing Public Reservations: 1900

evidently held architects in disdain. It was into these insensitive and not altogether capable hands that the task of replanning the Mall and enlarging the White House was thrust.[13]

Bingham already had completed and exhibited his own plans for the treatment of the Mall. Under what circumstances these were prepared is not entirely clear. One Washington historian states that Bingham learned of impending legislation which would have permitted the Pennsylvania Railroad to build a viaduct across the Mall to reach its station on the north side of the mall at 6th Street. Bingham, realizing that such a project would still further disfigure the Mall, began a campaign to block this development by quickly preparing plans for a great avenue from the Capitol to the Washington Monument and for other improvements coordinated with this proposal.[14] It is also conceivable that Senator McMillan may have conferred with Bingham concerning the treatment of the Mall, although McMillan's own scheme, revealed to the press and public on February 26, was both different from and inferior to the two Bingham plans of about the same time.

Bingham's two plans are dated March 1, 1900, and April 1, 1900. They were apparently first published only in July 1901, when they appeared, with no word of explanation, in his annual report for the fiscal year ending June 30, 1901.[15] At least one of them, however, had been publicly exhibited as early as April 30, 1900, and had been reproduced and discussed in the Washington *Post*.[16] Accompanying them and dated January 1, 1900, was an enlarged drawing of the central portion of L'Enfant's plan for Washington. While it incorrectly identifies the L'Enfant plan as dating from 1790 and includes some indications of trees not shown on the original, it is a generally faithful depiction of L'Enfant's concept of how the grounds stretching from the Capitol to the presidential mansion should be treated.

Bingham's two plans are similar, but with important differences. Both show a major boulevard leading from the Capitol to the Washington Monument. In the first, however, shown in Figure 43, the axis of the boulevard lies just to the north of the monument and terminates at what is identified as a "Colossal America Group," presumably a large sculptural mass. This was to be located in a military parade ground on the newly reclaimed tidal flats of the Potomac River. The second plan, reproduced in Figure 44, employed the Monument as the terminal feature of the avenue and modified the layout of the parade ground, omitting the sculpture group.

Both plans incorporated a new bridge across the Potomac River on the line of New York Avenue. The first plan shows two triumphal arches on either side of the river at the approaches to the bridge. The one on the west side lies on the Mall axis at the same distance from the White House as the Capitol. In the second plan the western bridge approach is omitted, and the arch on the eastern side is changed to a statue and fountain at the intersection of New York Avenue and 23rd Street. This latter street is shown as a boulevard connection to Rock Creek Park via Washington Circle.

[13] Bingham was to become better known as Police Commissioner of New York City, a post he held during 1906–09. His administration was stormy, although he introduced a number of important reforms and restored a measure of confidence in a police force then under attack as corrupt. At the time of his death in 1934 the New York *Times* remembered his services to the city as generally beneficial, but added this comment: "Theodore A. Bingham had his faults. He was a bluff soldier, unaware that discretion is sometimes the better part of valor. His judgement was not always unerring, his ideas of discipline may have been in some respects better suited to life in army cantonments than to the control of a police force in a metropolitan community." The New York *Times,* September 7, 1934. During the eventual remodeling of the White House in 1902, Bingham clashed with Charles McKim, whom President Roosevelt had selected to prepare plans and supervise their execution. For an account of this episode and the amusing "Treaty of Oyster Bay," which led to the removal of the Colonel's beloved greenhouses from the White House grounds, see Charles Moore, *The Life and Times of Charles Follen McKim,* Boston, 1929, pp. 215–17.
[14] H. Paul Caemmerer, *Washington The National Capital,* Washington, 1932, p. 224.
[15] *Improvement and Care of Public Buildings and Grounds in The*

District of Columbia—Washington Monument. Report of Col. Theo. A. Bingham, United States Army, Officer in Charge, for the Fiscal Year Ending June 30, 1901, Washington, 1901, Reports of War Department, 1901, Engineers, Part 5, pp. 3689–3760.
[16] The Washington *Post,* April 30, 1900. The small illustration reproduced in this article apparently incorporates features of both the plans published a year later. True to form, the Washington *Evening Star* objected violently to the Bingham plan on the same grounds that it had opposed McMillan's earlier proposal. The Washington *Evening Star,* May 2, 1900.

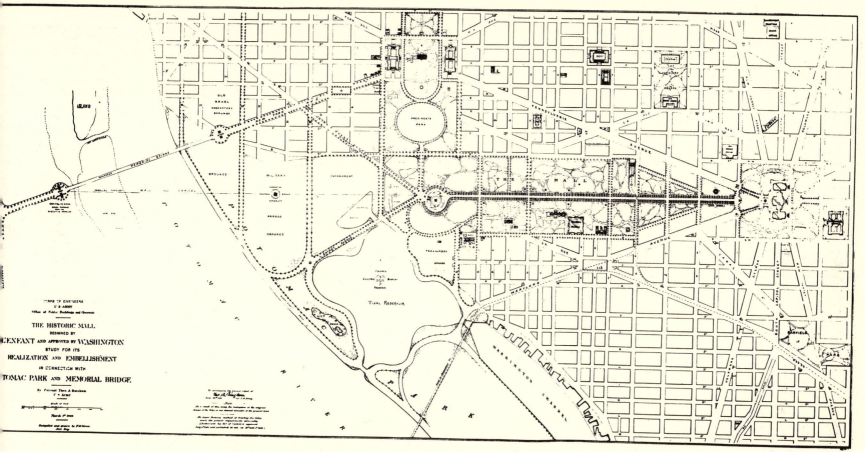

Figure 43. First Plan for Central Washington by Theodore Bingham: 1900

Both plans also show a continuation of Virginia Avenue through the Mall to the vicinity of the Monument and a corresponding diagonal avenue leading southwesterly from the Monument area bearing the name of L'Enfant. The second plan shows some kind of monument where these two diagonals intersect the axis of the White House, with a short, broad boulevard leading to it from B Street which bordered the Mall on the north.

The Mall itself, aside from the avenue down its center, is shown essentially as it then existed with all its winding and sinuous paths and drives. The building of the Agriculture Department and the various museums along its south side are also indicated. The first plan shows no additional public buildings. The second, however, reveals Bingham's recommendations for the location of building sites. They appear along Pennsylvania Avenue and in the triangular space between that thoroughfare and B Street. In this suggestion Bingham adumbrated the later recommendations of the Park Commission and others who were to study and suggest solutions for this problem.

Bingham also included in his report a suggested plan for the treatment of the newly reclaimed land beyond the Washington

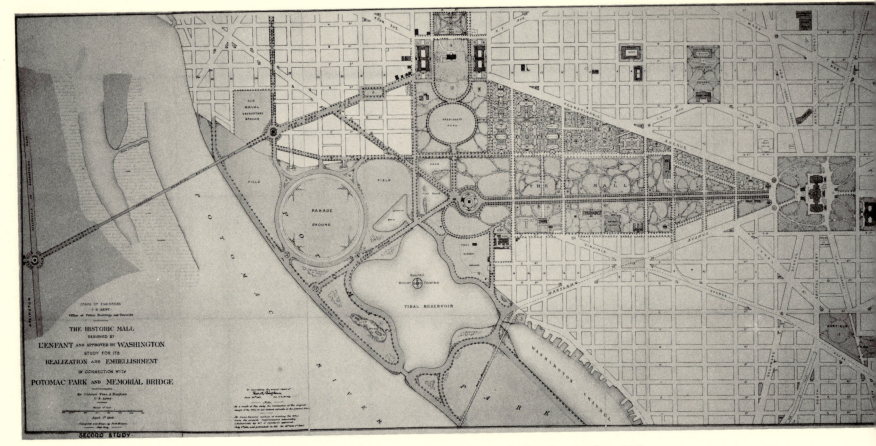

Figure 44. Second Plan for Central Washington by Theodore Bingham: 1900

Channel. His plan, which appears in Figure 45, shows a rather tortured design for a great park with drives along the shore, major athletic facilities near the north end, a "one mile straight away," a Japanese Garden, and a series of curling paths which evidently represented Bingham's interpretation of proper romantic landscape layout.

According to the Washington *Post* for April 30, 1900, Bingham showed his plans to President McKinley, who "greatly admired" them, and to senators, congressmen, governors, and members of the citizens' committee. However, he must have felt somewhat

chagrined at the lack of confidence in his abilities as city planner and civic designer implied in Congress's authorization in June for the employment of a landscape architect to prepare studies for this same area. Nevertheless, he immediately took the steps necessary to put this new venture under way.

By July 20, 1900, Bingham arranged a preliminary agreement with the firm of Parsons and Pentecost of New York to carry out the study. Samuel Parsons, Jr., the senior partner of the firm who was to undertake the work, was then in Europe. A month later he returned and began the job. Samuel Parsons was a competent

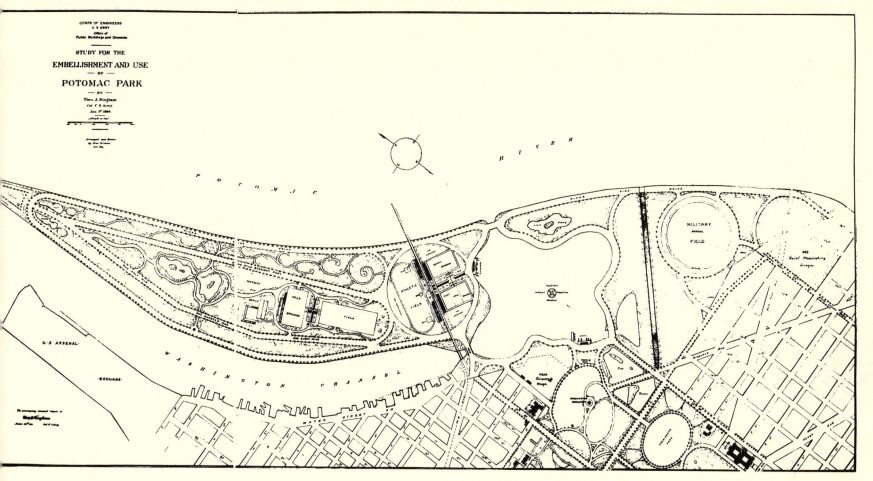

Figure 45. Plan by Theodore Bingham for East Potomac Park: 1900

landscape gardener. He had been closely associated with Calvert Vaux in developing the details of the plan for Central Park in New York City, which had been prepared by Vaux and Frederick Law Olmsted, Sr. His knowledge of plant materials and gardening was superior to his talents as a designer, and he had never faced the kind of problem now confronting him. However, for that matter, few architects or landscape architects in America could claim experience in civic design, and the choice of Parsons for this important assignment was at least defensible.

Parsons submitted his report to Bingham on November 14. At

the outset he stated the basic principles which had guided his design:

"I think that these propositions will not be denied by persons who have really considered the subject: (1) A park, as a pleasure ground, should be set apart and isolated as completely as art can contrive it from sound and sight of the surrounding city; and (2) On the same line of endeavor the interior of the pleasure ground should be made to suggest woodland and meadow scenery so laid out as to afford convenient and agreeable access, by means of

79

carriage and bridle roads and footpaths, to all points of interest and landscape charm." [17]

It is apparent that Parsons, like Downing before him, completely failed to comprehend the design requirements for an open space of the Mall's character in a baroque cityscape. He brought to the quite different setting of central Washington some of the concepts of romantic park layout that had been so rightly employed in New York's Central Park under markedly different circumstances. The strong axial relationships of the principal buildings and the formal plan of the city itself virtually dictated a formal design for this as yet unfinished central feature. While Parson's plan was symmetrical, its repeating curves in the main roadways betrayed his inclinations toward informality and failed to supply the needed concentrated visual focus along a major axis.

The rendering of his plan included not only the Mall as it then existed but all the land lying between Pennsylvania Avenue on the north and Maryland Avenue on the south. An insert plan showed the location of this area and also his proposed connecting drive between the Washington Monument and Rock Creek Park in the northwestern part of the city.

Parsons proposed connections across the Mall north and south by means of four transverse roads, as shown in Figure 46. These would be depressed at the points where they were crossed by the park drives. Here too can be seen the influence of Central Park, where an identical solution to a similar problem had been worked out. Instead of a boulevard down the center of the Mall, Parsons proposed an alignment that would include three great elliptical forms around which the road would lead on either side. Although the Monument was made the terminal feature of this indirect approach, it would be on axis only of the short stretches of bridged roadway over the transverse streets. The important secondary axis of the White House he ignored completely. Even the Bingham plans, with all their faults, were far superior to Parsons' scheme in their recognition of the reciprocal relationships of major existing elements and the potentials of grandeur and monumentality that formal treatment of this section of the city might provide.

The plan did include one bold and desirable feature. This was the proposed relocation of the Pennsylvania Railroad station from its disastrous location on the Mall at 6th Street to a new site south of the Mall at 7th Street and Maryland Avenue. This recommendation for the elimination of the railroad tracks across the Mall and for the removal of the station, which stretched across nearly half its width, was to be repeated in subsequent proposals by others until a final solution was found. Parsons' recommendation for the acquisition of land between Pennsylvania Avenue and the Mall, a feature of the second Bingham plan, is also found in later schemes, and this, too, was finally to be carried out.

The Parsons plan was endorsed by Bingham and approved by Brigadier General John M. Wilson, Chief of the Army Engineers. On December 5, 1900, Secretary of War Elihu Root sent the plan and Parsons' report to the Speaker of the House of Representatives recommending "favorable consideration and action." [18] The Parsons report was thus completed and submitted to Congress just prior to December 12, the day fixed for the centennial celebration.

One of the features of that day was a morning reception at the White House given by the President for the governors of the states and territories and the commissioners of the District of Columbia. They were presented to the President by Bingham himself. Then this group, together with members of the Cabinet, the Supreme Court, leaders of the House and Senate, high military officials, and other dignitaries and special guests gathered in the East Room. On display, resting on a raised platform, was a plaster model of the White House with the additions proposed by Bingham, who was then asked to address the assembly.

Bingham described his proposal, which he identified as having been prepared by Frederick D. Owen, architect. Owen's name had appeared on the two Bingham plans for the Mall, preceded by the words "compiled and drawn by," and he, rather than Bingham, may have been the actual designer of the proposals for central Washington. Owen had previously made some studies for enlarg-

[17] "Report of Mr. Saml. Parsons, Jr., Landscape Architect," *Plans for Treatment of that Portion of the District of Columbia South of Pennsylvania Avenue . . . ,* p. 5.

[18] Letter from Root to the Speaker of the House attached to Parsons' report and the endorsements of Bingham and Wilson, *ibid.,* p. 1.

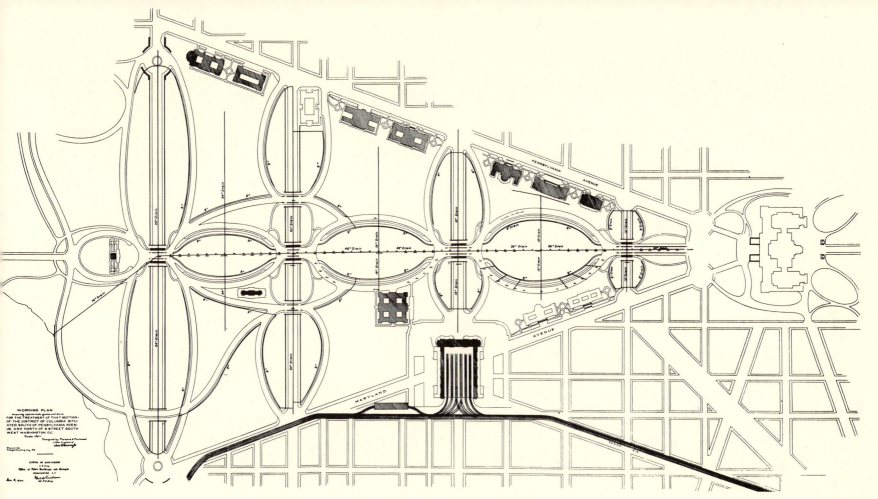

Figure 46. Plan for Central Washington by Samuel Parsons, Jr.: 1900

ing the White House under Mrs. Harrison. His later study was a modification of this earlier work.

The proposal, shown in Figure 47, incorporated two new wings, one on each side of the existing building and of the same height. Each was to be topped by a low dome surmounted by a lantern and around each wing was to run an elaborate colonnade. The effect of the proposed enlargement would be to change completely the appearance of the White House, to dwarf the original building, and to emphasize the elaborate and tasteless additions.

Bingham's plan brought a storm of protests, not only from local architects and citizens but from professional and citizen groups throughout the country. This opposition had been carefully organized by Glenn Brown, the newly elected Secretary of the American Institute of Architects and the author of a massive history of the National Capitol, who had learned of the proposals prior to their presentation in December. On the day following the centennial celebration he sent to President McKinley the official opposition of the Institute along with signed protests from nearly fifty art associations throughout the country. McKinley was impressed by these vigorous objections and subsequently had the model removed from

81

Figure 47. View of Model Showing Theodore Bingham's Proposals in 1900
for Remodeling the White House: 1900

the White House. The cellar of the Corcoran Gallery became its resting place.[19]

Parsons' plan for the Mall met a similar fate, for it, too, was opposed by the American Institute of Architects. This group, prodded by the energetic Brown, then took the lead in pressing for a comprehensive study of the needs of central Washington by an expert group. At their annual meeting, held in Washington in the same December as the centennial celebration, a committee on legislation was appointed to impress Congress with the need of a

professional commission to consider the subject of improvements to the city. This committee, working with the always sympathetic Senator McMillan, succeeded in obtaining the appointment of the Senate Park Commission, whose work will be described in a subsequent chapter. Because the role of the Institute was so important at this critical time, its activities will be reviewed in some detail.

Glenn Brown occupied the key role in these events. His exhaustive study of the Capitol had given him an understanding not only of that building but of L'Enfant's plan for the entire city and

[19] Brown, *Memories*, pp. 108–10.

the great possibilities for its full realization if its third dimension in architecture could be carefully guided.[20] As Secretary of the Washington Chapter of the Institute, Washington correspondent of the *American Architect,* and an active participant in organizing the Public Art League, Brown soon became involved in discussions with public officials in Washington over the selection of architects and sculptors for federal buildings and monuments. At a meeting of the Institute in Washington in 1898 he was elected Secretary and exercised his considerable influence and energies to involve the organization in attempts to bring about improvements in the capital city.

Sensing that the coming centennial celebration would revive general interest in the history of the city and its development, which would provide an informed base on which to build proposals for its improvement, Brown decided to prepare a plan of his own for central Washington. He may have been motivated as well by his dislike for Bingham and his feelings that the Colonel lacked the necessary training and taste to carry out the task. In any event, Brown's plan appeared in the August 1900 issue of the *Architectural Review,* together with an explanation of his proposals.

Brown's article contained a number of photographs of Washington accompanied by critical comments on the mistakes that had been made and the opportunities that had been lost during the preceding century. Other photographs showed great formal compositions from Europe, chiefly Paris, which Brown held up as examples that should be studied and followed in the development of Washington. Senator McMillan's proposed boulevard running obliquely through the Mall received the author's vigorous criticism. Brown contended that a modified version of the original L'Enfant plan for a formal mall flanked by major buildings would be the most satisfactory solution to the existing problem.

His own plan, reproduced in Figure 48, provided for a boulevard through the middle of the Mall, its axis tilted slightly so that the

[20] Glenn Brown, *History of the United States Capitol,* Washington, 1900. Charles Moore, himself one of the great leaders in the improvement of Washington for more than a quarter of a century, asserted that "Glenn Brown, more than any other one person, stimulated the architects of the country to take an interest in reviving the L'Enfant plan of Washington." Charles Moore, *Daniel H. Burnham,* Boston, 1921, I, p. 136n.

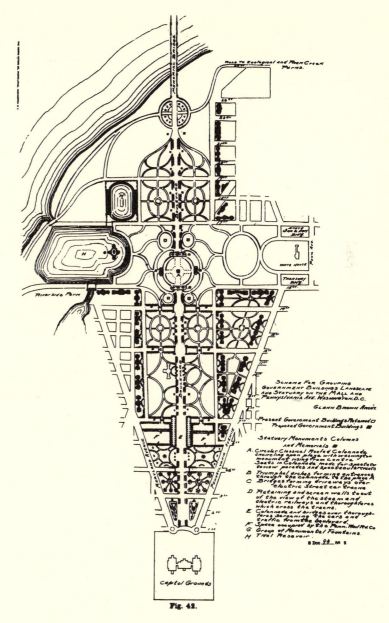

Figure 48. *Plan for Central Washington by Glenn Brown: 1900*

Monument would be at its center, continuing on to the west over a new memorial bridge to the Virginia side of the Potomac River. Brown reluctantly accepted the existing location of the Pennsylvania Railroad tracks and station, but he proposed that the tracks be depressed and the boulevard pass over them on a bridge whose sides would be lined by colonnades and dense planting to screen the tracks and the station from view. Transverse roads across the Mall from north to south would be similarly depressed and screened by dense planting. Around the Monument he proposed a great circular colonnade enclosing a plaza 700 feet in diameter. Along the boulevard leading from the Capitol to the Monument and in the formal gardens on each side, Brown suggested that statues, fountains, and other decorative and memorial devices should be located.

Sites for future public buildings appear on either side of the eastern end of the Mall, on the north side of its extension beyond the Monument area, and in the triangle between Pennsylvania Avenue and the Mall. Brown, for all his love of formal compositions with strong axial relationships, strangely enough did not make much of the White House axis. The only recognition of this appears in the proposed "group of fountains and statuary" directly south of the White House in the tidal basin near the river. Finally, as a connection to Rock Creek Park, he suggested a boulevard leading from a large circle at the bridge approach to 25th Street, from which Massachusetts Avenue would lead to the park.[21]

Brown's plan could hardly be called a masterpiece; yet it had a consistency that those of Bingham lacked, and in its undeviating use of formal design forms it was far more appropriate for the space than that of Parsons. Certainly Brown must have informed key legislators, officials, and those active in centennial preparations about his scheme, and doubtless it received more than passing attention. Brown's real influence on Washington's development was, however, to stem from his position as Secretary of the American Institute of Architects and his activities in connection with its convention in the year 1900.

Robert S. Peabody was then President of the Institute. Brown persuaded him to hold the annual convention in Washington and to announce as its theme the unified and artistic development of the city. Brown set to work to obtain the best qualified speakers in the country on this subject. As early as March he began writing and talking to those designers whom he felt were capable not only of presenting stimulating ideas but whose views might carry substantial weight.[22]

His persistence and persuasiveness were difficult to resist. To Cass Gilbert he wrote on March 24 asking him to present a paper. When Gilbert replied a few days later, hesitating to accept because he might not have time to prepare an address, Brown quickly answered with a short but forceful letter pointing out the importance of the occasion and that all members of Congress would be invited to the sessions. Gilbert still procrastinated on his decision, finally told Brown he would be willing to discuss other papers but could not prepare one of his own, but under the prodding of Brown at last appeared with a plan of his own for the improvement of Washington.[23] Other speakers were secured in the same manner, and Brown doubtless supplied many of them with maps and information about the city as he had offered to do for Gilbert.

The opening address to the convention in December by President Peabody set the stage for the remarkable performances to follow. Pointing out that one of the aims of the Institute was to "make our Government architecture more worthy of the greatness and intelligence of the Republic," Peabody stated:

"No city is more full of architectural warnings. None better exemplifies in its buildings what is and what is not architecture. One does not need a professional education to feel mortified at the sight

[21] Glenn Brown, "A Suggestion for Grouping Government Buildings, Landscape, Monuments, and Statuary," *The Architectural Review,* VIII, No. 8 (August 1900), pp. 89–94. This article also appears in Glenn Brown (comp.), *Papers Relating to the Improvement of the City of Washington, District of Columbia,* Washington, 1901, pp. 59–69.

[22] Brown, *Memories,* pp. 259–62.
[23] American Institute of Architects Letter File: Letters from Brown to Gilbert on March 24, April 2, May 15, May 21, July 6, November 22, November 27, and December 22, 1900; Letters from Gilbert to Brown on March 31, May 17, July 11, and November 26, 1900.

of certain buildings that have been thrust upon these beautiful highways in comparatively recent times. . . .

"If great Government buildings are to be scattered about the country, if a boulevard is to traverse the National Capital, if the future buildings for the Government are to be effectively placed in this beautiful city, if the White House, in which we all take such pleasure and pride, needs to be increased in size, we want each and all of these works carried out by the best artistic skill that the country can produce, and by nothing less efficient. Nor are we alone in this wish. So far as I have observed, the public aspires to even better things than our best talent produces. They want the very best. Now that architecture is a matter of active interest to great numbers of people in all parts of the country, it ought to be possible to bring to life again the admirable artistic spirit which one hundred years ago planned the city of Washington and built its earlier and best monuments." [24]

The papers that followed discussed the principles that should guide such public improvements. Several speakers—Cass Gilbert, Paul J. Pelz, George O. Totten, Jr., and Edgar V. Seeler—presented plans or sketches illustrating their concepts of how central Washington should be replanned. While space does not permit a detailed analysis of each plan, some comments are required. In each plan can be found the seed of ideas later to take root in the minds of the official Senate Park Commission, which itself grew out of the fertile ground prepared by the convention of architects.

Gilbert's plan, shown in Figure 49, was perhaps the most skillful of all. The proposed treatment of the central part of the Mall and the strengthening of the White House axis are noteworthy features. Gilbert proposed to locate an Historical Museum not far from the Monument as the terminal feature of the axis of the White House. This was to be emphasized by two elements: The erection of a great memorial to the founders of the nation directly across this axis from the Washington Monument and the symmetrical disposition of two building masses to the east and west of the White House area north of the Mall. Wishing to preserve the

White House in its present form but recognizing that additional space was needed for both residential and official purposes connected with the presidency, Gilbert suggested the construction of a new presidential residence near the intersection of New Hampshire and 15th Streets, somewhat more than a mile north of the present location. Gilbert's plan did not show any changes for the eastern end of the Mall except for the avenue leading from the Capital, which would widen gradually until it entered a plaza bordered on the north and south by new buildings for governmental departments. Beyond the Washington Monument and the new low but massive memorial to the founders of the country he proposed the development of a great reviewing ground for pageants and official ceremonies. Gilbert accepted the New York Avenue alignment of the proposed Potomac bridge, which he related to this central composition only by a rather unimpressive connection at the end of B Street.[25]

Far less imposing, although with some interesting features, was the plan advanced by Paul J. Pelz, which can be seen in Figure 50. This Washington architect was content to leave the Mall and Monument grounds much as they then existed. The area north and south of the Mall to Pennsylvania and Maryland Avenues he proposed for government acquisition, the sites to be used for govern-

[24] Robert S. Peabody, "The Need of Artistic Treatment of Government Work in Washington," in Brown, *Papers*, pp. 11–12.

[25] Cass Gilbert, "Grouping of Public Buildings and Development of Washington," in Brown, *Papers*, pp. 78–82. Cass Gilbert (1858–1934) was regarded in 1900 as one of America's finest young architects. After an apprenticeship in St. Paul, study in a special course at the Massachusetts Institute of Technology, several months of European travel, and 2 years of work in the firm of McKim, Mead, and White, Gilbert established his office in St. Paul with James Knox Taylor. His most important commission prior to 1900 was the design for the Minnesota State Capitol, awarded as the result of a competition. At 31 he had been elected a Fellow of the American Institute of Architects. His later career was distinguished. He served as President of the American Institute of Architects, the American Academy of Arts and Letters, the Architectural League, and the National Academy of Design. Theodore Roosevelt appointed him chairman of the Council of Fine Arts, and he later served as a member of its successor body, the Commission of Fine Arts. He designed major buildings throughout the country and also ventured into city planning work. For a list of his more important buildings see Henry F. and Elsie R. Withey, *Biographical Dictionary of American Architects,* Los Angeles, 1956. I have relied on this source for information about the other designers of plans for Washington presented at the convention of 1900.

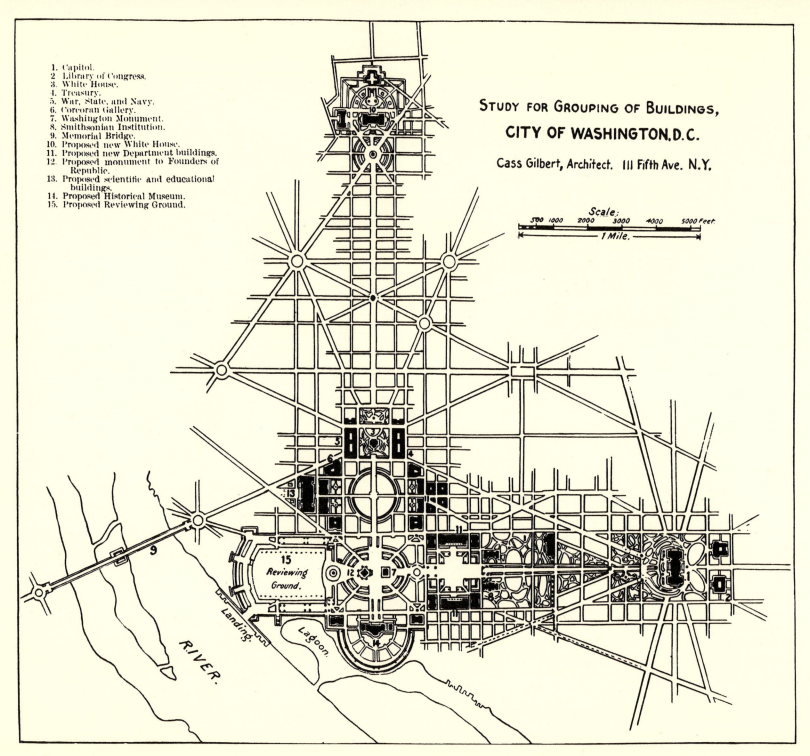

Figure 49. Plan for Central Washington by Cass Gilbert: 1900

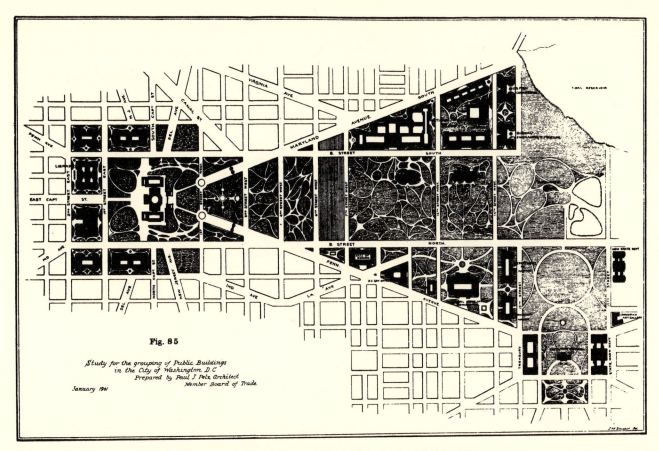

Fig. 85

*Study for the grouping of Public Buildings
in the City of Washington D.C.
Prepared by Paul J Pelz, Architect
Member Board of Trade.*

January 1901

Figure 50. Plan for Central Washington by Paul J. Pelz: 1900

mental offices. He, like Gilbert, accepted the present site of the Pennsylvania Railroad station, but in addition proposed its enlargement and the creation of a small plaza to its north between Sixth and Seventh Streets. His plan shows the eastern end of the Mall at the Capitol approaches widened to South B Street and North B Street. Pelz's otherwise uninspiring plan did contain one feature of merit, later to be echoed in the Park Commission plan and ultimately to be carried out. This was the group of buildings in the vicinity of the Capitol, which he described as follows:

"The Capitol and the Library are already in close relationship; a balance building will soon be built to form a trine of principal structures. As the Capitoline hill falls rapidly to the north and southward from the two C streets, an acropolis effect would indeed be had by the creation of such a group of seven or nine buildings, of which the Capitol would be the dominant feature." [26]

[26] Paul J. Pelz, "The Grouping of Public Buildings in Washington," in Brown, *Papers,* p. 89. Paul J. Pelz (1841–1918) received his early education in Germany, coming to the United States for his apprenticeship in a New

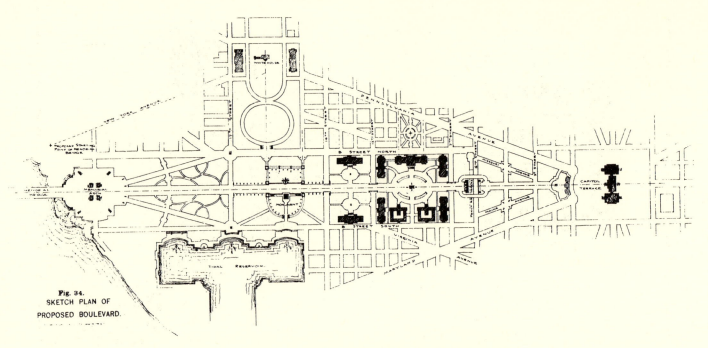

Fig. 34.
SKETCH PLAN OF
PROPOSED BOULEVARD.

Figure 51. Plan for Central Washington by Edgar V. Seeler: 1900

The proposal by Edgar V. Seeler, reproduced in Figure 51, was limited chiefly to the proper location of the proposed "centennial avenue." Seeler argued that tilting the axis of this to run from the

Capitol to the Washington Monument would be not only discernible but disturbing to the viewer. He therefore led it past the Monument, placing a lower structure on its north side opposite the shaft. He suggested bridging the railroad tracks, which were to be depressed. Between the Capitol and the Monument Seeler showed a large quadrangle of public buildings grouped around an oval plaza. He proposed to continue the avenue on a straight line across a new bridge over the river. To balance this formal composition at its western end Seeler advocated the construction of an enormous memorial arch to stand in the center of a monumental square as the approach to the new bridge. Seeler's plan was less important than his recommendations for some permanent body to study, review, and submit recommendations on development proposals.

York architectural firm. He moved to Washington as architect and engineer for the U.S. Lighthouse Board. In 1873 he formed a partnership with John L. Smithmeyer, and their joint submission won the competition for the design of the Library of Congress. The firm designed a number of other public and private buildings in Washington and other cities. Pelz was thus thoroughly familiar with Washington. Moreover, he had earlier become involved with plans for the city's improvement when he had volunteered his services as "advisory architect" to Franklin W. Smith, whose elaborate plans for the Mall area have already been described. Pelz designed for one of Smith's publications a new presidential residence, the drawing for which is reproduced in Smith, *National Galleries,* p. 41.

"No department of the Government should be permitted to choose a site or decide upon a building without the advice and consent of expert counselors. . . . But when the monumental reconstruction of the city of Washington is to be considered . . . the occasion is one which cries for the appointment of a special commission—a body of individual workers, with the power and means to employ the best talent in whatsoever lines their judgment shall direct, whose decisions shall command the respect of the nation, and shall be authoritative by reason of their feasibility and their artistic and practical excellence." [27]

George Totten prefaced a description of his plan by a discussion of what could be learned from the design of the great world's fairs and expositions of past years. He pointed out that in designing such groups of temporary buildings much had been discovered that could be applied to permanent civic design. As Totten stated,

"In our Chicago experience we learned lessons—what vistas mean, what uniform scale means, how effectively broad terraces, balustrades, and other accessories become, how the value of architecture is enhanced by reflection in suitably arranged water basins. . . .

"The grouping of government buildings would, though in a more restricted sense, follow the same natural laws as in the grouping of exposition buildings; the more important ones would be made the more monumental and dignified and given the most prominent locations—vista terminations where possible; lesser ones arranged along avenues somewhat according to their needs and

uses, leading up to the former or to other monuments of special interest." [28]

Totten lamented the fact that the World's Columbian Exposition had not been held in Washington, rather than Chicago. If built on the Mall it would have provided an unparalleled opportunity to experiment with full-size models. Totten's impression of what might be accomplished appears in Figure 52, which he termed a "hasty sketch" rather than a carefully studied plan. Perhaps this accounts for the depiction of the Washington Monument turned forty-five degrees from its true orientation. His paper does not describe the scheme, but the general nature of his proposals is clear. One aspect is worth noting: The treatment of the Washington Monument area as a plaza reached from the west by a broad and monumental flight of stairs, a feature, although much changed, to be found in the later official plan.

As important a contribution to the conference as any of these plans was the thoughtful and profusely illustrated address by Frederick Law Olmsted, Jr., who was rapidly succeeding to his father's position as the outstanding landscape architect of America. This essay was one of the first attempts by an American designer to define the role of landscape architecture in the planning and improvement of cities. It can be read with profit today because of the timelessness of most of the principles enunciated by the younger Olmsted.

Olmsted began by pointing out that landscape architecture was not limited to the creation of planned informality in apparent imitation of nature but dealt with the much broader subject of the relation of buildings to the space about them and the ordering of that space into an appropriate design. This design could be informal or formal, depending on the effect desired. The design of the

[27] Edgar V. Seeler, "The Monumental Grouping of Government Buildings in Washington," in Brown, *Papers,* p. 57. Edgar V. Seeler (1867–1929) was one of Philadelphia's leading architects. He was a graduate of the Massachusetts Institute of Technology and had studied at the Ecole des Beaux Arts in Paris. For three years he taught at the University of Pennsylvania before opening his office in Philadelphia. His recommendation for the appointment of a permanent commission to oversee important governmental buildings was not the first such suggestion. An earlier proposal for such a body had been made in 1899 by the Washington Board of Trade. The text of this may be found in "Action of the Washington Board of Trade in Relation to the Park System of the District of Columbia," in Charles Moore (ed.), *Park Improvement Papers,* Park Improvement Papers No. 1, Washington, 1902, p. 13.

[28] George O. Totten, Jr., "Exposition Architecture in its Relation to the Grouping of Government Buildings," in Brown, *Papers,* p. 84. George Oakley Totten, Jr. (1865–1939) studied architecture at Columbia University and at the Ecole des Beaux Arts. Totten established an architectural practice in Washington after two years of work in the office of the U.S. Supervising Architect. He was later to become better known in the city for his designs of many of the foreign embassy buildings, including those for France, Spain, and Poland.

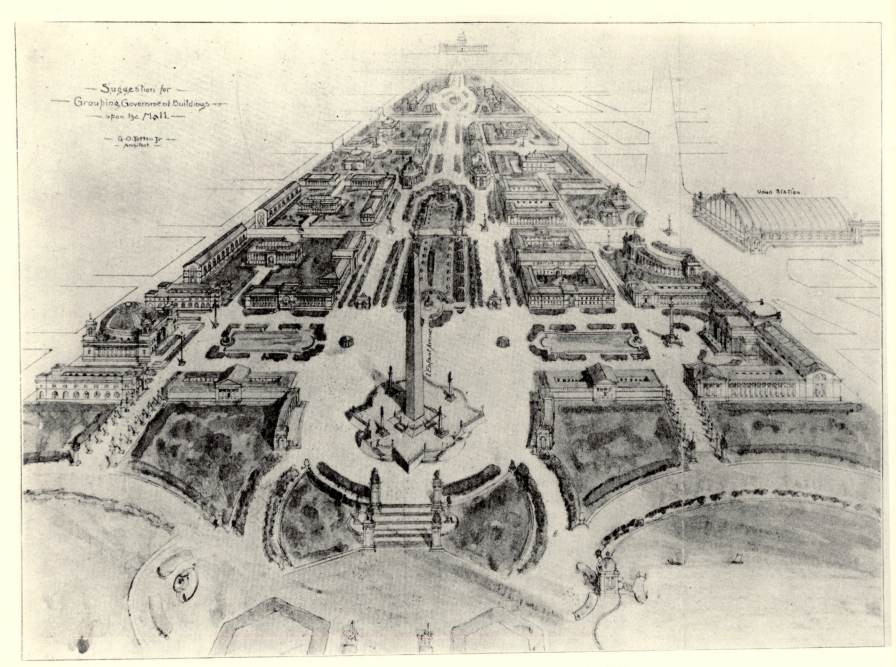

Figure 52. Plan for Central Washington by George O. Totten, Jr.: 1900

landscape, however, should be appropriate to the buildings themselves and to the plan of the city. Then, turning to the problem of government buildings in Washington, Olmsted asserted: "Great public edifices must be strongly formal, whether they are perfectly symmetrical or not, and this formal quality ought to be recognized in the plan of their surroundings if the total effect is to be consistent." [29]

Olmsted then discussed the problems of scale in formal landscape treatment, pointing out that "Where the scale of the general scheme is large, there should be a corresponding simplicity, and the formality need not be and should not be pushed so far into detail as in the case of projects of smaller scale." [30]

Attention should be directed to the over-all plan of the city in determining the appropriate landscape design of its major elements. In Olmsted's opinion the Mall as it then existed must be viewed as a failure by this test.

"The Mall was not laid out on the main axis of the Capitol without a reason. . . . It was laid out there because it was meant to relate directly and visibly to the Capitol; while it has been planned and planted for the most part in utter disregard of this primary purpose. Its details, some good in themselves and some bad, instead of being subordinated to the considerations that fixed its position, have arrogated to themselves the control of the design." [31]

Then, becoming specific on how he would treat this great open space, Olmsted offered a suggestion that was later to be incorporated in the official plan for the city and eventually to be carried out:

"When I speak of the importance of treating the Mall in such a way as to relate strongly and visibly to the Capitol, I do not mean merely, or necessarily, that a straight road should be slashed down the middle of it. . . . A different and more agreeable treatment would be a sort of compound "boulevard," marked by several parallel rows of trees with several pavements and turf strips. Such

an avenue is that of the Champs Elysées. . . . The axis of the Capitol should neither be ignored by the use of a wiggling road and confused informal planning, nor should it be marked by a mere commonplace boulevard, but by an impressively broad and simple space of turf, with strong flanking masses of foliage and architecture and shaded driveways." [32]

Olmsted touched on other points of importance. He would deal with the railroad problem by combining a bridge over the tracks with a great elevated terrace reached by roadways from each side. He suggested that part of the planting on the Smithsonian grounds, the result of Alexander Downing's design half a century earlier, could be retained. He felt that, in replanning the Mall, the off-axis location of the Washington Monument could be tolerated, fearing that an adjustment of this axis would be detected by and have an unfortunate effect on the viewer. He also rejected the idea of continuing the Capitol axis across the Potomac over a bridge, stating that the effect created would not be proportional to its length. As to the construction of buildings on the Mall itself, Olmsted defended this not only because it was part of L'Enfant's original concept but because this treatment of the Mall could provide the greatest "artistic success" in establishing "the effect of grandeur, power, and dignified magnificence which should mark the seat of government of a great and intensely active people." [33]

Olmsted closed with a moving plea for following the original plan designed by L'Enfant and approved by President Washington:

"In great undertakings requiring centuries to mature the one hope of unity and harmony, the one hope of successful issue, is the establishment of a comprehensive plan and the consistent adherence to it.

"In any great plan time must develop features which seem under the conditions of the present moment capable of improvement, but unless the plan appears upon thoughtful and conservative judgment distinctly bad the one safe course is to adhere steadfastly to its fundamental features. Once open the plan to a radical change,

[29] Frederick Law Olmsted, Jr., "Landscape in Connection with Public Buildings in Washington," in Brown, *Papers*, p. 25.
[30] *ibid.*, p. 26.
[31] *ibid.*, p. 28.

[32] *ibid.*, pp. 29–30.
[33] *ibid.*, p. 34.

once establish the precedent of seriously altering it to meet the ideas of the moment, and the bars are thrown down for caprice and confusion.

"Here is a plan not hastily sketched, nor by a man of narrow views and little foresight. It is a plan with the authority of a century behind it, to which we can all demand undeviating adherence in the future. . . ." [34]

This remarkable paper by Olmsted has been summarized at such length not only because of its intrinsic value but because of the important role he was soon to play in designing the Washington of the future. Not all of his ideas prevailed, as will be seen in future chapters, but his powerful statement of the principles that should govern the replanning of Washington served as a guide through many of the design difficulties that confronted those in whose hands the task of replanning central Washington was thrust. It seems likely, also, that he must have stirred his listeners to a new awareness of the need to approach such a responsible assignment with respect for the past and for the national importance of the city as both a seat of federal government and a symbol of the spirit of a mighty nation.

In these and other papers of the Institute convention can be found most of the ideas that were later to be used by those charged with the responsibility of working out Washington's renewal. No single plan advanced at that time fully met the challenging requirements that had to be faced. And as yet the circumstances under which a comprehensive plan could be prepared had not been determined.

Doggedly, Senator McMillan once again attempted to provide the means. The American Institute of Architects committee on legislation, which had been the first tangible result of the convention discussion on improvements in Washington, met with the Senator and other members of the senate Committee on the District of Columbia. Following this meeting, on December 17, 1900, Senator McMillan introduced a proposed Joint Resolution authorizing the President to appoint a commission of two architects and one landscape architect to study and report on the location

and grouping of public buildings and the development of the park system in the District of Columbia. [35]

According to Brown, McMillan's attempts to secure House consent to the joint resolution failed because of Representative Cannon's opposition. He, it was said, regarded the spending of public funds on "anything of an artistic character a raid on the Treasury." [36] A different but risky strategy was therefore decided on. At an executive session of the Senate on March 8, 1901, McMillan secured the passage of the following Senate Resolution:

"That the Committee on the District of Columbia be, and it is hereby, directed to consider the subject and report to the Senate plans for the development and improvement of the entire park system of the District of Columbia. For the purpose of preparing such plans the committee may sit during the recess of Congress, and may secure the services of such experts as may be necessary for a proper consideration of the subject. The expenses of such investigation shall be paid from the contingent fund of the Senate." [37]

Two features of this resolution should be noted: First, the expenses were to be paid from Senate contingent funds. House approval was thus not required, and Cannon's opposition would be to no avail. While this parliamentary device succeeded in getting the necessary studies under way it was later to cause great difficulties. Members of the House, led by Cannon, who were opposed to the subsequent recommendations of the Senate Committee's experts could and did argue that the House had not been consulted in the matter.

Second, the resolution called only for the development of a plan for the District's parks. Perhaps Senator McMillan was guilty of concealing the true intent of the measure, for it was obvious from his actions in the following weeks that what he had in mind was nothing less than a comprehensive development plan for all of

[34] ibid.

[35] Charles Moore, "Introduction," in Brown, *Papers*, p. 9.
[36] Brown, *Memories*, p. 264.
[37] *Report of the Senate Committee on the District of Columbia on the Improvement of the Park System of the District of Columbia,* Washington, 1902, p. 7.

central Washington in addition to certain studies of Rock Creek and Potomac Parks.

After the passage of the resolution McMillan conferred with his secretary and Clerk of the District Committee, Charles Moore. Moore had followed the activities of the past year with increasing interest. McMillan asked him to suggest whom the committee might employ as experts to carry out the study. Moore proposed Daniel H. Burnham, the well-known Chicago architect who had been in charge of the board of design of the Chicago Fair of 1893 and had been the architect for numerous important buildings in Chicago and other large cities. McMillan proposed Frederick Law Olmsted, Jr., whom he did not know but whose father had designed Belle Isle Park in Detroit when the Senator was a member of the Detroit Board of Park Commissioners.[38]

On March 19 a subcommittee of the Senate District Committee, consisting of McMillan and Senators Gallinger and Martin, met with the legislative committee of the American Institute of Architects. The Institute committee chairman, William A. Boring of New York, was asked to recommend persons to undertake the contemplated studies. Boring suggested that two architects should be selected, one of whom should be Daniel Burnham. He also put forward the name of Olmsted as landscape architect. McMillan agreed, saying "I think that is a very practical suggestion, and I may say that you could not suit me better personally. . . . The men you speak of would be the men I myself would have selected, if I were asked to select them." [39]

Actually, McMillan, acting through Moore, had already asked Burnham and Olmsted to meet him in Washington. Olmsted was present at the meeting just described. Burnham, arriving two days later, met with Moore and accepted the chairmanship of the expert group on the understanding that the other members would consist of Olmsted and a third man to be selected by them. Burnham inquired if there had been suggestions for the other architect. Moore replied that the choice was up to Burnham and Olmsted, "but if your choice should fall on Mr. McKim it would be very gratifying." [40] Burnham stated that Charles McKim "is the man I had in mind. He was the one I most relied upon in the Chicago Fair work. I will talk with Olmsted and will see McKim in New York and report." [41]

The following day Burnham conferred with McMillan and Olmstead. The three men, together with Moore, then drove through Rock Creek Park, as one newspaper recounted, "behind a pair of fast-moving bays . . . for the purpose of acquainting the park commissioners with the work which has already been accomplished . . . and both gentlemen expressed their pleasure at the progress made." [42] The same newspaper story mentioned that not only would plans be prepared for the parks of the city by this group but that they "will also have authority to suggest a general plan for continuing the erection of public buildings in Washington, the idea being to avoid, as far as possible, incongruities in architecture, and also the construction of buildings without surrounding ground. . . ."

A few days later Burnham visited McKim and talked to him at length about the proposal. McKim conferred with his partners and on March 25 sent Burnham and Olmsted a letter agreeing to join them in the assignment.[43] Burnham reported this to Moore and also asked him to send copies of "everything we can use" and specifically requested the plan for the Mall prepared the previous year by Samuel Parsons.[44] The preliminaries were over, the amateurs retired from the scene, the professionals of the Senate Park Commission set to work.

[38] Moore, *Burnham,* I, p. 137; Charles Moore, "Sketch of Senator McMillan's Life," Michigan Senate and House of Representatives, *In Memory of Hon. James McMillan,* East Lansing, 1903.

[39] "Informal Hearing Before the Subcommittee of the Committee of the District of Columbia, United States Senate," in Moore, *Park Improvement Papers,* Park Improvement Papers No. 5, p. 4.

[40] Moore, *Burnham,* I, p. 139.

[41] *ibid.*

[42] The Washington *Post,* March 23, 1901.

[43] Moore, *McKim,* p. 182. Moore states that Burnham first talked to McKim on March 21, but this is clearly an error.

[44] Moore, *Burnham,* I, p. 140.

CHAPTER 4
The Senate Park Commission at Work

The first meeting of the Senate Park Commission, as the group consisting of Burnham, McKim and Olmsted, came to be called, took place early in April 1901. In the three days these men, Moore, McMillan, and other interested persons conferred, they reached a number of preliminary decisions about the division of the work and the scope of the project. The Commission members also were taken by Secretary of War Elihu Root to meet President McKinley. McKim, normally rather reserved, became enthusiastic about the possibilities of significant accomplishments. To Wendell Garrison he wrote: "The Washington business opens with great promise, and the probable support of the President and of Secretaries Root and Gage. Opposition will doubtless develop as work proceeds, but I am satisfied that we shall have strong friends. . . . The President received us cordially and spoke without hesitation in favor of preserving the works of Washington's time." [1]

And to Prescott Butler he stated: "I have just returned from Washington after three most interesting days with Burnham and Olmsted over the District of Columbia problem. If half of what is talked of can be carried through it will make the Capitol City one of the most beautiful centers in the world." [2]

Burnham had a surprise for his colleagues. On their way back to Washington with Moore after luncheon at Cabin John Bridge, Burnham suddenly announced: "I have talked the matter over with Senator McMillan. The four of us are going to Europe in June to see and discuss *together* parks in their relations to public buildings —that is our problem here in Washington and we must have weeks when we are thinking of nothing else." [3]

Five days later Burnham wrote McKim stating how important he thought it was for them to visit Europe and to have a long period, uninterrupted by any other work, to develop in broad concept the general plan for Washington. He asked McKim to handle the necessary arrangements for a departure shortly after the first of June. The itinerary remained to be established. Doubtless Burnham, with typical enthusiasm, had suggested a long list of places that should be visited. McKim, more cautious, less rugged of constitution, and more experienced in European travel, had rather more modest ideas. On May 10, he wrote to Moore stating that arrangements had been made for a Cooks travel assistant to meet the party in Cherbourg and to accompany them until they departed from London, and then added:

"As regards our itinéraire, we are, I fear, undertaking altogether too much, in endeavoring to see so many places in so short a time. I feel sure that we should not only leave out St. Petersburg, but make a considerable further contraction, in order to form any intelligent idea of the ground to be gone over. In the thirty days at

[1] Letter from McKim to Wendell Garrison, April 10, 1901. Charles F. McKim Papers, Manuscript Division, Library of Congress, Letterbooks, 1900–1901.
[2] As quoted in Charles Moore, *The Life and Times of Charles McKim*, Boston, 1929, p. 185, no date given.
[3] Charles Moore, *Daniel H. Burnham*, Boston, 1921, I, p. 142.

our command, it seems madness to spend so large a proportion of it on the railroad." [4]

At a meeting of the Commission on May 17 the subject was again discussed. In the end the members agreed on a somewhat more limited list of cities to be visited over a period of five weeks. In addition, the Commission would have an extra six days on board ship on each voyage. During this period of approximately seven weeks they hoped to sketch out the general plan which would then be revised and detailed in the remaining months of 1901. Moore, the trusted aide of Senator McMillan and whose knowledge of Washington was extensive, was to accompany them.

Before their departure date of June 13 the Commission decided to visit and inspect some of the Virginia towns and estates that had been familiar to L'Enfant, Washington, Jefferson, and others who had been involved in the original planning of the city of Washington. Lyman J. Gage, Secretary of the Treasury and formerly chairman of the board of directors of the Chicago Fair, arranged for the party to use the lighthouse tender *Holly* for this purpose.

Stratford Hall on the Potomac River was the first stop on April 20. The following day the group landed at Yorktown, drove to Carter's Grove, and then to Williamsburg, where they spent the night. Here they examined the axial plan of the former Virginia capital. They visited other estates, including the majestic Westover, the seat of the Byrd family. While the scale of the developments differed greatly from that of Washington they provided examples of axial planning and formal treatment which may have stimulated the thinking of the group. Moreover, the trip provided an opportunity for them to discuss many of their ideas about the future of Washington that had occurred to them since they had last met. A later meeting in Washington and on board the *Holly* in the middle of May offered other chances to review their thinking about the possible treatment of the national capital.[5]

One more detail remained before they left for Europe. On June 1 McKim wrote to Burnham suggesting that Augustus Saint-Gaudens, the noted sculptor with whom both had worked during the development of the Chicago Fair, should be made a member of the Commission. Burnham gladly and promptly agreed and so suggested to Senator McMillan.[6] Because of the lateness of the date and Saint-Gaudens' recent illness, he was not able to accompany the other members to Europe. He was, however, asked to meet with the Commission on the day before its departure. McKim's letter to Saint-Gaudens on June 11 regarding this meeting reveals how much the Commission had already accomplished in its preliminary plans:

"I hope you will be able to join us on Monday, as the skeleton of the general scheme for the Mall will be discussed, and if possible accepted as the basis for future development. It is of the utmost importance that the question of the establishment of permanent sites for the Lincoln and Grant [memorials] especially should be reached at this meeting, and to do this effectively your presence and authority are most needful." [7]

Although the European expedition by the Commission was unusual, since summer junkets by congressional committees and staff members had not at that time become common occurrence, it proved to be enormously useful for the task at hand. This was to be no idle inspection of great monuments of the past; instead it was intended as a systematic exploration of the sources of inspiration that had guided L'Enfant's original plan and an examination of current European treatment of civic architecture in its relationship to open spaces. Moreover, the Commission expected to use much of its time in discussing specific solutions to the problems of modern Washington. Some of these had already been reviewed and tentative and general plans for the future prepared in sketch form. The party hoped to return from Europe with all major decisions reached, leaving only the details to be worked out as specific design studies were pursued.

The Commission lost no time in beginning. Olmstead had

[4] Letter from McKim to Moore, May 10, 1901. Charles Moore Papers, Manuscript Division, Library of Congress, Park Commission Correspondence, Mr. McKim.
[5] Details of the Commmission's trip and extracts from Burnham's diary of this period appear in Moore, *Burnham,* I, pp. 144–46.
[6] *ibid.,* pp. 147–48; Moore. *McKim,* pp. 185–86.
[7] Letter from McKim to Saint-Gaudens, June 11, 1901, as quoted in Moore, *McKim,* p. 186.

brought with him a tin cylinder containing maps of the city. Doubtless the other members of the group had brought along previous notes, studies, and sketches completed by them or by others containing suggestions for the treatment of central Washington. Moore records that as soon as the *Deutschland* had cleared New York harbor and the pilot had been taken off,

"Burnham piped all hands to conference and work began that day. The party had staterooms on the boat-deck; and the quartette lunched and usually dined in the little upper-deck grill-room, where the food was as light as it was good, and talk was uninterrupted. . . . Every day the maps were spread and the Washington projects were discussed." [8]

Moore also described the varied approaches and philosophies of the three men as they worked:

"Burnham's mind worked on a grand scale. He saw things in the large. McKim always acquiesced; he never contradicted; but when his logical mind began to work, quite hesitatingly he would offer suggestions which seemed only an expansion of the original idea, or perhaps a little better way of arriving at the intended result. Olmsted, being younger and possessing a brain fertile in expedients, offered many variations on the themes." [9]

When Moore suggested that some of the ideas advanced by the Commission were too grandiose to be accepted by Congress, Burnham retorted that only "the very finest plans their minds could conceive" would be adequate; even these might one day prove to be too modest, and if compromises were to be made they should come later after the plans were submitted and not at the outset.[10]

Neither Burnham nor McKim was a good sailor. Fortunately, however, the crossing was smooth, and much work was accomplished during the six days on board. On the afternoon of June 19 they arrived at Cherbourg and took the boat train for Paris. At 3:30 the next morning they gathered on the balcony of Burnham's room on the fifth floor of the Hotel Continental overlooking the Tuileries to watch the sun rise over Paris. Then, after a continental breakfast they retired for some much needed rest.[11]

Later that day they visited the Ecole des Beaux Arts and drove around the city. The next morning the party walked in the Tuileries and spent the afternoon in the Bois de Boulogne, returning to the center of Paris by a Seine steamer. Shortly before midnight they boarded a train for Rome, arriving there early on the morning of June 24, where they installed themselves at the Quirinal Hotel. Burnham, conscious of the summer heat, ordered two carriages with large umbrellas, and it was in these rather conspicuous vehicles that they made their way about the city.

McKim and Burnham had been instrumental in the establishment of the American Academy in Rome, and this was the first point to be visited. In the absence of the Director, S.A.B. Abbott, they were greeted by George W. Breck, a painter who later became the school's director, and Louis W. Pulsifer, an architectural student from Harvard and the Massachusetts Institute of Technology. Both men accompanied the party on many of its trips and acted as informal guides.

In the city and its surrounding country the Commission absorbed the former glories of ancient Rome and the great monuments of the Renaissance and baroque periods. Olmsted had brought a camera and tripod and special lenses, and here and elsewhere he busily recorded the details of architectural and landscape treatment for future reference. The young designer also filled his notebooks with dimensions of stairways, balustrades, and other features of buildings and gardens which he measured with his steel tape.

At Saint Peter's they admired the great piazza and its fountains surrounded by the noble colonnades of Bernini. The Villa Medici, occupied by the French Academy, the Baths of Caracalla, Hadrians's Villa, the Villa d'Este, the Villa Madama, the Villa Albani, and the Vatican Gardens were all included in their visits, along with the great piazzas and buildings of the central city. Everywhere they discussed the problems of Washington and how

[8] *ibid.*, pp. 187–88.
[9] *ibid.*
[10] *ibid.*

[11] *ibid.*, p. 189; Moore, *Burnham,* I, pp. 149–50.

the ancient buildings, squares, gardens, and fountains they were examining could be adapted to fit the requirements of a younger capital city.

Rome has always been a great teacher, and the members of this eager group proved willing students. Of their deliberations and conclusions, Moore, who participated in them, says:

"Some things seemed to them self-evident; that the problems in Washington must be worked out along Roman rather than Parisian lines; that simplicity, directness and subordination of ornament to structural uses should prevail; and that modern French work should not be allowed. Also that the effects produced by tree-crowned terraces should be sought where the configuration of the land permitted. . . . More than this, it was determined that the fountain and not the man-on-horseback is the proper ornament for Washington, and that the heat of our capital requires that the city should be filled with running water even as is Rome." [12]

Several decisions were reached during this period. Moore tells how, as they sat on the steps of the temple of the Villa Borghese, they agreed that the bridge across the Potomac should be a low structure leading from the Lincoln Memorial, whose site had evidently already been determined, on an axis whose western terminus would be the Lee Mansion high on a hill in Arlington Cemetery.[13] They also talked about the troublesome problem of the railroad station and tracks on the Mall and the coming meeting in London of Burnham, who had already been designated as the architect of the new station, with President Alexander J. Cassatt of the Pennsylvania Railroad. Burnham had been informed that he was not to concern himself with the station's location, which the railroad officials regarded as fixed on the Mall site, but they all agreed that a new attempt should be made to persuade Cassatt to agree to move it south of the Mall.[14]

Reluctantly the party left Rome for Venice, which they reached on July 1. They had included this city on their itinerary because

L'Enfant had been furnished a plan of it by Thomas Jefferson at the time he was working on the design of Washington. There was little here that could have helped the members of the Commission in their plan for the city of Washington, but the four days they spent in exploring this subtle and charming city furnished welcome relaxation from their busy days in Rome the previous week. Much of their time was spent on the canals. Burnham noticed that one of the gondoliers had a familiar face and, on inquiring, learned that he had been employed at the Chicago Fair, where he had once rowed Burnham about the lagoon. One night they realized that McKim was missing. " 'How shall we find McKim?' Olmsted asked. 'That is easy,' returned Burnham. 'We will go to the Piazza di San Marco and find him on the axis.' And the plan worked." [15]

On the afternoon of July 4 the party left for Vienna, where Charles Herdliska, the secretary of the American legation, had arranged for them to visit the palace and gardens of Schoenbrun and to drive around the Ringstrasse to see that impressive boulevard with its noble buildings standing in park-like settings. On July 7 they departed for Budapest, where they arrived that evening after a glorious train ride along the Danube River and through the Carpathian Mountains. Here they enjoyed the contrast between the ancient town on the Buda side and the modern city on the Pesth bank divided by the majestic Danube with its informal island park that reminded them of the senior Olmsted's design for Belle Isle Park at Detroit.[16]

At midnight on July 8 they boarded the Orient Express for Paris for a more extended visit in that city prior to their departure for England. Three great chateaux and their gardens were on their itinerary as well. At Versailles, Vaux-le-Vicomte, and Fountainebleau, they inspected the work of the great French landscape designer, André Le Nôtre. These magnificent formal gardens were of the scale of Washington itself. They knew that L'Enfant, who had spent his boyhood at Versailles, had been inspired by their *rond-points, allées,* and tree-lined symmetrical stretches of water in devising his design for the city which they must now replan. The imposing vistas with their main and cross axes furnished a vivid

[12] Moore, *McKim,* p. 192.
[13] *ibid.,* p. 193.
[14] *ibid.,* 192.

[15] *ibid.,* p. 194.
[16] *ibid.,* pp. 194–95; Moore, *Burnham,* I, pp. 152–53.

image of what the Washington Mall might one day become if their plans could be carried out.[17]

In Paris they also revisited the monumental central axis of the city stretching from the Louvre through the gardens of the Tuileries, the Place de la Concorde, and up the Champs-Elysées to the Arc de Triomphe standing boldly in the center of the Place de l'Étoile. Here stood in reality a monumental and formal composition similar in concept and scale to what the Commission members envisaged for the center of Washington. Doubtless it was at this time they resolved to prevail on President Cassatt, then waiting for Burnham in London, to visit Paris with them and experience with them this splendid urban scene if he remained adamant about the location of the new railroad station. The comparison which they hoped would convince Cassatt was summarized by Moore:

"The Palace of the Tuileries as the Capitol, the Tuileries Gardens as the Mall, the Obelisk in the crossing of two Paris axes as the Washington Monument centers the Capitol and White House axes; and then a Lincoln Memorial as a national monument in location at the termination of the composition, and also as a center of distribution comparable to the Arc de Triomphe de l'Étoile." [18]

On July 14 Burnham left the group to visit Frankfurt, where Cassatt wanted him to inspect what he regarded as the finest railroad station in the world. From there he went to Berlin for a day, then by train to Holland and by boat to England, where he rejoined McKim, Moore, and Olmsted at the Berkeley Hotel in London late on July 17. Burnham's interview with Cassatt occurred the next day. His colleagues prepared for a long and suspenseful wait, but Burnham returned after only a brief period—so short, in fact, that the other members felt certain that this signaled their defeat. Burnham, however, jubilantly reported Cassatt's words, as here recorded by Moore:

"Since you gentlemen left the United States a community of interests between the Baltimore and Ohio and the Pennsylvania Rail-

roads has been brought about. We are willing to build a Union Station north of the Capitol, provided Senator McMillan will secure from Congress an appropriation of a million and a half toward tunneling Capitol Hill to make the connections with the south." [19]

Immediately they sent a cable to Senator McMillan, informing him of what they rightly regarded as the key to replanning the city. Certainly if they had been weary from their travels and constant discussions of the previous weeks, they now felt considerably invigorated. During the next few days they approached their studies with renewed zest. In London, at Oxford, at Hatfield House, Bushy Park, Hampton Court, and Windsor they walked, talked, photographed, and measured, in what by then must have become a routine but still stimulating succession of experiences.

Aboard the *Deutschland* once again on July 26 on their homeward voyage from Southampton, the Commission resumed its round of shipboard discussions. Much remained to be accomplished, but the seven-week period had proved tremendously productive. By the time they docked on the morning of August 1 the major elements of the Washington plan had been laid down. Now the Commission faced the difficult and painstaking task of testing the feasibility of its decisions by more precise design studies of individual elements in the great scheme. Now, too, was the time for others to be brought into the planning process and for preparations to be made for a great exhibition of the final design.

It would have been ideal if the Commission could have set up its staff in drafting rooms and offices in Washington and, as a group, directly supervised the final design work. Already, how-

[17] Moore, *McKim*, pp. 195–97; Moore, *Burnham*, I, pp. 153–54.
[18] Moore, *McKim*, p. 198.

[19] *ibid.* Cassatt's offer was a splendid gesture, and his role in the replanning of Washington should never be forgotten. He may well have been motivated by simple engineering considerations, since there were economies to be realized by the two lines sharing a common terminal and the Mall site was too small for this purpose. I prefer to believe that other reasons were paramount. His sister was Mary Cassatt, the prominent Impressionist painter. Perhaps he shared her artistic talents and realized the potential beauty of the Mall if once freed from the baneful effects of the railroad. He was himself familiar with similar European developments, since he received part of his education at Heidelberg and had traveled widely on the continent. Moreover, his wife was a niece of President James Buchanan, and this family connection with Washington may have stimulated his concern for the welfare of the capital city.

ever, they had neglected their own affairs for the seven weeks they had spent in Europe, and their professional obligations made it impossible to conduct the work in this manner. Instead, they established three centers of activity, in Boston, in New York, and in Washington.

In Washington Moore and McMillan arranged for a portion of the Senate Press Gallery to be turned into a drafting room. There James G. Langdon was in charge of assembling maps of Washington, compiling data on existing parks, and preparing new and more accurate base maps of the Mall, the Capitol, and the White House grounds.[20] This work had started in April. Later, as final plans were being prepared in New York, the Washington office received and answered a great many queries about the exact location and height of certain buildings, street widths, and other tedious but essential details. It was also here and in the office of Moore and McMillan that the Commission members met to review their designs.

Most of the creative design efforts took place in New York under the direct supervision of McKim. On the floor above his partners' architectural offices, McKim set up a large studio. William T. Partridge, a recent architectural graduate of Columbia University, was given responsibility for organizing the work here under McKim's immediate direction. The members of the Commission agreed that McKim should have the assignment of redesigning the Mall and the buildings connected with this central composition which was the heart of public Washington.

Olmsted's professional office was located in Brookline, a suburb of Boston. He assumed primary responsibility for the design of the parks in the District of Columbia and for matters relating to landscape architecture generally. He also took over what proved to be the exasperating task of prodding and supervising the Boston model maker who was to prepare two large topographical models of central Washington as it existed and as planned by the Commission.

Burnham's role was far from limited, although in his Chicago office he did not attempt to produce plans for any specific segment of the over-all scheme. McKim and Olmsted sent him studies and

[20] Moore, *Burnham,* I, p. 166.

plans for information and comments, and the members of the Commission or two or three of them arranged to meet from time to time in Washington, New York, and Boston.[21] Burnham found much of his time taken up with settling the many details connected with the location of the new railroad station. True, Cassatt had agreed in London to a new location of the station, but there were many engineering problems to solve, the exact site had not been finally determined, congressional approval for the expenditure of federal funds remained unsecured, and Burnham was concerned that the final arragements should permit the design of a monumental structure to serve as a fitting entrance to the city without detracting from or clashing with the nearby Capitol Building.

In Philadelphia on September 26 Burnham and Cassatt met to review the situation. The site then under consideration was at C Street and New Jersey Avenue, the existing location of the Baltimore and Ohio station, only one block from the Capitol grounds. Cassatt's position, speaking for the railroad, as Burnham reported to Senator McMillan the following day, was that this site would be acceptable if certain actions by the government could be assured. As Burnham put it:

"This scheme involves a tunnel under the Government plaza lying between the Capitol and the Congressional Library; it also involves the condemnation of the two blocks lying between the said plaza and C Street North, on which latter the new station will face. This condemnation is necessary because the station and its surroundings should be treated in a monumental manner, as they will become the vestibule of the city of Washington, and as they will be in close proximity to the Capitol itself." [22]

[21] The following meetings, among others, took place: Burnham and McKim in New York on August 17; Burnham, McKim, and Olmsted on August 19 in Boston and with McMillan on August 20 in Manchester, Massachusetts; Burnham and McKim in New York on September 15; Burnham, McKim, and Saint-Gaudens in New York on September 25; Burnham and McKim in Washington on September 29; Burnham, McKim, and Saint-Gaudens in Washington on October 20, 23, 24, and 25, joined by Olmsted on October 21 and 22; and Burnham, McKim, and Olmsted in Washington on December 3. Moore, *Burnham* I, pp. 157–63.
[22] Report from Burnham to McMillan, September 27, 1901, as quoted in *ibid.,* I, p. 160.

The site, however, had several disadvantages. The length of the required train shed would put this structure across the line of Massachusetts Avenue, and a tunnel for this important thoroughfare would be required to avoid the creation of a major traffic block. In addition, the location so near the Capitol would make it difficult to design a monumental building which would not rival the Capitol in importance.

Early in December McKim and Olmsted joined Burnham and McMillan in an inspection of the site. They agreed that a location to the north of Massachusetts Avenue would be preferable. Burnham, probably seconded by McMillan, was able to convince Cassatt that the Massachusetts Avenue location should be chosen. This was finally agreed on, although much fill would be required to bring the plaza in front of the station to the proper elevation. As Burnham reported to Moore on December 13,

"The engineers made some difficulty because of the fill required. But . . . everything is now in good shape. I again beg that the District engineers shall raise no questions, and that they shall heartily assist in carrying through the design.

"The Government is to fill and finish the Grand Court in front of the depot. Of course, this will cost some money, but it is for the adornment of the city, to produce a vestibule in keeping with the Capitol, and is as important as the work around the Monument in the Mall.

"The railways can get along without this Grand Court, but we cannot. It is essential to the broad scheme of improvement, and is for the dignity and beauty of the city, and should be provided for in the railroad bill, so that work on it can proceed early this year." [23]

Once again Burnham's great capacity for bringing together and reconciling conflicting views had brought a solution to a difficult problem. Now the matter was in the hands of Senator McMillan, who had the responsibility of preparing, introducing, and steering through the Senate the necessary legislation. While there was some opposition to this action, the merits of the proposal seemed obvious to all, and by the end of 1901 congressional support appeared assured. [24]

Meanwhile work proceeded on the Mall plan and other aspects of the Commission's work in New York, Boston, and Washington. The members began to consider the manner in which their recommendations should be presented. Obviously a report containing a full description of the plan and the reasons for each proposal would be needed. Burnham had employed W. H. Harper of Chicago to do the necessary writing. Harper's unfamiliarity with Washington proved to be a disadvantage, however, and it was finally decided that Olmsted and Moore should undertake this important responsibility. [25]

McKim felt strongly that additional publicity was needed. In September he suggested to Senator McMillan that the best commercial artists and illustrators be engaged to prepare large color renderings showing the Commission's proposals. These, he felt, would be in a style more familiar to laymen and would be more readily understandable than the usual architectural plans and drawings. The Senator immediately agreed, offering to pay the cost himself if he could not secure government funds for the purpose. [26]

More than a dozen artists were eventually drawn into the project on this basis. Editors of the magazines for which they worked were asked to release part of their time for a matter of national importance. These drawings were also reproduced in black and white in the printed report as well as in newspaper and magazine stories when the recommendations were made public. They did much to render comprehensible to public officials and the public at large the real nature of the Commission's proposals for the capital city. Some of them have been preserved in the office of the Commission of Fine Arts, but unhappily most of them have

[23] Letter from Burnham to Moore, December 13, 1901, as quoted in *ibid.,* I, p. 164. There were a number of other conferences about the troublesome matter of grades. A final decision was reached on March 16 at a meeting in Philadelphia attended by Cassatt, the President of the Baltimore and Ohio Railroad, the chief engineer of the Pennsylvania Railroad, the Engineer Commissioner of the District of Columbia, Burnham, Moore, and several others. See *ibid.,* I, pp. 176–77.

[24] The Senate approved the bill on May 15, 1902, but Congress adjourned before the House could act. Final approval by Congress occurred in February 1903.

[25] Moore, *Burnham,* I, p. 159n.4.

[26] *ibid.,* p. 165.

been lost or destroyed by later generations who did not realize either their historic importance or their artistic merit.[27]

The Commission also resolved that there should be a public exhibition of its plans. On October 22 former Senator and Mrs. John B. Henderson invited the members of the Commission and the trustees of the Corcoran Art Gallery to dinner. At that time the trustees offered the use of several rooms of the Corcoran Gallery as an exhibition space, and the Commission eagerly accepted this invitation.[28]

Earlier in the course of its work the Commission had decided that two large topographic models at a scale of 1 foot to 1000 feet should be prepared for both study and presentation purposes. One model was to show central Washington as it then existed; the other was to present the Commission's recommendations. Each measured about 9 by 17 feet and was to be complete down to the last building and tree. The Commission employed George C. Curtis of Boston to prepare these models. Another model, showing the suggested treatment of the area around the Washington Monument, was built in McKim's office.

Mr. Curtis was to cause the Commission a great deal of trouble. He complained constantly about the lack of time to complete the two projects. He repeatedly wrote to McKim asking for funds which were slow in coming from Washington, and at the last minute he threatened not to send one of the models to Washington unless he was paid in advance. Despite an extension of 15 days when it became evident that the models could not be completed and delivered by January 1, they remained partially unfinished as the time for opening of the exhibition approached. McKim, desperate and angry, telephoned McMillan, who sent Curtis a wire directing him to ship one of the models being built in Boston to Washington immediately regardless of its condition.[29]

Part of the difficulty was caused by the decentralized activities of the Commission and its staff. The original agreement with Curtis had called for him to construct both models in the New York office. He argued, and McKim reluctantly agreed, that he could work better and faster if part of the job was carried out in his Boston shop. The model of the Commission proposals was ultimately shipped to New York, and Curtis was supposed to send along some of his employees to complete it there. The other model of existing Washington, a photograph of which appears in Figure 53, remained in Boston. Olmsted there and McKim in New York spent much of their time and doubtless all of their patience in urging Curtis and his men to greater speed. In the end both models arrived in Washington in time for the exhibit, and, although McKim felt that their "condition of incompleteness" would endanger "the success of the whole work of the Commission," they served their purpose well, and their flaws apparently were magnified by McKim, who could tolerate nothing less than perfection.[30]

The other problem with Curtis concerned money. In this he was not alone. The artists who had been retained by McKim were requesting payment for their work, and money from Washington was slow in coming. McKim, using funds from a special account set up by his firm, met the payroll as best he could. He obviously hesitated to bother Moore, but on several occasions he had to remind Moore that funds were due and that Curtis and the artists were demanding payment.[31] Moore, himself, evidently encountered difficulties in securing government funds to meet the costs of the

---

[27] Efforts to trace these drawings in the Commission of Fine Arts, the Library of Congress, and the Archives of the United States have proved fruitless. The few that remain are framed and hang in the office of the Commission of Fine Arts. The Commission's photographic files contain black and white reproductions of most of the drawings no longer extant. Several color reproductions appear in Moore, *Burnham*.

[28] *ibid.*, I, p. 162n.2; p. 167.

[29] Commission correspondence with and about Curtis is extensive. See, for example, the following letters from McKim: to Moore, December 23, 1901;

to Moore, December 24, 1901; to Moore, January 2, 1902; telegram to Olmsted, January 3, 1902; to Moore, January 15, 1902, in Charles Moore Papers, Park Commission Correspondence, Mr. McKim.

[30] The quotations are from a handwritten note from McKim to Moore the evening of the exhibition, January 15, 1902, Charles Moore Papers, Park Commission Correspondence, Mr. McKim. The letter referred to the proposed public buildings on the model as "huge unbaked blocks—wholly out of scale & character with their environment." McKim added, "Unless these bldgs are immediately finished Congress will form at the start an erroneous & adverse opinion—which once established will be impossible to overcome. . . . In my opinion this *unfinished* model is at this moment almost an argument against us."

[31] Letter from McKim to Moore, December 6, 1901; Letter from McKim to Moore, December 23, 1901. Charles Moore Papers, Park Commission Correspondence, Mr. McKim.

Figure 53. View of Senate Park Commission Model Showing Existing Conditions in Washington: 1901

Commission's work. At one point he had to advance money from his private account, an action which brought the following letter from McKim:

"Your cheque for $1,000, to be applied to the Washington account, was received this morning. We should be very unwilling to accept it, were the calls from all sides less urgent, but just now every penny counts, and I am so anxious to avoid delays and complications arising from any cause, that I do not return it, as I should prefer. The mysterious dispensation, which obliges you, rather than Senator McMillan, to put up money to prosecute his pet hobby, is one of those things which no fellow can find out! However, we all have the greatest confidence in the Senator, and Uncle Sam too, and these remarks are not intended seriously." [32]

The financial arrangements for the Commission's activities had not been carefully thought out. The informal and rather free-wheeling attitude of men such as Burnham and McKim, accustomed to dealing with private clients of substantial means, conformed not at all to the orderly, cautious, and exceedingly slow procedures apparently followed by governmental clerks charged with the payment of Senate committee funds. But it was not only the speed, or rather the lack of it, that became a matter of concern, but the total amount that threatened to exceed by far the original estimate of $15,000. [33] Senator McMillan became mildly alarmed. He had agreed as early as June 1 to Burnham's request that the models be prepared, when he and Burnham conferred in the Senator's private railway car at the Michigan Central Station in Chicago. [34] He did not have much enthusiasm for this aspect of the Commission's work, however, and what little he was able to muster must have dwindled as Moore reported from time to time

on the mounting expenses. However, McMillan's love for Washington and his growing understanding of the Commission's basic concepts led him to approve additional funds when needed. He wrote to Moore on September 12 in reply to his secretary's request for his signature to authorize a further payment:

"Very sorry that matters are not in satisfactory shape so far as the financial end of the Commission is concerned. You will remember that I objected most strenuously to any agreement or arrangement for the expenditure of a large sum of money for the model, although Mr. Burnham seems to have got the impression that I assented to it provided the depot was taken from the Mall; anything I did say was rather in the nature of a remark than an agreement. Possibly I did say that if he could get the Mall cleared we could do most anything. However, we will have to make the best of it, and therefore, I have signed the receipt and letter which you enclosed. . . ." [35]

In this same letter McMillan cautioned Moore to keep Senator Jacob H. Gallinger of New Hampshire of the District Committee closely informed of the progress of the work. McMillan had invited Gallinger to a meeting with him at his summer home at Manchester, Massachusetts, late in August when he met with Burnham, Olmsted, and McKim to hear of their trip to Europe and to examine the preliminary plans. Gallinger had been unable to attend, but Senator William B. Allison of Iowa, Chairman of the Senate Appropriations Committee was present. McMillan obviously was looking beyond the technical report itself and considering how political support for its recommendations could be assured. [36] It is quite likely that McMillan at this time may have suggested that senators, congressmen, and high executive officials

[32] Letter from McKim to Moore, December 24, 1901, Charles Moore Papers, Park Commission Correspondence, Mr. McKim.

[33] This figure is from Moore in his *Burnham,* I, p. 137n.1, where he states, "Had the expenses incurred been limited to $15,000 as anticipated, the contingent fund would not have been depleted as it was, several times over." I have not been able to find a record or even make a close estimate of what the total costs were. Many years later Elihu Root told his biographer that the cost "ran up to fifty or sixty thousand." Philip C. Jessup, *Elihu Root,* New York, 1938, I, p. 279.

[34] Moore, *Burnham,* I, p. 147n.2.

[35] Letter from McMillan to Moore, September 12, 1901. Charles Moore Papers, Park Commission Correspondence, James McMillan Letters.

[36] Moore tells that at this meeting on August 20, McMillan continually addressed the chairman of the Commission as "General Burnham." Later, at dinner, he explained ". . . that a man who could persuade President Cassatt to take the Pennsylvania Railroad out of the Mall *deserves* to be a general.'" Moore comments: "There was much more than a joke in the remark: it was the Senator's method of impressing upon his all-powerful colleague his own high appreciation of the work Mr. Burnham had already accomplished." Moore, *Burnham,* I, p. 158.

should be consulted and given an opportunity to see some of the Commission's proposals prior to their official release. The Senator possessed an astute political brain, and he knew that if early support could be obtained from leading members of Congress and key executive officers the rocky legislative road that lay ahead could be smoothed. Moore, the members of the Commission, and doubtless McMillan himself engaged in several activities of this kind.

McKim, on August 26, for example, journeyed from New York to Washington to see Secretary Root, returning the same day by the midnight train. Root's department had jurisdiction over most of the public grounds of the capital aside from those occupied by the Capitol, the Smithsonian, and the Agriculture Department. Obviously his support for the Commission's proposals would be needed. McKim sent a full account of the meeting to Burnham reporting that Root had approved the site then being considered by the Commission for the Grant Monument. He also had agreed to their proposals for the Lincoln Memorial near the Potomac River at the end of a great reflecting basin stretching westward from the Washington Monument. McKim also stated that Root strongly favored the acquisition of land between Pennsylvania Avenue and the Mall, pointing out that "the fear that the value of property on Pennsylvania Avenue would be diminished, by making a great public centre of the Mall, will be thus dispelled." [37] Root also advanced an idea for securing public support which was later to be followed by the Commission. This was to enlist the support of influential newspapers and magazines throughout the country. Root, stated McKim, ". . . mentioned the names of a dozen newspaper men, in different sections of the country, who should be properly seen, and fully informed and prepared, in advance, on the subject." [38]

Finally, Root also urged McKim to include in the Commission's report an introductory chapter dealing with

". . . conditions as we found them, with the history of the inception of the plan and the laying out of the City by Washington, as proof that the scheme proposed by the Commission was in consequence of what had been already done, and a natural development of his (Washington's) aims and views. Mr. Root said he felt that if the Commission could prove their case in this regard, that it would go far towards winning it; that, in this way public acceptance would be assured, and opposition removed." [39]

In this respect, in its frequent mention of historical precedents and references to the work of President Washington, the Commission's report was to follow closely the suggestions made to McKim by the Secretary of War.

Evidently McKim, other members of the Commission, or Moore held additional meetings with Root or his assistants at which time the details of many aspects of the plan were revealed. In the Secretary's annual report for 1901 he referred to their work in these words:

"In admirable spirit that Commission seeks to restore and develop the original designs of President Washington and L'Enfant, and the plans which they are about to present for the work to be done hereafter in making the capital city more beautiful have the hearty approval and sympathy of the War Department, and will, if they shall happily be adopted, have that Department's cordial cooperation." [40]

This quotation appeared in Senator McMillan's committee report to the Senate when he formally presented the Commission's recommendations. Similar statements were quoted from the reports of the Attorney-General and the Commissioners of the District of Columbia, indicating that these officials had also been consulted and informed of at least the general nature of the Commission's proposals. It seems likely that Moore, thoroughly familiar with Washington officialdom, arranged for the meetings between Com-

[37] Memorandum enclosed in a letter from McKim to Burnham, August 28, 1901. Charles Moore Papers, Park Commission Correspondence, McKim Letters.
[38] *ibid.*

[39] *ibid.*
[40] *Report of the Senate Committee on the District of Columbia on the Improvement of the Park System of the District of Columbia,* Washington, 1902, p. 13.

mission members and government officials, in many of which he also participated.

It should not be thought that at the time these political activities were being undertaken all final decisions on the details of the plan had been made. As late as November 21 the proposed location of the Grant Monument, then under consideration by an official government committee, had not been fixed. On that date McKim wrote to Moore suggesting the site that was ultimately recommended and on which the statue was eventually erected: "In the great Square, at the foot of the Capitol Hill, heading the Mall—Washington's Place de la Concorde. . . ." [41]

McKim's letter also requested a plan of the rooms in the Corcoran Gallery that were to be used for the exhibition, a project on which he now began to concentrate. Olmsted also wrote to Langdon in Washington a few days later, giving the dimensions of the maps, plans, cross-sections, and photographs that he proposed to exhibit showing the recommendations for parks and parkways. [42] Olmsted sent a copy of this to McKim and later conferred with him in New York about the details of the exhibit. McKim became concerned over the amount of space that would be needed and wrote to Moore on December 10 inquiring if additional room could not be made available. [43] The following day McKim sent to Moore plans showing how the models should be installed in the gallery theatre along with a description of how he proposed to have them placed and lighted. [44]

Newspaper stories about some aspects of the Commission's proposals aroused public and official anticipation in the coming exhibition. Moore and the Commission followed a calculated policy in releasing to the press just enough information to maintain interest while withholding data on most of the details and some of the major proposals. A three-column story in the *Evening Star,* for example, described the essential elements of the plan so accurately that it would appear unlikely the information had been obtained without the assistance of those engaged in its preparation. [45]

Shortly before the opening of the exhibition on January 15, 1902, McKim came to Washington to supervise its installation. He had already arranged for the ceiling of the gallery theatre to be draped with unbleached muslin to lower its level and provide better acoustical effects. The still partially unfinished models, finally secured from a reluctant Curtis, were mounted on long tables in the center at eye-level height. Work on them continued until the last minute as shown in Figure 54, apparently the only surviving photograph of the exhibit. At one side stood a raised platform from which viewers could obtain a bird's-eye vision of the future Washington and compare it with the Washington of the day shown on the model along side. The room was darkened; the only light was that illuminating the models. The effect must have been dramatic—exactly the atmosphere that McKim wished to achieve.

In New York the meticulous McKim had prepared plans and wall diagrams showing the exact location of every item that was to be displayed. However, when these were hung as planned McKim saw that the sizes and colors of many of the drawings clashed. Glenn Brown, who, along with other local architects and the Commission's staff, assisted McKim, records that, in the hectic final hours of preparation,

". . . we all went earnestly to work changing and rehanging the drawings under McKim's directions as to color and scale, and this rearrangement was finished in the early morning hours to his satisfaction. . . . In the morning the value of the artificial lighting was studied and modified to suit each drawing.

"The time of the opening was upon the party and the rooms were not cleared of paper and other débris. The building force was actively engaged in this work, but could not apparently get through in time. McKim, several prominent architects and a noted physi-

[41] Letter from McKim to Moore, November 21, 1901, Charles Moore Papers, Park Commission Correspondence, McKim Letters.

[42] Letter from Olmsted to Langdon, November 27, 1901, Charles Moore Papers, Park Commission Correspondence, Frederick Law Olmsted Letters.

[43] Letter from McKim to Moore, December 10, 1901. Charles Moore Papers, Park Commission Correspondence, McKim Letters.

[44] Letter from McKim to Moore, December 11, 1901, Charles Moore Papers, Park Commission Correspondence, McKim Letters.

[45] The Washington *Evening Star,* November 16, 1901.

Figure 54. View of Preparations for the Senate Park Commission Exhibit in the Corcoran Gallery: 1902

cian, a friend of McKim, all lent a hand clearing the trash out of one door as Roosevelt entered with many of his Cabinet and Senators at another door." [46]

While McKim took charge of arranging the exhibition, Moore and McMillan were busy with legislative matters. On the morning of January 15 they presented the final draft of a proposed committee report to the members of the Senate Committee on the District of Columbia, together with the report of the Park Commission. This received unanimous approval, and at noon Senator McMillan submitted the reports to the Senate. [47] Then Moore and McMillan drove to the Corcoran Gallery to await the presidential party. Moore, who acted as guide for the President and his Cabinet, recalls how President Roosevelt was "interested, curious, at first critical and then, as the great consistent scheme dawned on him, highly appreciative." [48] The President's eyes had first fallen on the small model of the proposed treatment for the Washington Monument terrace and gardens, which he called "fussy." But McMillan insisted that he examine the renderings of this project by Jules Guerin and Charles Graham, after which the President admitted that he had been wrong in his initial judgment. [49] Roosevelt then mounted the viewing platform from which he could see the large model of the Commission's proposals, shown in Figure 55, alongside the other which depicted the city as it then existed.

Secretary of State John Hay, that remarkable combination of poet and politician, showed particular interest in the proposal for the memorial to Abraham Lincoln, whom he had once served as personal secretary. Moore describes his reactions:

"When he realized the meaning of the conception—that Lincoln, standing with Washington in the history of this country, should also stand with him in memorial symbolism in the nation's capital —the Secretary said that the reasoning was sound in both logic and sentiment. Then and there he accepted the location and design

Figure 55. View of Senate Park Commission Model Showing Proposed Development of Washington: 1902

[46] Glenn Brown, *Memories,* Washington, 1931, pp. 269–70.
[47] Moore, *McKim,* p. 201.
[48] Moore, *Burnham,* I, p. 167.
[49] Moore, *McKim,* p. 201.

of the Lincoln Memorial on the axis of the Capitol and the Washington Monument, saying that he regarded it as inevitable." [50]

After the President's party departed, the exhibition was visited by members of the Senate and House Committees on the District of Columbia and by the District Commissioners. Moore and Glenn Brown acted as guides, and the gallery remained open until 9:00 in the evening to accommodate the visitors. The next day the exhibition was opened to the public. Initial official reaction seemed favorable. On January 16 one Washington newspaper reported as follows:

"All of those who saw the exhibit yesterday were greatly pleased at the manner in which the commission had executed the big order given it for fulfillment. District Commissioners Macfarland and Biddle . . . expressed themselves as pleased with what they had seen. This view was also taken by Senators McMillan, Clark of Montana, and Foster of Washington, members of the Senate District Committee, and Representative Babcock, of Wisconsin, chairman of the House District Committee." [51]

It was a moment of triumph for the members of the Commission. Oddly enough, they were not all present at the same time during the great day. McKim, exhausted and, as always, retiring, had slipped away from his labors of the last three days and had taken a train for a much needed and well deserved vacation in South Carolina.[52] Burnham had not arrived in Washington until

the evening, at which time he had his first look at the exhibition.[53] Olmsted presumably was present to help explain his park proposals.

Burnham, Moore, and others adjourned to the Cosmos Club after the gallery closed to review the events of the day. Doubtless, too, they must have discussed the future and how their plans could be turned into reality. Still warmed by the many words of congratulations and encouragement spoken by those who had seen the exhibit, they may have been lulled into the belief that the force and persuasiveness of their great design would alone be sufficient to insure its execution. They could hardly have foreseen the years of controversy and the attempts to subvert their plan that lay ahead. But for the moment, at least, they could relax in the conviction that a great task had been carried out with dispatch and skill.

---

[50] *ibid.,* p.202.

[51] The Washington *Post,* January 16, 1902.

[52] From Garnett, South Carolina, McKim sent a brief penciled note to Moore on January 24 thanking him for newspaper accounts of the Park Commission report and exhibit, adding: "After two or three first days of weariness I have enjoyed everything gluttonously—sleep, food, wood fires, the absence of petticoats—abstention from shaving—flannel shirts—all the luxuries of a semi-savage existence!" Charles Moore Papers, Park Commission Correspondence, McKim Letters. McKim also received a letter from Burnham praising the exhibition. Letter from Burnham to McKim, January 22, 1902, quoted in Moore, *Burnham,* I, p. 168.

[53] Moore, *McKim,* p. 202. Burnham arrived in time to help explain the proposals to visiting congressmen. Brown remembers an amusing and typical anecdote: "I was standing by Burnham who was describing the principles of the plan to a Congressman who wished to know why the Supreme Court should not extend across Maryland Avenue, as the Congressional Library extended across Pennsylvania Avenue. Burnham very gravely and emphatically said: 'It would destroy one of the contemplated vistas of the Capitol, a most important element in the original plan. It is so important that the Congressional Library should be removed to reestablish the vista.' The Representative was shocked but impressed with the idea that a vista might be more important than their Library, the pride of Congressmen." Brown, *Memories,* p. 282.

CHAPTER 5

The Senate Park Commission Plan
for Central Washington

On January 15, 1902, Senator McMillan presented the report of the Park Commission to the Senate. This was accompanied by a report from his Committee on the District of Columbia which summarized the circumstances under which the Park Commission plan had been prepared. The Senator pointed out the necessity of following a long-range plan for the city's development as individual buildings were approved from time to time. Realistically he stated that "the task is indeed a stupendous one; it is much greater than any one generation can hope to accomplish," but if the plan were adhered to over the years, "the city which Washington and Jefferson planned with so much care and with such prophetic vision will continue to expand, keeping pace with national advancement, until it becomes the visible expression of the power and taste of the people of the United States." [1]

Three drawings showing the entire comprehensive plan for central Washington appeared in the report. Figure 56 shows the rebuilt city as seen from the air looking northeast from above the Virginia shore of the Potomac. Figure 57 is a rendered plan of

the area. Figure 58 shows existing and proposed buildings and streets for the great composition envisaged by the Park Commission.

Briefly, the Commission proposed to surround the Capitol square with a series of monumental buildings for congressional use and for the Supreme Court. These, together with the existing Library of Congress, would form a frame for the Capitol and its towering dome. Extending westwards on a rectified axis, a broad mall with four carriage drives would lead to the Washington Monument. Lining the mall on both sides would be major cultural and educational buildings.

The Washington Monument grounds were to receive equally formal treatment. A broad terrace on the east would provide the base on which the shaft would rest. A great stairway would lead down to a sunken garden centered on a pool and fountain marking the intersection of the White House axis. To the west a long reflecting pool would extend to a monument to Abraham Lincoln set in a circular site from which roadways would lead to Rock Creek Park and to a new bridge across the Potomac to Arlington Cemetery.

Forming the terminal feature of the southern end of the White House axis would stand a group of memorial buildings to national

---

[1] Report of the Senate Committee on the District of Columbia on the Improvement of the Park System of the District of Columbia, *The Improvement of the Park System of the District of Columbia*, Washington, 1902, p. 19.

Figure 56. Perspective View of Washington Showing Proposals of Senate Park Commission: 1902

Figure 57. General Plan for Central Washington by the Senate Park Commission: 1902

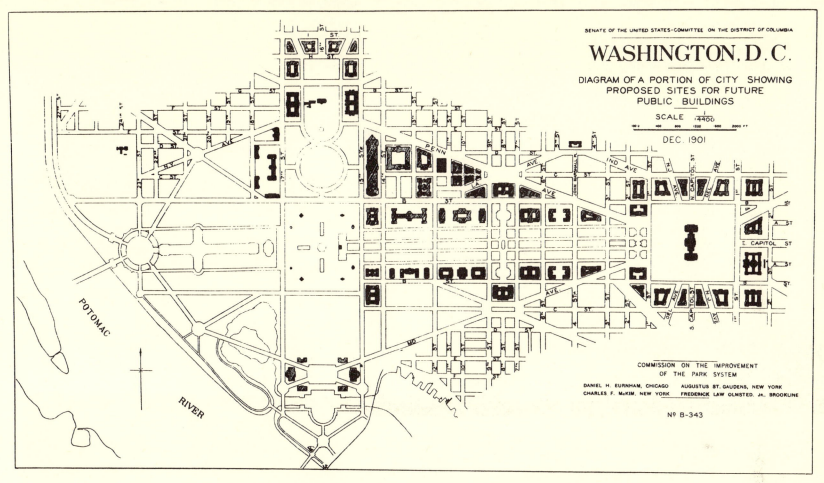

Figure 58. Public Building Sites in Central Washington Proposed by the
Senate Park Commission: 1902

heroes. The area between this complex and on either side of the reflecting pool was to be treated as a formal park. North of the Washington Monument, on the west side of the Ellipse in front of the White House, the Commission proposed for sites of semi-public buildings facing 17th Street. To the north of the White House, surrounding Lafayette Square, executive department buildings were to be located in symmetrical fashion. Between B Street (now Constitution Avenue) and Pennsylvania Avenue, in the triangle extending east from 15th Street, the Commission proposed

the erection of buildings for the District government, a great armory and auditorium, a new market, and other buildings of a municipal character.

The written report of the Park Commission, prepared by Moore and Olmsted, described in detail the Commission's proposals for central Washington. Moore, with his training as a journalist, was probably responsible for the text of this portion of the report. Olmsted doubtless chose the illustrations and wrote the section of the report dealing with the plans for parks and recreation areas

111

outside the central area of the city. Mere paraphrase could not do justice to the clear and convincing style of the report. Moreover, its text has not been reprinted, and copies of the report are no longer readily available. For these reasons and because of its importance as a document of significant interest, the entire part of the report concerned with central Washington is quoted in the pages to follow. Here, then, is the description of the Park Commission's plan as it appeared in the original report, a statement unique in American city planning and one which was to have a profound effect on the future of the Capital City.[2]

The Mall System

"The City of Washington, during the century since its foundation, has been developed in the main according to the plan made in 1791 by Major Charles L'Enfant and approved by President Washington. That plan the Commission has aimed to restore, develop, and supplement.

"The 'Congress house' and the 'President's palace,' as he termed them, were the cardinal features of L'Enfant's plan; and these edifices he connected 'by a grand avenue four hundred feet in breadth, and about a mile in length, bordered by gardens, ending in a slope from the houses on each side.' At the point of intersection of two lines, one drawn through the center of the Capitol the other drawn through the center of the White House, L'Enfant fixed the site of an equestrian statue of General Washington, one of the numerous statues voted by the Continental Congress but never erected.

"When, in 1848, the people began to build the Washington Monument, the engineers despaired of securing on the proper site a foundation sufficient for so great a structure; and consequently the Monument was located out of all relations with the buildings which it was intended to tie together in a single composition. To create these relations as originally planned was one of the chief problems of the Commission.

"Again, the reclamation of the Potomac Flats, prosecuted since

[2] The text of the report does not refer specifically to the illustrations interspersed in the text. I have included many of them, inserting the figure numbers in parentheses where they seeem most appropriate.

1882, has added to the Monument grounds an area about one mile in length from east to west; so that where L'Enfant dealt with a composition one and a half miles in length, the Commission is called upon to deal with an area two and a half miles long, with a maximum breadth of about one mile. (Figure 59)

"By the inclusion of the space between Pennsylvania and New York avenues on the north, and Maryland avenue and the Potomac River on the south, the new composition becomes a symmetrical, polygonal, or kite-shaped, figure bisected from east to west by the axis of the Capitol and from north to south by the White House axis. Regarding the Monument as the center, the Capitol as the base, and the White House as the extremity of one arm of a Latin cross, we have at the head of the composition on the banks of the Potomac a memorial site of the greatest possible dignity, with a second and only less commanding site at the extremity of the second arm. (Figure 60)

"So extensive a composition, and one containing such important elements, does not exist elsewhere; and it is essential that the plan for its treatment shall combine simplicity with dignity.

THE CAPITOL DIVISION

"The Capitol, located by Washington and L'Enfant on a site which seemed to the latter as 'a pedestal waiting for a monument,' was constructed in accordance with plans prepared by Thornton and selected by the first President and his Secretary of State, because among the number of designs submitted Thornton's alone displayed the dignified simplicity which should characterize the legislative halls of a nation. Under the personal direction of President Fillmore, the Capitol was extended by the addition of the Senate and the House wings, and the edifice was surmounted by a soaring dome, all designed by Thomas U. Walter. Distinguished alike for its historic associations and for its architectural merits, the Capitol stands in the midst of ample grounds, indeed, but is surrounded in the main by private buildings, many of them of the most squalid character, or by neglected stretches of land used as dumping grounds. From the Mall system the grounds are cut off by the Botanic Garden, walled and fenced so as to block the way. (Figure 61)

Figure 59. View of Senate Park Commission Model Showing Existing Conditions in Central Washington: 1902

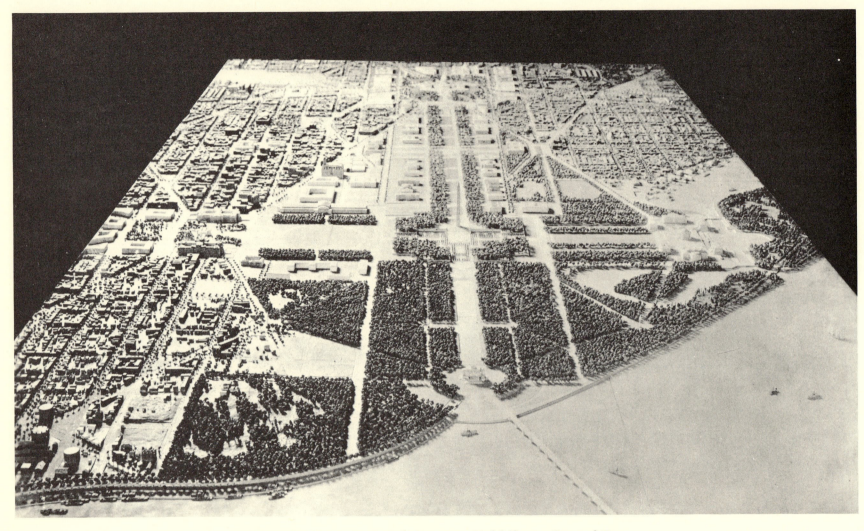

Figure 60. View of Senate Park Commission Model Showing Proposed Development of Central Washington: 1902

"Facing the Capitol grounds on the east stands the Congressional Library; and it is contemplated that at no distant day the Supreme Court of the United States shall be accommodated in a building constructed for the exclusive use of that tribunal, on the square directly north of the Library; and that the Senate and the House of Representatives will have constructed for the uses of their members buildings respectively on the north and on the south of the grounds of the Capitol.

"The construction of the above-mentioned buildings as planned will make it in the highest degree appropriate that fronting the entire square occupied by the Capitol grounds only public buildings bearing a common relation to legislative work shall be erected. If the reciprocal relations of the new buildings shall be studied carefully, so as to produce harmony of design and uniformity of cornice line, the resulting architectural composition will be unequaled in magnitude and monumental character by any similar group of legislative buildings in the modern world.

"The successful development of this proposed series of buildings inclosing the Capitol square is to be assured only by strict adherence to that system of radial avenues laid down by Washington and L'Enfant, upon which the Capitol depends for its dominating character. Any invasion of these historic arteries representing the original States and centering upon the Dome must be fatal, because inconsistent with fundamental principles upon which the city is built. The location of the Library of Congress partly in Pennsylvania avenue is a perpetual mutilation of L'Enfant's plan, and inflicts incalculable injury to the Capitol, which the Library in part conceals. Other similar instances are the extension of the Treasury and the construction of the State, War, and Navy buildings so as to close forever carefully planned vistas of the White House. These discordant notes should warn future generations that sites for public buildings are dearly purchased at the cost of those essential elements which give to Washington its unique advantage over all other American cities.

"In 1803 Thornton marked the boundaries of the Capitol grounds to correspond with the rectilinear system of streets, and these lines were maintained until the latest addition to the grounds brought about innovations, resulting in various curved projections,

Figure 61. View of Portion of Senate Park Commission Model Showing Existing Conditions in Central Washington: 1902

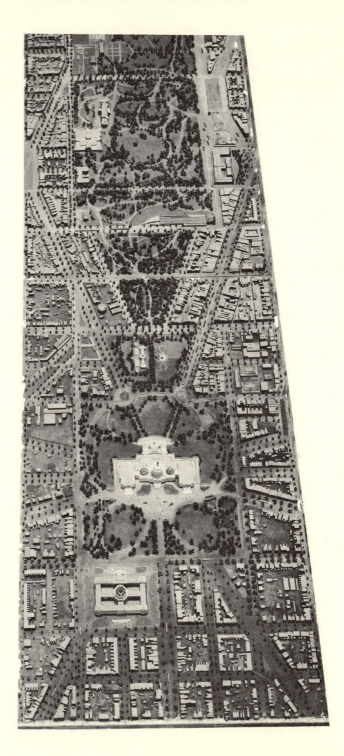

*Figure 62. View of Capitol and East End of Mall Showing Development
Proposed by the Senate Park Commission: 1902*

especially on the western side. This complication of the early plans banished the Bulfinch gates and fence which so strongly emphasized the frontage of sixteen hundred feet that corresponds to the width of the Mall. The recovery of this original feature of the Capitol design, supplemented by the construction of a central terrace one thousand feet in width, will give the broadest possible support to the Capitol, which, resting upon this base as on a plinth, will gain an additional height of forty feet.

"The western slope of the Capitol grounds should be relieved and enriched by basins and fountains in which the water, falling from one level to another, is poured finally into a great central pool at the level of First street. So L'Enfant intended in his plan for 'a grand cascade formed of water from the sources of the Tiber,' which was to mitigate the heat of the sun-baked hill. (Figure 62)

"Several of the great radial avenues extending from the Capitol and the White House climb the hills encircling the city, and on the crests of these hills superb sites are found for shining memorials standing out against the sky. Often these vistas terminate on some far-off hill, where a simple white shelter will prove the most effective treatment. In other instances the hill crests are in the midst of a populous region, and in these cases the treatment should be on a more comprehensive scale. For example, at the head of North Capitol street a monumental entrance to the Soldiers' Home should be built; and the sharp rise of Sixteenth street should carry an imposing arch, such as the one projected as a memorial to William McKinley.

UNION SQUARE

"On the western side of the Capitol grounds, where Pennsylvania and Maryland avenues converge, the L'Enfant plan shows 'a publicwalk, through which carriages may ascend to the upper square of the Federal house.' Having restored the true north and south line of the Capitol grounds, it is proposed to treat the space now occupied by the Botanic Garden as a broad thoroughfare, so enriched with parterres of green as to form an organic connection between the Capitol and the Mall.

"The exceptional opportunities for monumental treatment offered by the commanding location of this area leads the Commission to suggest that the Grant memorial already provided for shall be the chief decoration of the square; and that associated with the Grant monument shall be the figures of his two great lieutenants, Sherman and Sheridan, standing independently, yet so as to form a single composition.

"The placing of the defenders of the Union at this great point of convergence doubly justifies the name of 'Union Square.'

"Brilliantly illuminated, embellished with fountains, and commanded by terraces, this square would compare favorably, in both extent and treatment, with the Place de la Concorde in Paris. (Figure 63)

THE MALL

"Having considered the Capitol grounds and the areas related thereto we come now to that long stretch of territory designed to furnish the park-like means of communication between the legislative and the executive departments. It is interesting to note that although this space has been cut into pieces, some of which have been highly developed according to the landscape art of the day, as for example the grounds of the Smithsonian Institution and the Agriculture Department, and while other portions have been diverted from their original purposes, as in the case of the sections given up to the Botanic Garden and the Baltimore and Potomac

Railroad, still the L'Enfant idea of treating the entire space as a unit has never been entirely lost sight of. Indeed, during the very months of 1871, when the right of way across the Mall was bestowed upon a railroad, one branch of Congress agreed to a proposition to combine the scattered areas into a single park, but was deterred from so doing largely by the objection that such treatment would divide Washington into two parts.

"The gradual development of the city and its growth toward the north, together with the location in the Mall of public buildings for scientific purposes, have resulted in a steady improvement in the character of the Mall, which during the past thirty years has been changed from a common pasture into a series of park spaces unequally developed, indeed, and in places broken in upon by being put to commercial or other extraneous uses, but nevertheless becoming more and more appreciated from year to year. With this gradual improvement has sprung up a general desire that the L'Enfant plans be reverted to, and that the entire space south of Pennsylvania avenue be set apart solely for public purposes.

"In order to realize this natural and most laudable desire, two things are essential: First, the railroad must be removed from the Mall, and, secondly, axial relations must be established between the Capitol, the Monument, and the White House. Happily, as has been explained elsewhere in these reports, the opportunity is presented to Congress to secure not only the exclusion of the railroad, but also the construction of a union station, a consummation which, long agitated, has heretofore seemed beyond the possibility of accomplishment.

"Fortunately, also, the location of the Monument does not preclude the establishment of such relations as will bring that structure into organic connection with the monumental buildings above mentioned, so that Capitol, White House, and Monument shall become constituent parts of one composition. The plan of the Commission contemplates the extension of B street northeastward to Pennsylvania avenue, whence it continues on the north side of the Capitol grounds, thus securing for the Mall a uniform width of sixteen hundred feet throughout its entire extent. Within these boundaries it becomes possible to develop the Mall area in accordance with the general distribution of the L'Enfant plan, with

117

Figure 63. View of East End of the Mall from the Capitol Showing Development Proposed by the Senate Park Commission: 1902

such enlargements as the conditions of to-day have made possible and desirable.

"Thus areas adjoining B street north and south, averaging more than four hundred feet in width from the Capitol to the Monument, afford spacious sites for buildings devoted to scientific purposes and for the great museums. The structure to be erected for the Department of Agriculture on the site of the present building marks at once the building line and the type of architecture which should be adopted throughout the Mall system; while the buildings of the National Museum and the Fisheries Commission building, both of which are inadequate and unsuited for their respective purposes, serve to show the class of the service that may well be accommodated with new structures located within a park area.

"The axis of the Capitol and Monument is clearly defined by an expanse of undulating green a mile and a half long and three hundred feet broad, walled on either side by elms, planted in formal procession four abreast. Bordering this green carpet, roads, park-like in character, stretch between Capitol and Monument, while beneath the elms one may walk or drive, protected from the sun. Examples of this treatment abound in England and on the Continent of Europe, and also may be found in our own country in those towns, both North and South, which were laid out during the colonial era. Moreover, these two plantations of elms traversed by paths are similar in character to the Mall in Central Park, New York, which is justly regarded as one of the most beautiful features of that park. (Figure 64)

"The American elm was chosen not only because of the architectural character of its columnar trunk and the delicate traceries formed by its widespreading branches, but also because in the District of Columbia this tree is at its best, notable examples being found in the city parks and in the grounds of the Capitol.

"The streets leading southward from Pennsylvania avenue are to cross the Mall at their present grades, no attempt being made either to exclude street car and other traffic or to hide it. Indeed, the play of light and shade where the streets break through the columns of trees, and the passage of street cars and teams give needed life to the Mall, while at the same time those persons most interested in the area maintained as a park will obtain the full enjoyment from it. As the Garden of the Tuilleries, besides performing its artistic function of uniting the palaces of the Louvre with the Arc de Triomphe, furnishes a pleasing passageway for tens of thousands of persons who cross it going to and from their work, so the Mall will afford variety and refreshment to those going and coming between the "Island" and the other sections of the city.

"By extending Ninth street through the Mall, an opportunity occurs to emphasize these very necessary north and south connections, and at the same time to relieve from monotony the meadow-like stretch a mile and a half long. The entire space between Seventh and Ninth streets should be treated in a manner similar to the proposed Union Square in front of the Capitol, with parterres of green and large basins of water, with frequent seats tempting the passer-by to linger for rest.

THE WASHINGTON MONUMENT DIVISION

"From this cross axis the carpet of greensward of the Mall stretches westward. The bordering columns of elms march to the Monument grounds, climb the slope, and, spreading themselves to right and left on extended terraces, form a great body of green, strengthening the broad platform from which the obelisk rises in majestic serenity. The groves on the terraces become places of rest, from which one gets wide views of the busy city; of the White House, surrounded by its ample grounds; of the Capitol, crowning the heights at the end of the broad vista; of sunny stretches of river winding at the foot of the Virginia hills. (Figure 65)

"Axial relations between the White House and the Monument are created by the construction of a sunken garden on the western side of the great shaft, the true line passing through the center of a great round pool, to which marble steps three hundred feet in width lead down forty feet from the Monument platform. Surrounded by terraces bearing elms, laid out with formal paths lined by hedges and adorned with small trees, enriched by fountains and temple-like structures, this garden becomes the gem of the Mall system. Seen from the lower level, the Monument gains an additional height of nearly forty-five feet, while at the same time nothing

119

*Figure 64. View of the Mall Showing Development Proposed by the Senate
Park Commission: 1902*

is suffered to come so near as to disturb the isolation which the Monument demands. (Figure 66)

"At present the immediate surroundings of the Monument are so inadequate as to cause the beholder near at hand to lose that very sense of grandeur which it inspires when seen from a distance; and the lack of harmonious relationship between it and the great structures with which it comes into juxtaposition disturbs one's sense of fitness. No portion of the task set before the Commission has required more study and extended consideration than has the solution of the problem of devising an appropriate setting for the Monument; and the treatment here proposed is the one which seems best adapted to enhance the value of the Monument itself. Taken by itself, the Washington Monument stands not only as one of the most stupendous works of man, but also as one of the most beautiful of human creations. Indeed, it is at once so great and so simple that it seems to be almost a work of nature. Dom-

*Figure 65. View of the Washington Monument, the Monument Gardens,
and the Mall Showing Development Proposed by the Senate
Park Commission: 1902*

inating the entire District of Columbia, it has taken its place with the Capitol and the White House as one of the three foremost national structures. (Figure 67)

THE WASHINGTON COMMON

"Taking the Monument garden as a center, one looks northward over the White Lot, which is retained as the great drill grounds of the District. On the east and on the west, along Fif-

teenth and Seventeenth streets, walks shaded by four rows of lindens tempt one from the hot and busy streets of the city to the cool and quiet of the gardens or to the field of sports beyond. (Figure 68)

"The space south of the Monument is to be devoted to the people as a place of recreation—the Washington Common it might be called. Here should be constructed a great stadium arranged for athletic contests of all kinds and for the display of fireworks on festal occasions. Ball grounds and tennis courts, open-

Figure 66. View of the Washington Monument from the Monument Garden Showing Development Proposed by the Senate Park Commission: 1902

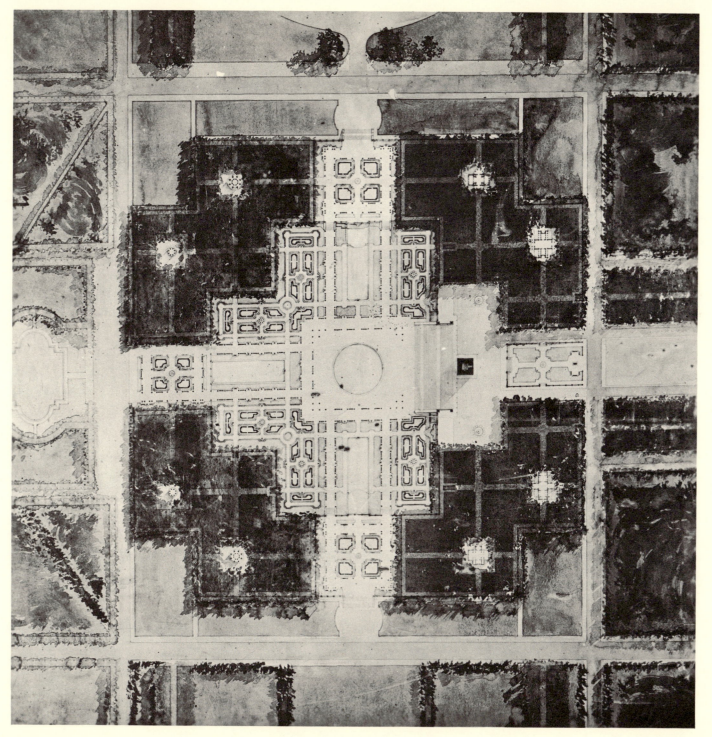

*Figure 67. Plan of the Washington Monument, Terrace, and Garden, Show-
ing Development Proposed by the Senate Park Commission:
1902*

Figure 68. View North to the White House from the Monument Garden
Showing Development Proposed by the Senate Park Commission: 1902

Figure 69. View South from the White House Showing Development Proposed by the Senate Park Commission: 1902

air gymnasiums for youths, and sand piles and swings for children, all should be provided, as they are now furnished in the progressive cities of this country. The tidal basin should have the most ample facilities for boating and for wading and swimming in summer, as well as for skating in winter. To this end boat pavilions, locker houses, and extensive bath houses should be constructed with all the conveniences known to the best-equipped institutions of like character. The positive dearth of means of innocent enjoyment for one's leisure hours is remarkable in Washington, the one city in this country where people have the most leisure. (Figure 69)

"Where the axis of the White House intersects the axis of Maryland avenue a site is found for a great memorial. Whether this memorial shall take the form of a Pantheon, in which shall be grouped the statues of the illustrious men of the nation, or whether the memory of some individual shall be honored by a

125

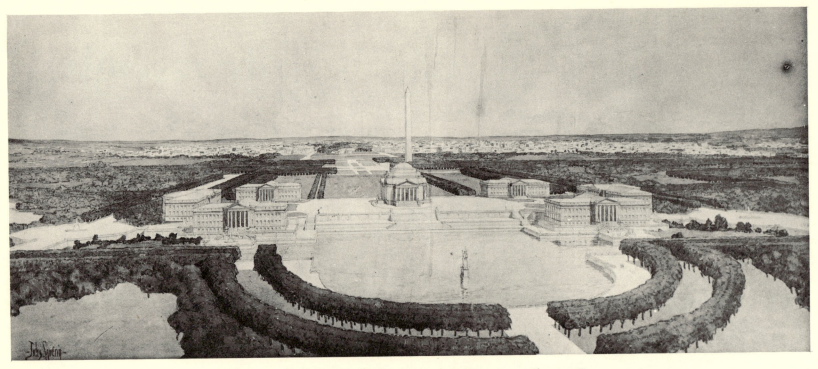

Figure 70. View North from the Memorial Building Group Showing Development Proposed by the Senate Park Commission: 1902

monument of the first rank may be left to the future; at least the site will be ready. (Figure 70)

THE LINCOLN MEMORIAL

"The area extending westward for a mile from the Monument to the bank of the Potomac—land reclaimed from the river flats—remains to be considered. For the most part this area from New York avenue to the river should be treated as a wood, planted informally, but marked by formal roads and paths, much as the Bois de Bologne at Paris is treated. If the plans as laid down by this Commission shall be observed by the army engineers in the remaining work of flats reclamation, and by the District engineers when they come to complete the sewage-disposal system, this

portion of the Potomac Park can be made ready for planting without appreciable expense.

"The central portion of this area, still adhering to the Mall width of sixteen hundred feet, has a special and particular treatment. From the Monument garden westward a canal three thousand six hundred feet long and two hundred feet wide, with central arms and bordered by stretches of green walled with trees, leads to a concourse raised to the height of the Monument platform. Seen from the Monument platform, this canal, similar in character and general treatment to the canals at Versailles and Fountainebleau, in France, and at Hampton Court, in England, introduces into the formal landscape an element of repose and great beauty. At the head of the canal a great *rond point,* placed on the main axis of

126

Figure 71. View of the Lincoln Memorial from the East Showing Development Proposed by the Senate Park Commission: 1902

the Capitol and the Monument, becomes a gate of approach to the park system of the District of Columbia. Centering upon it as a great point of reunion are the drives leading southeast to Potomac Park and northwest by the Riverside drive to the Rock Creek system of parks. From this elevation of forty feet the Memorial Bridge leads across the Potomac directly to the base of the hill crowned by the Mansion-house of Arlington.

"Crowning the *rond point,* as the Arc de Triomphe crowns the Place de l'Etoile at Paris, should stand a memorial erected to the memory of that one man in our history as a nation who is worthy to be named with George Washington—Abraham Lincoln. (Figure 71)

"Whatever may be the exact form selected for the memorial to Lincoln, in type it should possess the quality of universality, and also it should have a character essentially distinct from that of any monument either now existing in the District or hereafter to be erected. The type which the Commission has in mind is a great portico of Doric columns rising from an unbroken stylobate. This portico, while affording a point of vantage from which one obtains a commanding outlook, both upon the river and eastward to the Capitol, has for its chief function to support a panel bearing an inscription taken either from the Gettysburg speech or from some one of the immortal messages of the savior of the Union.

"The portico contemplated in the plans, consisting of columns forty feet in height, occupies a space of two hundred and fifty feet in length and two hundred and twenty feet in width; it is approached by flights of stairs on the east and the west, is embellished with appropriate groups of sculpture, and is surmounted by a central crowning group of statuary. At the head of the canal, at the eastern approach to the memorial, it is proposed to place a statue of Abraham Lincoln, while surrounding the memorial and framing it are linden trees, planted four rows deep, to form a peristyle of green, from which radiate various avenues centering upon the memorial itself.

The Memorial Bridge, Analostan Island and the National Cemetery at Arlington

"On the occasion of laying the corner stone for the extension of the Capitol, on the Fourth of July, 1851, Daniel Webster, in the course of an impassioned plea for preservation of the Union, which in his prophetic vision seemed even then on the verge of dissolution, exclaimed:

'Before us is the broad and beautiful river, seprarating two of the original thirteen States, which a late President, a man of determined purpose and inflexible will, but patriotic heart, desired to span with arches of ever-enduring granite, symbolical of the firmly established union of the North and the South. That President was General Jackson.'

"The struggle which the orator and the statesman were powerless to avert brought about the perpetuation of the Union; and to-day the survivors of that war, both those of the North and those of the South, using the words of President McKinley, urge the building of the Memorial Bridge as a monument to American valor.

"For the past seventeen years the Memorial Bridge project has been before Congress constantly. In response to the Senate res-

olution of May 24, 1886, Major Hains, of the Corps of Engineers, reported in favor of a bridge of four spans, each about three hundred feet in length, to extend from the Washington bank of the Potomac to Analostan Island, the island itself and the bed of Little River to be crossed partly by an embankment and partly by an open trestle, the cost for the entire work to be about $650,000. About the same time Captain Symons submitted a plan for a more elaborate structure, to extend from Observatory Hill to the National Cemetery and Government estate at Arlington, at a cost of $1,500,-000. On February 20, 1890, the Senate again called for a study of the subject, and in response Colonel Hains proposed a bridge four thousand five hundred and eighty feet in length, extending from New York avenue to the Arlington estate, at a cost of $3,591,-000.

"Subsequently several reports were made on bills to provide for a Memorial Bridge, but the first legislation on the subject is found in the sundry civil act approved March 3, 1899, which appropriated $5,000, 'to enable the Chief of Engineers of the Army to continue the examination of the subject and to make or secure designs, calculations, and estimates for a Memorial Bridge from the most convenient point of the Naval Observatory grounds, or adjacent thereto, across the Potomac River to the most convenient point of the Arlington estate property.'

"Acting under the authority so conferred, four bridge engineers, Messrs. L. L. Buck, William H. Burr, William R. Hutton, and George S. Morrison, were invited to prepare plans. These plans were submitted to a jury composed of Lieutenant Colonel Charles J. Allen, Major Thomas W. Symons, Captain D. D. Gaillard, of the Corps of Engineers, and Mr. Stanford White and Mr. James G. Hill, architects, who reported in favor of a combination of the designs submitted by Professor Burr. The cost was estimated at $4,860,000, and the structure proposed was a highly decorated bridge eighty-four feet in width, adapted for street-railway tracks, and fitted with a steel bascule draw. These plans were submitted to Congress by the Secretary of War on April 9, 1900, but thus far no action upon them has been taken.

"Up to the time this report was submitted no study had been made for the development of the Potomac Park, and for this reason, doubtless, favorable consideration was given to bridge plans which contained in themselves features unusually elaborate. The studies which the Park Commission has made for the improvement of Potomac Park, and the introduction in the park proper of memorials of the largest type, have led the Commission to recommend certain modifications in both the location and the character of the Memorial Bridge.

"The proposed Lincoln memorial, located on the bank of the Potomac, on the axis of the Capitol, and the Washington Monument, and occupying an elevation forty feet above the level of the water, makes a starting point for the bridge that becomes especially convenient when this *rond point* is considered as the point of divergence and reunion of the driveways leading to the Rock Creek park system on the northwest and the Potomac system on the southeast. Moreover, the establishment of this concourse allows the bridge to cross the river at the angle most convenient, taking into consideration both the channel of the river and the main objective point—the mansion house at Arlington.

"Inasmuch as the comparatively flat topography of the country makes undesirable a high bridge under which vessels could pass, the decreased length of bridge required under the new plans is in itself a weighty consideration. At the same time the necessity of placing a draw in the bridge calls for such a treatment of the spans as shall not result in an apparent weakening of the structure at its central and vital point.

"All these things considered, the Commission recommends that the Memorial Bridge proper begin at the proposed Lincoln memorial and extend to Analostan Island; that the supports be masonry piers of monumental character; that the spans be so arranged as to present a uniform appearance, the character of the draw used being such as to bring about this result. Also, that a concourse suited to memorial treatment be established on Analostan Island, and that the extension of the passageway from the island to the Virginia shore be distinctly subordinate to the bridge proper. (Figure 72)

"The competition already mentioned having resulted in the selection of one of the leading bridge builders of the country, it is not considered necessary to do more than to have the subject restudied in the light of the new conditions and to have such modifications made in the plans as shall adapt them to the principles above laid down, all of which may be accomplished under the direction of the Secretary of War when the necessary appropriations shall be made. Such modifications would call for the removal of the central ornamental towers, which would conflict with the proposed Lincoln memorial, and which are not considered as in themselves desirable features for the central portion of a bridge structure.

"In connection with the Memorial Bridge, the acquisition and development of Analostan Island becomes an important consideration. The island proper is about eighty-eight acres in extent; and to this should be added the flats at the eastern end, which must be reclaimed eventually. The western portion, separated from Georgetown by the narrow channel of the river, is in part covered by trees and in part by sedges and water plants. Forming an important and beautiful part of all the views over the Potomac, the island should not be permitted to come into disagreeable occupancy, but at the earliest convenient opportunity it should be purchased and developed as a river park for the use of that portion of Georgetown which is now entirely without park facilities. Inasmuch as the island will be crossed by the Memorial Bridge, it will be accessible, and at its present offered price it would form a very desirable and inexpensive addition to the park system.

"The broader and simpler the treatment of the bridge to Arlington the closer will be the connection between the reservations now separated by the Potomac, and the more vital will be the relation between the Potomac Park and the Arlington estate. Such a result becomes desirable in the highest degree when one considers the immense numbers of people who resort not only to Fort Myer, but also the Arlington Cemetery.

"The interest excited by the drills at the cavalry post, the superb view from the heights, and the feelings of patriotism awakened by the vast field of the hero dead, known or unnamed, all call for such a treatment of the entire reservation as shall not diminish but rather enhance the effect produced on the visitor.

"There is nothing that needs proper supervision and planning more than the modern cemetery, for there is certainly nothing that

Figure 72. View of the Lincoln Memorial and Riverside Drive Showing
Development Proposed by the Senate Park Commission: 1902

suffers more from vulgarity, ignorance, and pretentiousness on the one side, and grasping unscrupulousness on the other; and instead of being a place to which one may go with a sentiment of respect and peace, as into a church or sacred place, the eye and the feelings are constantly shocked by the monstrositities which dominate in all modern cemeteries.

"There is no doubt that the feeling which pervades the majority of people who erect monuments to their dead is one of the tenderest; a sincere desire to do nothing even in the simplest form which is not fitting and in entire harmony with the feeling that prompts the erection of the memorials. This feeling, if properly protected and guarded, would lead to the harmonious and sober treatment so necessary for such places. A great example of the effectiveness of such restraint and guidance is the extraordinary dignity, impressiveness, and nobility of the Soldiers' Cemetery at the Soldier's Home in this city, and also in that part of the Arlington Cemetery set apart for the privates and unknown dead. This is not attained by any large monuments, but by the very simplicity and uniformity of the whole.

"The trouble is that the majority of monuments now in the cemeteries are produced by firms who make it merely a business affair, the greater portion of them having not the slightest idea of what is good or bad, and possessing not even an elementary knowledge of architecture or even good taste. To remedy this it is absolutely necessary that the designs for all the monuments in all the cemeteries, from the most modest to the most costly, should be made by or subject to the approval of a commission composed of two or three architects and a landscape architect of the highest possible standing. They should lay out and design the cemeteries and establish rules for their proper supervision, and should control the designs for future monuments in the cemeteries already existing.

"Nothing could be more impressive than the rank after rank of white stones, inconspicuous in themselves, covering the gentle, wooded slopes, and producing the desired effect of a vast army in its last resting place. Those spaces reserved for burials of officers and their families, however, exhibit all the heterogeneous forms which disturb those very ideas of peace and quiet which should characterize a spot sacred to the tenderest feelings of the human heart. In particular, the noble slopes toward the river should be rigorously protected against the invasion of monuments which utterly annihilate the sense of beauty and repose. This is one of the most beautiful spots in the vicinity of Washington; it should not be defaced or touched in any way, and a law or rule should at once be passed forbidding the placing of any monument on this hill.

The Grouping of the Buildings of the Executive Departments

"The location of the buildings connected with the Legislative and Judicial Departments of the Government having been discussed in another portion of this report, attention should be given to the buildings of the Executive Department. Of these the first to be considered is the White House, the corner stone of which was laid on October 13, 1792, and which was first occupied by President and Mrs. John Adams in 1800. The building was burned by the British in 1814, and both its construction and reconstruction were superintended by its architect, James Hoban.

"For a number of years past the White House has been overcrowded by reason of the rapid increase in public business, which has encroached seriously upon the private apartments of the President. The larger receptions and other social functions are now so inadequately provided for as to cause serious discomforts to the guests, and a consequent loss of that order and dignity which should characterize them. State dinners can not be served adquately; and all the conditions surrounding the home life of the President are primitive to the last degree.

"Three methods of overcoming the present unfortunate conditions have been suggested: First, the enlargement of the White House by additions on the east and west of the present building. The plans and model prepared for such enlargement prove conclusively that the historic White House can not be enlarged without destroying its individuality, thus causing the loss of those characteristic features which endear the edifice to the American people. Second, it has been urged that the White House be given up entirely to public business, and that a residence for the President be built on one of the commanding hills overlooking the city. This plan, however, has not as yet commended itself to popular opinion.

The third alternative is that the Executive offices be removed from the White House, and that the Presidents House (as the White House was termed officially until about 1860) be devoted entirely to residence purposes. This latter plan is favored by the present Chief Executive; and to the Commission it seems to be the best solution of the problem possible at this time.

"The location of the building to contain the Executive offices is a more difficult matter; but the Commission are of the opinion that while temporary quarters may well be constructed in the grounds of the White House, a building sufficient in size to accommodate those offices may best be located in the center of Lafayette Square. This suggestion must be taken in connection with the full development of the plan outlined below.

"There is a present and pressing need for new buildings for existing Departments. The Department of Justice is without a home, and the site selected for a new building (a portion of the square opposite the Treasury Department) is admitted to be inadequate for the erection of a suitable structure. The State, War, and Navy Departments, now housed in a single building, are in so crowded a condition that they are occupying additional rented quarters. For the sake of convenience these Departments should be accessible to the White House, which is their common center. The proper solution of the problem of the grouping of the Executive Departments undoubtedly is to be found in the construction of a series of edifices facing Lafayette Square, thus repeating for those Departments the group of buildings for the Legislative and Judicial Departments planned to the Capitol grounds. Certainly both dignity and beauty can best be attained by such a disposition of public edifices.

"The execution of this plan may best begin by erecting on the entire square bounded by Pennsylvania avenue, Jackson place, H, and Seventeenth streets a building for the use of the Departments of State and of Justice. The square opposite the Treasury Department will be required before many years by the Post-Office Department, now most unworthily and inadequately housed in rooms over the local postoffice; and by the Department of Commerce, soon to be created. It is quite possible also that the Interior Department may find it most convenient to give up to the growing needs

of the Patent Office its present noble building, and to come into closer physical relations with the other Executive Departments. The Agricultural Department, however, being the nucleus of a great number of laboratories requiring a maximum of light and air, may properly have its new building located, as at present proposed, on the grounds in the Mall, now set apart for its uses.

"Such a group of buildings, with the Executive offices for a center, as the Capitol is the center of the Legislative group, will result in a composition of the greatest possible dignity and impressiveness.

The Area South of Pennsylvania Avenue

"During the past two decades a sentiment has developed both among the residents of the District and also in Congress, that the area between Pennsylvania avenue and the Mall should be reclaimed from its present uses by locating within that section important public buildings. The avenue itself is one of the historic thoroughfares of the world, a preeminence attained by reason of the fact that it connects the Executive Department with the Legislative and Judicial Departments of Government, and so has become the route of those processions which celebrate great occasions in peace and war, or which from time to time mark the change of Administrations. Although within recent years imposing buildings devoted to business purposes have been erected on the north side of the avenue, nevertheless, for the most part, the thoroughfare, spacious as it is in itself considered, is lined by structures entirely unworthy of the conspicuous positions they occupy. The upbuilding of Pennsylvania avenue, therefore, must of necessity have consideration in any comprehensive plan for the treatment of Washington.

"The extension of B street north eastward to Pennsylvania Avenue, and the inclusion within the Mall of the space south of that street, as extended, will in part solve the problem. Furthermore, the present location of the city post-office and of the great central market, together with the fact that the business of the city is concentrated largely along this avenue, both suggest that within this area the public buildings of the municipality, as distinct from the General Government, may well be located. The Commission have the more confidence in making this recommendation for the reason that, by common consent and by positive action as well, a site for a District building was set apart in front of the present Center Market, and for nearly thirty years the District of Columbia virtually has been paying an annual rental for that site, in the decreased rents charged the market company in consideration of the relinquishment of a portion of their property to be used as the site of a municipal building. Inadequate as to size, the location of the site is especially adapted to the end sought. Occupying a position midway between the White House and the Capitol, situated at the point of convergence of wide avenues, located in the very center of business activity, placed on a line with the dignified building of the Department of the Interior and of the new Carnegie Library, the site selected would give to the District building and to the municipality it represents a distinction and a dignity all its own. No other site would so assert the individuality of the District of Columbia. This individuality would be still further enhanced by grouping within the same general area other buildings municipal or semi-municipal in character. In this connection the axial relation existing between the proposed site and the present location of the District courts should not be overlooked.

"The location of the District building at the point named would bring about a much-needed change in market conditions. As at present conducted, a large portion of the market business is conducted in public thoroughfares, to the inconvenience of travel and to the disturbance of municipal good order. Congress having retained an option of purchase, the market may well be removed to a location west of the present one, where could be provided a sufficient area, within which territory the business could be conducted within the market itself without encroaching upon the public thoroughfares. This new market should be constructed with streets running through it, as in the case in the admirable examples at Paris, Budapest, and other cities of continental Europe.

"Within the same general area should be constructed an armory sufficient in size to accommodate the brigade of District militia; and since the inauguration of the President of the United States is regarded as a municipal and not as a national function, the armory should be of a character to accommodate the inaugural balls now,

given in the Pension Bureau, to the disturbance of public business.

"Also the much-needed new police court, the police and fire headquarters, an enlarged emergency hospital, and other like divisions of civic administration should find local habitations in immediate proximity to the District building.

"In such manner, gradually, and as municipal needs become insistent, the entire space should be occupied, transformed from its present unworthy conditions into a section having a distinct character, and also being closely related to its environment." [3]

Thus did Olmsted and Moore describe and analyze the plans and proposals advanced by the Senate Park Commission for the central portion of Washington. The balance of the report dealt with outlying parks and reservations. This, too, was masterfully presented, and although the scope of the present study does not include this aspect of the 1902 plan, this section of the report is well worth examination by modern planners. The younger Olmsted, under whose responsibility this aspect of the work fell, was a worthy successor to his illustrious and talented parent, the father of the American park movement.

The Commission's plan, as is obvious from the text of the report and the drawings and models that illustrated its features, amounted to a firm endorsement and extension of L'Enfant's original concept of a great city designed on baroque planning principles. L'Enfant's earlier work obviously exercised an enormous influence on the members of the Commission. The framework for a monumental, formal pattern already existed, the result of L'Enfant's plan of 1791. The placing of the Capitol, the White House, and the Washington Monument—even if the Mall itself had not existed— strongly suggested the solution that was eventually recommended. With the Mall area still miraculously almost undeveloped, with the extensive system of diagonal boulevards laid down by L'Enfant more than a century earlier, with the numerous open spaces and urban squares that had survived through the nineteenth century, and with the inviting area of newly reclaimed land stretching west-

[3] Report of the Park Commission to the Senate Committee on the District of Columbia, *The Improvement of the Park System of the District of Columbia,* Washington, 1902, pp. 35–71.

ward from the Washington Monument, it was almost inevitable that the Commission's plan would be some version of a formal and symmetrical design.

For the Commission to have planned otherwise would have meant the destruction of the essence of the unique plan on which the city had been founded. It would, moreover, have required the designers to reject a noble opportunity to establish in three dimensions what L'Enfant had succeeded in creating in two. Downing, less sensitive to the urban environment that had been created even by the middle of the last century, had ignored the underlying elements of the L'Enfant plan in his attempt to reduce the Mall to a romantic garden. Frederick Law Olmsted, Sr., in his planning of the Capitol grounds in 1874 had also used many of the devices of romantic landscape gardening. His design, however, had a symmetry and restraint more appropriate to the neoclassic structure for which he provided the approaches. Now, in 1902, the buildings, the avenues, and the central open space of the capital city were at last drawn into a single unified plan possessing an underlying design harmony.

The authors of the plan were, of course, firm advocates of this school of design. McKim, trained at the famed l'Ecole des Beaux Arts in Paris, naturally leaned in this direction. Burnham, despite his own early accomplishments with contemporary design in Chicago office buildings, obviously felt more at home with the neoclassic. Olmsted, in his remarkable address before the convention of the American Institute of Architects a year earlier, clearly and forcefully announced that the principles of romantic landscape design, almost synonymous with the Olmsted name, patently were inappropriate in such a setting as Washington. Saint-Gaudens, too, favored formal settings for grand sculptural compositions.

It seems likely, however, that even if designers with less committed tastes had been retained for the task of replanning central Washington, the strong elements of the L'Enfant plan and the existing major structures with their axial relationships would have dominated in the end. This comes close to asserting that the plan of 1902 was almost foreordained, which was not the case. In less skilled or sensitive hands the plan of 1902 might have been disastrous, even though in superficial harmony with the original L'Enfant composition. The rather shallow and conventional scheme produced by Glenn Brown, the unimaginative proposal of Colonel Bingham, and the characterless plan of Samuel Parsons in the years immediately preceding are examples of what planners of less ability might have produced.

In short, this first and greatest essay in civic design of the American twentieth century emerged almost inevitably from the background of its authors and under the strong influence of the environmental setting. There was yet another influence—the prevailing attitude toward architecture in America. The architectural revolution that had begun in Chicago in the 1880's or earlier and which had been challenged by the imitative classicism of the World's Fair of 1893 was, by the turn of the century, almost stilled. All over the country major buildings followed classical designs—city halls, banks, office buildings, libraries, etc. Louis Sullivan's grim prediction that the effect of the Chicago Fair would last half a century or more was beginning to come true. Only Sullivan and a few architectural iconoclasts such as the young Frank Lloyd Wright continued to struggle with the problems of creation rather than imitation in architectural design. The taste of the entire country had been re-directed by the Fair. Burnham, McKim, and Saint-Gaudens, who had been associated in that enormous project, were perhaps more responsible than any others for the new style that had now become standard. So in their formal composition proposed for Washington they symbolized the taste of the entire nation. In other cities, lacking the type of plan for which this kind of civic design was appropriate, the results might have been unfortunate. For Washington, the plan of 1902 proved an especially fitting combination of two-dimensional plan and three-dimensional design.

The plan of 1902 was, however, not beyond criticism, and some of its flaws must be mentioned. There were, first of all, two rather strange discrepancies between the descriptive text and the models and drawings. One concerned the recommendation for separating the executive office from the White House, leaving the latter to serve only as the residence of the chief executive. According to the report, the executive offices were to be housed in "a building sufficient in size" which was to be "located in the center of Lafayette Square."

The plans and drawings presented by the Commission, however, show no such building. Was this an oversight on the part of the designers? Or, was the text in error, possibly including a passage written at an earlier date when the plans had been different and which the authors had neglected to delete? Happily, no such building or any other has been erected in that square which forms such an important part of the entire White House composition. That the Commission could even contemplate placing a structure in the center of this significant open space seems incredible. Such a building would have been ridiculous if made to look insignificant, while, as the site demanded, if it had been developed as a building of major architectural importance, it would have rivaled the White House itself. The deftness and assurance with which the Commission solved other design problems was here unaccountably lacking, but, fortunately, no harm resulted.

The second discrepancy concerned the Smithsonian Institution. The plans for the Mall do not show this romantic, crenelated structure. Yet nowhere in the text is its removal discussed. Possibly the authors simply hoped this might go unnoticed, for a clearly worded statement advocating its demolition would surely have raised a storm of protest. Certainly for the designers this structure, intruding into the broad expanse of the proposed Mall, was an awkward feature with which to cope. Doubtless they expected its exhibits and research facilities to be transferred to one or more of the new buildings they proposed along the sides of the Mall, but the omission of any discussion of this feature of the plan was a serious flaw in their presentation.

Far more important was the failure of the Commission to address itself to the problems of design on both sides of Pennsylvania Avenue. The plan did recommend the acquisition of land south of that important artery and the construction of buildings related to local government in the triangle formed by the avenue and what is now Constitution Avenue (then B Street). A building for the District government, an armory, a police court, police and fire department headquarters, a new and entirely enclosed market, and similar uses were to be housed in this area.

The plans and model of the Commission show a number of very substantial buildings on this site. One can question whether they really expected all of these to be occupied by municipal activities, for the area of these structures appears to exceed that set aside around Lafayette Park for the administrative offices of the national government itself. One could question also the wisdom of retaining the central market in this area at all, even in new quarters as they recommended. This building was to be built on the south side of Pennsylvania Avenue between 9th and 11th Streets, with city streets running through the building, which, they pointed out, was common in the newer European market buildings.

Unaccountably, the Commission neglected to make any proposals whatsoever for the north side of Pennsylvania Avenue. Perhaps it felt that this area lay beyond its jurisdiction, but this omission marked a failure to comprehend the unique opportunities which lay within its grasp. The Commission had, after all, gone well beyond its presumed duty of planning for the park system of the District, and it should have realized that the omission of any proposals for the north side of the avenue constituted a serious shortcoming in the scheme.

Subsequent developments have proved this criticism to be just. Even after the construction of the imposing federal buildings in the triangle area during the 1930's, the north side of Pennsylvania Avenue remained a hodge-podge of buildings of varying height, use, and architectural treatment. Nor have recent years brought any significant changes in conditions. What L'Enfant clearly intended as the most important boulevard of the city remains an architectural disgrace to the District and to the nation.

Only in 1964, with the publication of the report of the President's Commission on Pennsylvania Avenue, has there been a comprehensive plan for the unified architectural treatment of this important artery—the link between the massive governmental buildings in the triangle and along the Mall and the commercial heart of the city to the north.[4] It was scarcely sufficient for the Park Commission report to refer to the historic role of the avenue and the necessity for its "upbuilding." What was needed as a minimum was some design concept on which more detailed plans eventually could have been based.

[4] U.S. President's Council on Pennsylvania Avenue, *Pennsylvania Avenue*, Washington, 1964. See Chapter VII below for a description of this proposal.

There were other deficiencies as well. Perhaps the most obvious is the failure to express symbolically the three fundamental divisions of the national government. Here the Commission perpetuated, where they might have remedied, a deficiency in the L'Enfant plan. L'Enfant saw the Executive and Legislative branches of the new government as clearly the most important. He provided each with its physical symbol: The Capitol on the crown of Jenkins' Hill and the presidential mansion on a somewhat less prominent elevation. Only once did L'Enfant mention a site for the "Judiciary Court," and this was in his preliminary report to the President on August 19, 1791. Certainly no one at that time could have foreseen the position which the Court would eventually attain. No such comparable institution existed in Europe, and L'Enfant may have felt that the Supreme Court would never exist as more than a minor appendage to the other two dominant branches of government.

As early as 1803, in its famous decision in *Marbury* v. *Madison,* the Supreme Court asserted its authority to invalidate an act of Congress as unconstitutional, thus foreshadowing its ultimate increase in importance.[5] While the Court did not again invoke this power until 1857 in the Dred Scott case, by the turn of the century its role in the national government had greatly expanded.[6] In a series of cases dealing with the power of state and federal governments to regulate such matters as railroad rates and business monopolies, the Court began to assume a new and powerful status.

Even before the Park Commission began its work there had been discussions concerning the need for a separate building for the Court, which then met in chambers in the Capitol. Mere space needs were doubtless paramount in this projected move, but there was also at least a partial recognition that the Court had become an important instrument in the scheme of national government.

One wonders why this was not clearly realized by the members of the Commission, who in other ways proved to be so prophetic in their plans and in their vision of the eventual space needs for the federal establishment. Their recommendation that the Supreme Court should be provided with a building to the north of the

Library of Congress and facing the east front of the Capitol was scarcely more perceptive than L'Enfant had been. It seems likely that the Commission, having rightly decided that the Capitol grounds needed a frame of imposing buildings, seized upon the desire for a new structure for the Court as a means to provide an occupant for one of the fifteen new buildings they showed grouped around Capitol Square. They did not foresee that the need for additional library space or, more important in terms of building requirements, for office space for Senators and Representatives that was to develop during the coming decades would furnish sufficient demand to justify these proposed buildings.

The obvious site for a Supreme Court building which would have provided the visual expression of the triad of powers comprising the national government was that chosen for the Lincoln Memorial. An almost equally satisfactory alternative would have been the site now occupied by the Jefferson Memorial, which the Commission's plan referred to rather vaguely as a future memorial site for one or more national heroes. To the extent that capital cities should in some way symbolize the form and style of government, the planners of 1902 failed to grasp one of their greatest opportunities, now forever lost.

The Commission's treatment of the Mall is also open to criticism. Although its report states that the plan constituted a reestablishment of the original L'Enfant proposal, the proposal for the Mall in 1902 differed from the earlier scheme in both concept and execution. L'Enfant's "Grand Avenue" running down the center of the Mall became, in the hands of the Park Commission, the *tapis vert* of Versailles or Compiègne, both of which are illustrated in the report, or of Schoenbrunn, which the members visited in Vienna. One could argue that the Commission's plan was a less "urban" solution to the problem of how to treat this vital portion of monumental Washington than that suggested by L'Enfant. The text of the report describes this as "an expanse of undulating green," the appearance of which is shown in Figure 64. Perhaps here is where the tradition of romantic landscape gardening, represented by the junior Olmsted, asserted itself. The case for the *tapis vert* concept was at least defensible, but in these surroundings the "undulating green" was as out of place as a rumpled green

[5] *Marbury* v. *Madison,* U.S. Supreme Court (1803), 1 Cranch 137.
[6] *Dred Scott* v. *Sandford,* U.S. Supreme Court (1857), 19 Howard 393.

carpet would be at a White House reception. Fortunately, in the eventual execution of the scheme, the Mall was developed as a plane surface from the foot of Capitol Hill to a point near the Monument grounds.[7]

The Commission's plan for the Mall may be criticized as well for its failure to call for underpassing of the principal north-south streets, a defect which is only now partially remedied and which is currently under further study. The report suggested that "the play of light and shade where the streets break through the columns of trees, and the passage of street cars and teams give needed life to the Mall." Possibly in this pre-automobile era this statement may have had some justification. Yet it is difficult to understand even under those circumstances. Almost a half-century earlier the elder Olmsted, faced with a similar long and narrow park site in the middle of a great city, had provided four sunken transverse roads in his magnificent design for Central Park in New York. It is strange indeed that his son did not insist on similar treatment in a situation where aesthetic as well as functional reasons dictated this solution.

Finally, one of the plan's major recommendations which was insufficiently studied was for the treatment of the grounds surrounding the Washington Monument. The importance of this feature was clearly indicated by the fact that the Commission had prepared a separate model showing this area and had displayed this in a prominent part of the Corcoran Gallery. Many of the rendered drawings in that exhibition showed the Monument rising from a great terrace, reached from the west by a monumental stairway extending upward from the formal gardens at its foot.

[7] For an extended criticism of this portion of the Commission's plan and an alternative proposal of considerable merit see Elbert Peets, "New Plans for the Uncompleted Mall," Baltimore *Sunday Sun*, Magazine Section, March 3, 1935, pp. 1–2. Peets' proposal was for a broad paved pedestrian promenade to run down the center of the Mall, lined with benches and flagpoles. Automobiles would be confined to drives along the north and south edges. This and other articles by Peets in the same journal contain unusually perceptive commentary on the orginal and later plans for the central part of the city. See his "Ancestry of the Washington Plan," February 10, 1929, p. 3; "The New Washington—a Sharp Complaint," January 26, 1930, pp. 1–2; and "The Lost Plazas of Washington," April 24, 1932, pp. 4–5, all in the Baltimore *Sunday Sun* Magazine Section.

What the Commission report referred to as the "sunken garden" on the west was 40 feet lower than the base of the shaft. To accomplish this design would require the removal of much of that side of the natural hillock on which the monument rests. The planners were here confronted with two problems: To provide a setting that would enhance the height and isolation of the monument, and to reinforce the axis between the White House and the proposed "Pantheon" facing the presidential mansion which is now the approximate location of the Jefferson Memorial. The intrusion of the western slope of that hill, then, as now, prevented full realization of that axial placement.

Apparently the Commission did not investigate the engineering feasibility of this recommendation. In later years, when studies were conducted, it was found that, unless extensive and very expensive underpinning of the monument was carried out, the stability of the great shaft would be reduced beyond the point of reasonable safety by the removal of earth for the sunken garden. This portion of the Commission's plan was therefore abandoned. No fully satisfactory plan for the development of this portion of the Mall has yet been devised. What the Commission would have proposed had it made itself aware of these difficulties is, of course, unknown. One possible solution would have been to advocate extending the terrace to the west of the Monument by extensive filling of the ground and the erection of a massive but low structure at the intersection of the two main axes. One could argue that some device of this kind was necessary, since the size of the White House and Pantheon grouping to the south was insufficient for the vast distance between these two ends of the north-south axis of the Mall System.

But with all these objections considered, the Park Commission plan still emerges as a composition of civic design unmatched in American history and surpassed by few comparable efforts elsewhere in the world. This sweeping and noble plan carried the stamp of those who created it in the belief that a distinctive image of urban grandeur could be achieved in the nation's capital by underlining and reemphasizing the original baroque character of the L'Enfant design. There are those who feel, perhaps like Jefferson, that this is not the appropriate atmosphere for the capital of a democracy. Yet few can deny the power and majesty of this plan which, as largely realized today, seldom fails to move those who experience its disciplined monumentality. "Make no little plans; they have no power to stir men's souls," Burnham was often heard to remark. That motto was to be frequently derided in later years by younger planners in other cities who rightly appreciated the inappropriateness of neo-classical designs sought to be imposed on the grid cities of America. Yet for Washington in the year 1902 the Park Commission plan for the country's civic center could scarcely have been improved.

One final comment should be made. The plan as presented by the Commission was simple as well as bold. The models and numerous drawings in the report and the effective description and explanation written by Moore and Olmsted aided immeasurably in understanding what was proposed. But the plan itself was straightforward and its essentials were easily grasped even by laymen. In this quality the Washington plan resembled most of the great civic design concepts of the past. Some strong unifying ele-ment, in this case the majestic Mall, nearly always has served as a key to understanding the essential features of noteworthy plans. At Washington the designers seized the splendid opportunity originally foreseen by L'Enfant and happily still largely available after a century of neglect and partial misuse.

The modern generation of architects, civic designers, and urban planners developed professionally in an era when monumental design, axial planning, and symmetrical grouping of buildings was scorned and rejected by their leaders. The central portion of Washington was often pointed to as the major example of what should be avoided. Yet Washington has continued to move deeply countless visitors, domestic and foreign, of perhaps less sophisticated taste and training. There are now signs that we have once again begun to appreciate the use of formal design where appropriate and feasible. As we rediscover the pleasures and delights of a more disciplined urban order, the words of the Senate Park Commission, quoted at such length earlier in this chapter, may at last attain the stature they deserve.

CHAPTER 6

The Plan, the Press, and the Politicians

The journalistic reaction to the Park Commission's plans for Washington was overwhelming both in its extent and in its approval. There were a number of reasons for this response.

The plan appeared at the time when many efforts were being expended throughout the country in various aspects of municipal reform. Attempts to eliminate or reduce graft and corruption in local government, to replace the spoils system by the merit system of employee selection, and to cut down on crime and vice in the cities of America were all examples of this movement. Part of this reform concept was civic beautification and the provision of recreation and park grounds. The Washington plan seemed to many the ideal toward which other cities might strive. True, Washington was no ordinary metropolis, but to those concerned with the improvement of cities the differences between the nation's capital and other communities did not seem significant. Most of the "enlightened" journals of opinion of the day supported reform activities. The appearance of the Washington plan thus provided them with an excellent opportunity to further their existing editorial policies.

The plan attracted much attention, too, simply because it was for the capital of the country. Washington was the second city of every American wherever might be his place of residence. National political news called attention to the city, and even in that day it was a tourist attraction of some considerable importance. Every taxpayer in the country also contributed to the construction of public buildings and other improvements in the District of Co-

lumbia, and it was only natural that they should be interested and concerned in what had been proposed for its future. Located here, too, were correspondents of the major newspapers of the country, who were able to report at first hand what the Commission recommended and how senators, representatives, and members of the Cabinet reacted.

The Commission's plan also attracted widespread comment because of its scope and novelty. The report submitted by Burnham, Olmsted, McKim, and Saint-Gaudens may fairly be regarded as the first city planning document of its kind. While the idea of planned improvements was, of course, not new, the idea of relating them to one another so that the eventual result would be something far more impressive than the sum of individual projects had rarely been considered. And the scale of the proposals, which if carried out would accomplish nothing less than the virtual redesign of an entire central city, stirred the imagination of all who considered the matter.

The high quality of expository writing in the report also served to draw attention to it. Moore, who had once worked as a newspaper reporter and had already written several books, possessed the gift of a clear, direct prose style. Olmsted obviously had inherited much of his father's journalistic skill. The two, working together on the text of the report and utilizing as illustrations the drawings and renderings of the best commercial artists in America, produced a document of unusual persuasiveness and clarity.

A further reason for national interest in the work of the Park

Commission stemmed from the personalities involved. Burnham, McKim, and Saint-Gaudens were widely known throughout the country for their artistic accomplishments. Their contributions to the Chicago Fair had been well publicized, and their individual buildings or, in the case of Saint-Gaudens, pieces of sculpture and monuments, had received much favorable comment. The younger Olmsted, not so widely known himself, bore the name of one who had planned the most important parks in the country. McMillan, of course, was a public figure of some importance. The fact that these men came from different parts of the country meant that reports of their activities which appeared in the newspapers of their home cities served to broaden the interest in the Park Commission undertaking.

Finally, the Commission adopted what was for the time an unusually advanced policy toward public relations. Here they followed Elihu Root's wise suggestions of releasing information on and drawings of the recommendations to leading newspapers and magazines well in advance of the date on which their report would be submitted to the Senate. Just three days after his meeting with Root, McKim was writing Moore about the "feasibility of simultaneous publication, of articles on the work of the Park Commission, in the three New York magazines. . . ."[1] Moore found himself in full agreement with this idea. He wrote a two-part article for *The Century Magazine,* the first portion of which appeared in its February 1902 issue, followed by the second section the next month.[2] McKim's office arranged with the editor to reproduce several of the views being prepared by the artists working under Partridge's direction. There was also a plan of the Mall proposals, which was more detailed and more clearly drawn than the one used in the official report, and evidently this was prepared especially for magazine use.[3] This same plan, together with repro-

ductions of many of the views, also appeared in an article in *The Outlook* early in April.[4] There were other articles as well.[5] It was only natural, in addition, that the men responsible for the plan were called upon to speak or write on numerous occasions about the nature of their recommendations. This, too, served to keep interest in the plan before civic groups around the country.[6]

The first and fullest newspaper accounts were published in Washington. The most complete coverage was provided by the Washington *Post.* The entire first page of its second section on January 16 was devoted to a description of the plan, its background, and the opening of the exhibit by the President. A large, three-column drawing, shown in Figure 73, showed the presidential party viewing the large models from the raised platform, Senator McMillan pointing out some of the features to President Roosevelt, and Secretaries Long and Wilson looking at the drawings. A two-column box summarized the chief recommendations of the Commission. The editorial page of the same issue contained a brief but highly favorable statement about the Commission's proposals, ending with these words:

"Hitherto our public improvements have had no definite scheme including the entire system and making each feature harmonious with all the rest. Now, however, we appear to have done with the haphazard and fitful and to have started on a scheme that time cannot render obsolete. The exhibition at the Corcoran Gallery of Art is tangible proof of good work accomplished and a bright promise of great results to follow."[7]

---

[1] Letter from McKim to Moore, October 29, 1901. Charles Moore Papers, Park Commission Correspondence, McKim Letters, Library of Congress. See also a similar letter dated November 4, 1901.

[2] Charles Moore, "The Improvement of Washington City," *The Century Magazine,* LXIII, Nos. 4 & 5 (February and March, 1902), pp. 621–28, 747–57.

[3] McKim's letter to Moore, dated November 20, 1901, refers to a plan that would soon be returned from *The Century Magazine* as one "made for

reproduction." Charles Moore Papers, Park Commission Correspondence, McKim Letters, Library of Congress.

[4] Elbert F. Baldwin, "Washington Fifty Years Hence," *The Outlook,* LXX, No. 14 (April 5, 1902), pp. 817–29.

[5] "The Beautifying of Washington," *Harper's Weekly,* XLVI, No. 2354 (February 1, 1902), pp. 144–46; "The Improvement of Washington," *Scientific American,* LXXXVI, No. 7 (February 15, 1902), pp. 108–09; and Carroll D. Wright, "The Embellishment of Washington," *The Independent,* LIV, No. 2815 (November 13, 1902), pp. 2683–87.

[6] See, for example, Daniel Burnham, "White City and Capital City," *The Century Magazine,* LXIII, No. 4 (February 1902), pp. 619–20; and Frederick Law Olmsted, "Beautifying a City," *The Independent,* LIV, No. 2801 (August 7, 1902), pp. 1870–77.

[7] The Washington *Post, January* 16, 1902, editorial entitled "Beautifying Washington."

THE
PRESIDENTIAL
PARTY
VIEWING THE
MODELS.

THE PRESIDENT
AND SEN. MC MILLAN

(SECRETARIES
LONG AND WILSON

Viewing the Exhibit in the Hemicycle.

Figure 73. View of Theodore Roosevelt and his Party at the Exhibition of the Senate Park Commission in the Corcoran Gallery: 1902

The Washington *Evening Star* also gave extended coverage to the new plan. On Wednesday, January 15, the evening of the opening of the exhibition, the paper published a full column editorial. It began with a statement similar to the passage just quoted from its rival, indicating a belief that "the old, haphazard, hit-or-miss methods of capital making" would no longer be followed. Along with a summary of the principal recommendations of the Commission, the *Star* included warm praise for the quality of the plans and the manner in which they had been prepared. They were, asserted the editorial,

"Broad and comprehensive, respectful of the principles underlying the original plans of the founders yet daring in the proposal of new projects in harmony with the old, regardful of only the single precept to make the most of Washington's opportunities for beauty and impressiveness." [8]

And, calling for action by Congress to implement this vision of the new city, the *Star* concluded: "By adopting this scheme now, leaving its components to be worked out in detail as necessities and opportunities arise, Congress will demonstrate its foresight and its wisdom as well as its intelligent pride in the national capital." [9]

The next day the *Star* carried a story about the exhibit, with photographs of Burnham, Olmsted, and McKim. While this appeared as a news story, it included many comments of commendation.[10] The Friday issue contained another news article with a cut of one of the illustrations, and the Saturday issue summarized the plans for the Lincoln Memorial, accompanied by an illustration.[11] On the back page of the Saturday issue appeared a three-column cartoon showing the figures of Uncle Sam and Columbia gazing at a list of the major proposals. Uncle Sam is saying, " 'That's a fine program. Now I must get to work and carry it out.' " [12]

Newspapers in other cities were quick to take note of the proposals for Washington. The Philadelphia *Press,* after describing the exhibit and what it advocated, also suggested official adoption of the plan, stating:

"The sensible thing for Congress to do is to make the plan the new artistic datum, as it were, by which and about which the future improvements of the capital shall crystallize into orderly advance, with utility and beauty the main objects in view. As things go, it is unlikely the work of Senator McMillan can come to naught, and at all events the exhibition now on is in itself a victory for common sense, as well as a triumph of art." [13]

The most authoritative words in the press appeared in the New York *Times.* Here Montgomery Schuyler, the respected architectural critic, dwelt at some length on the historical basis of the plan and the underlying concepts of baroque city plans and architecture. His article included a full account of what the Commission proposed and an analysis of the plan which strongly supported the recommendations. Schuyler also addressed himself to the matter of cost, stressing that, while no one could estimate the ultimate cost of executing the plan, this was unimportant. Then, he added:

"The point is to have a plan that you believe in, that is based upon study of what has been found most admirable in its kind in the world, in those examples of the art of city making which 'have pleased many and pleased long.' That without doubt the commission have triumphantly attained. Whatever it may cost Uncle Sam to do all this, it will cost him nothing to say now that he believes in it, that he means to do it in good time, and that in the meantime whatever he does in the way of public architecture or public embellishment he will do in accordance with it." [14]

Schuyler, too, called upon Congress to adopt the plan. He also advocated "that the commission which have devised such a plan shall be perpetuated to supervise its execution." This recommendation and similar proposals from other sources were ultimately to be followed.

[8] The Washington *Evening Star,* January 15, 1902, editorial entitled "The Grander Washington Plan."
[9] *ibid.*
[10] The Washington *Evening Star,* January 16, 1902.
[11] *ibid.,* January 17 and 18, 1902.
[12] *ibid.,* January 18, 1902.

[13] The Philadelphia *Press,* as quoted in *ibid.,* January 16, 1902.
[14] Montgomery Schuyler, "The Nation's New Capital," The New York *Times* Supplement, January 19, 1902, pp. 4–5.

Professional journals were equally responsive. The *American Architect and Building News* for February 1 contained an editorial commenting favorably on the proposals. A two-part article on the Commission's work began in the same issue and continued in the March 8 issue. The first part concluded with these words:

"The whole is a masterly presentation of the most important work of artistic significance ever projected in the United States. It marks an epoch in our national progress. It educates. It calls aloud for realization. It crowns gloriously the labors of the Commission and should effect their retention as a permanent board to inaugurate the plan they have conceived and to direct what the nation should do in the arts which they so honorably represent before the country." [15]

The most thorough and painstaking review of the Commission's plans written for professional circles appeared in the *Architectural Record*. Here Montgomery Schuyler expanded his remarks written for the lay readers of the New York *Times*. No fewer than 13 illustrations, many of them full-page, accompanied this long and detailed article. Schuyler, who never hesitated to level withering criticism at that which he disliked, could scarcely find sufficient terms of admiration for the Washington plan. After analyzing the recommendations and repeating his suggestion for a permanent body to have control over the design of both public and private buildings, he concluded: "We can have nothing but praise for the magnificent scheme of Messrs. Burnham, McKim, Olmsted and St. Gaudens. Their part in the making of a beautiful city has been so well done that they already deserve to be ranked with L'Enfant in the gratitude of Washingtonians and of all Americans who wish to be justified of their pride in the Capital." [16]

Public and professional acceptance of the plan and acclaim for its boldness was thus widespread. Nor were indications of official support long in coming. Elihu Root, whose advice had been sought by McKim and who in turn had been convinced of the merits of the Commission's plans which had been divulged to him, became one of the plan's staunchest supporters. On the very day that the exhibition opened he replied to an invitation to express his opinion on the proposed memorial bridge across the Potomac, then projected as a continuation of New York Avenue:

"The bill commands my hearty approval, with the exception of one matter of detail; that is, the limitation of the Washington end of the bridge to the old naval observatory grounds. I think the bridge should be located in accordance with the very admirable plans prepared by the Commission consisting of Messrs. D. H. Burnham, Charles F. McKim and Frederick L. Olmsted, jr. . . . which are the development of the original plans of Washington and L'Enfant for the Capital City." [17]

And three months later, in a letter to Senator McMillan asking for his support for an appropriation to make possible further work on Potomac Park, Root added, "Of course you understand correctly that I want to see every peg possible driven in to fasten the future development of the city down to the lines of the Commission's plan." [18]

Moore records how one actual peg was driven. On March 22, 1902, Senator Cullom of Illinois, a supporter of the plan, arranged a meeting with Secretary Hay, Secretary Root, and Senators Wetmore and McMillan. McMillan proposed that McKim attend the conference, and McKim brought Saint-Gaudens down from New York with him. As Moore tells it, "Before the meeting, McKim, Saint-Gaudens, and Moore explored the wastes of Potomac Park until they got the Monument on a line with the dome of the Capitol, and there, on the bank of the Potomac, they drove a stake to mark the site of the Lincoln Memorial; and there, after many vicissitudes, it was finally placed." [19]

Secretary Hay expressed his unqualified approval of the Commission's plans. According to Moore, he stated that his feelings

[15] "Washington: The Development and Improvement of the Park-System," *American Architect and Building News*, LXXV, No. 1362 (February 1, 1902), pp. 33, 35–36; LXXV, No. 1367 (March 8, 1902), pp. 75–77.

[16] Montgomery Schuyler, "The Art of City Making," *The Architectural Record*, XII, No. 1 (May 1902), pp. 1–26.

[17] Letter from Root, January 15, 1902, as quoted in Philip C. Jessup, *Elihu Root*, New York, 1938, I, pp. 282–83.

[18] Letter from Root to McMillan, April 11, 1902, as quoted in Jessup, *Root*, I, p. 282.

[19] Charles Moore, *The Life and Times of Charles Follen McKim*, Boston, 1929, p. 203.

were so strong on the subject that "even my house can go to carry out the scheme of having Executive Department buildings around Lafayette Square." [20] McKim was asked to prepare sketch plans and rough cost estimates for the Lincoln Memorial, and Senator Cullom shortly thereafter revised his bill for a memorial to Lincoln so that the site proposed corresponded with that recommended in the Washington plan.[21]

While these indications of executive and legislative support for the plan were highly encouraging to the members of the Commission and their friends, this attitude proved to be by no means unanimous. Joseph Cannon's contempt for their work already had become widely known. Cannon's background as a smalltown lawyer in Illinois had provided little opportunity for contact with the arts. He had been elected and reelected by his constituents partly because of his outspoken criticism of governmental expenditures for elaborate buildings or, indeed, for any governmental programs involving substantial sums of money. He was deeply conservative politically, and his convictions in this area were paralleled by his hostility toward any but the most spartan building plans.

Moreover, Cannon felt deeply about the prerogative of the House of Representatives to initiate appropriations measures. He bitterly resented Senator McMillan's stratagem of arranging for the expenses of the Commission to be paid out of Senate contingent funds, an action which had been taken without reference to the House. While perfectly legal, the strategy was perhaps politically unwise and, in any event, it almost proved the undoing of the Commission's plans by arousing the enmity of a powerful and implacable foe. Cannon's hand was strengthened when he was elected Speaker of the House in 1903 and began his long and virtually single-handed rule of that body.[22]

In August 1902 another event occurred which was to hinder the acceptance of the plan as a guide for the future. Senator

McMillan died suddenly at his summer home in Massachusetts, and with his passing the Capital lost the most influential and best informed proponent of the plan in the Senate. While other members of the Senate District of Columbia Committee and a few additional senators especially interested in Washington had been kept informed of the work of the Commission as it progressed, the entire project was properly regarded as McMillan's. No other member of Senate, in or out of the committee, possessed his energy and enthusiasm for the plan or his intimate knowledge of its details and the reasons for many of the recommendations. The fight for the plan, which was to last many years, was at once made immensely more difficult because of his loss.

Problems were not long in arising. Many departments of government urgently needed new buildings. Their needs had existed and were recognized before the Park Commission had been created, and individual building plans for some of them had been under consideration. One involved a proposed hall of records, or archives. Congress had passed legislation authorizing the purchase of a site bounded by Eighteenth and Nineteenth and E and F Streets. The proposed location was thus only two blocks from the White House. The Commission's plan had not proposed public buildings in this tier of blocks. Moreover, the Commission's report specifically recommended a site for a Hall of Records between Pennsylvania Avenue and the Mall.

The Secretary of the Treasury, Leslie M. Shaw, the former Governor of Iowa whom Roosevelt had appointed to the Cabinet, wrote to Burnham on July 24, 1903, asking his advice. Apparently President Roosevelt had requested that Burnham be consulted, although the Park Commission no longer had any official standing after its report had been submitted. They began a lengthy correspondence which grew increasingly more vehement.[23]

Burnham first replied to Shaw stating that the Commission's plan or some other plan for the entire central area must be followed if orderly development were to be attained. Shaw answered that he did not think that the Commission's plan could be carried out if each proposed building had to be sited in conformity with

[20] *ibid*. Moore adds that Hay then commented "with a smile, 'probably my house will not be needed during my lifetime.' "
[21] *ibid*.
[22] For biographical information about this colorful and tyrannical legislator see the following: William Rea Gwinn, *Uncle Joe Cannon*, New York, 1957; and Blair Bolles, *Tyrant from Illinois*, New York, 1951.

[23] The text of Burnham's letters and a portion of two of Shaw's appear in Charles Moore, *Daniel H. Burnham*, Boston, 1921, I, pp. 206–13.

it. He then asked Burnham for an opinion whether the presently proposed site for the hall of records would be regarded as a substantial departure from the plan. Burnham's answer followed and expanded on his previous letter. He pointed out that, if the first buildings to be erected by the government after the preparation of the plan did not follow it, then almost certainly it would not be followed when future buildings were constructed. In Burnham's words,

"If the Executive yields now, it will be much more difficult to refuse in the future, because it will then have not alone the urgency of personal interest, but precedent as well to contend with. On all future occasions the claim will be set up that the Plan was abandoned by the administration and was dropped definitively. Therefore, I believe that unless you now adhere to the general plan it will be lost and the work done upon it thrown away. It will never again be so easy as it now is to stem the tide." [24]

Shaw seized on Burnham's use of the word "Executive" in his rejoinder. He pointed out that Congress had authorized the building for a particular site and the President had no discretion to change it. The only course open to the President was to decide whether or not to construct the building. Shaw then inquired if Burnham felt the location of a hall of records as contemplated would "do such violence to the report as to render it inadvisable to carry out the remaining suggestions." [25]

Burnham replied, assuring Shaw that he understood the President's position. He stated that the site under consideration might be satisfactory in itself as a convenient location for a hall of records, but added, "I feel that the failure of the Government to carry out our plan when the first opportunities arise for doing so will be a practical abandonment of it." [26]

Shaw's answer was brief and caustic: "Personally, I do not believe that any Congress will ever pay the least attention to the report of the Commission. Personally I would follow any plan rather than erect buildings with no general plan, but Congress is a practical and not a theoretical body." [27]

Burnham answered this with a long and vigorous statement. He insisted that, even if the hall of records must be erected on the controversial site, the Commission's recommendations on other buildings should be pressed "upon the attention of Congress." Then Burnham declared that he was much more concerned about the location of the new building for the Department of Agriculture, expressing the fear that if it was not built on the "true axis" of the Mall "then a state of disorder will have been made permanent and a systematic arrangement of this public space will have been made impossible thereafter." [28] He pointed out that President Cassatt of the Pennsylvania Railroad had agreed to surrender the Mall location of the station in the belief that nothing should stand in the way of the development of the Mall as originally conceived.

With this letter and its allegation that the Agriculture Building might violate the plans for the Mall, Burnham opened up a new and even more bitter struggle. Shaw showed the letter to the President, who passed it on to Shaw's fellow Iowan, Secretary of Agriculture James Wilson, who served in this post from 1897 to 1913, and whose political influence was substantial.

In a highly charged letter to Burnham, Wilson demanded to know what axis Burnham was talking about and continued: "Some busybody who meddles in other people's affairs has been giving you a great deal of misinformation. We have not come to the location of the building and will not for several months. Who has told you that anybody proposes to have the Agricultural building go on without reference to any future plan . . . ?" [29]

Burnham, perhaps appalled at the turn matters had taken, replied courteously and enclosed a large plan of the Mall with a tracing paper overlay showing in red lines the eight-hundred-foot distance between the rows of buildings proposed to border it on

[24] Letter from Burnham to Shaw, July 16, 1903, as quoted in *ibid.*, I, p. 208.

[25] Letter from Shaw to Burnham, July 18, 1903, as quoted in *ibid.*, I, pp. 209–10.

[26] Letter from Burnham to Shaw, July 21, 1903, as quoted in *ibid.*, I, pp. 210–11.

[27] Letter from Shaw to Burnham, as quoted in *ibid.*, I, p. 211, no date given.

[28] Letter from Burnham to Shaw, July 24, 1903, as quoted in *ibid.*, I, pp. 212–13.

[29] Letter from Wilson to Burnham, August 3, 1903, as quoted in *ibid.*, I, pp. 213–14.

each side. He could not resist adding this sly paragraph in an attempt to turn Wilson's angry protest into a statement of support for the Mall plan: "It gives me great pleasure to know that you resent the implication that you might be a party to placing the Agricultural building anywhere else than in its proper relationship with the plan for the future development of the city." [30]

The President also received a copy of the map from Burnham, sent in the hope that it would clarify the issue over which the Commission had spent so much time but which seemed to be so misunderstood. [31]

This constituted only the preliminary skirmish in the battle over the location of the Department of Agriculture building. Soon it was resumed, the first of a series of major conflicts in which the supporters of the plan of 1902 were to find themselves engaged over the years. The details of attack, counterattack, thrust, and parry are instructive.

On February 6, 1904, B. T. Galloway, an official of the Department of Agriculture who had been made chairman of the building committee of the department, wrote to the architects who had been selected to design the new structure, Rankin, Kellogg & Crane of Philadelphia. He informed them that in their studies for the building they could disregard the eight-hundred-foot distance between buildings on the Mall specified by the Park Commission and could assume that the building might be located within three hundred feet of the center line of the Mall. He cited as authority a decision reached at a meeting of the President, Secretary Wilson, and the sixteen members of the House Committee on Agriculture. [32]

The architects sent McKim a copy of Galloway's letter, and he immediately wrote to President Roosevelt requesting that he be allowed to explain the reasons why the Commission felt the eight-hundred-foot width was important to establish and maintain. [33] Meanwhile Glenn Brown arranged for McKim to confer with Secretary of War William H. Taft to determine if he had jurisdiction over this area of the public grounds. Taft found himself in sympathy with McKim's arguments and agreed that he would maintain the building line as originally recommended by the Park Commission. But as McKim was reporting this welcome news to Brown a telephone call from Taft's office informed them that jurisdiction over the location of the building had been vested in the Secretary of Agriculture and that only the President could interfere. [34]

McKim then met with Roosevelt to explain how important it was to uphold the original planned width of the Mall. Glenn Brown records the President's reaction:

"I wish," Roosevelt said, "I had known this before, but I have given my assent to the six hundred feet scheme, as the engineers told me it would be 'wide enough for anything," and only a slight modification of the park plan.

"Now, if you will take this up with the Senate and get them to approve the nine hundred feet between buildings, I will have an opportunity to reconsider." [35]

Brown, McKim, and others conferred with Senator Francis Newlands of Nevada, who had indicated his interest, and with Senator Jacob Gallinger of New Hampshire, who had succeeded McMillan as Chairman of the District Committee. Newlands agreed to introduce a bill providing that all buildings erected on the Mall should observe the proposed four-hundred-foot setback from its center line. [36] Gallinger, on the other hand, stated that the members of his committee had viewed the Mall and decided that a three-hundred-foot setback was sufficient. Nevertheless, at Senator

[30] Letter from Burnham to Wilson, August 5, 1903, as quoted in *ibid.*, I, p. 214.

[31] Burnham mentions the map sent to the President in a letter to Moore, September 17, 1903, in which he enclosed copies of his correspondence with Shaw and Wilson. The text appears in *ibid.*, I, p. 215.

[32] The contents of this letter are described in *ibid.*, I, p. 217. According to Glenn Brown, the proponents of this scheme had small red flags placed on the mall to mark the 600-foot width, and the President, after viewing the Mall as so marked agreed that the space was "wide enough for anything." Glenn Brown, *Memories*, Washington, 1931, p. 274. Brown states that it was the Senate District of Columbia Committee that met with the President on this occasion, rather than the House Committee on Agriculture. It seems likely that two meetings with different legislative groups were held.

[33] Letter from McKim to Roosevelt, February 10, 1904, as quoted in Moore, *Burnham*, I, p. 218.

[34] Brown, *Memories*, p. 275.

[35] *ibid.*, p. 276. Brown quotes the President as saying "nine hundred" feet, rather than the eight hundred recommended by the Commission.

[36] Moore, *Burnham*, I, p. 219.

Newlands' insistence, Gallinger agreed to hold a hearing on the matter.[37]

The hearing on March 12 was well attended. Appearing before the District Committee were eight members representing the American Institute of Architects; Senator Newlands and Senator George Wetmore of Rhode Island, who supported the measure; officials of the Department of Agriculture; Thomas Kellogg, the architect of the proposed structure; Burnham, McKim, Olmsted, Saint-Gaudens, and others.

Burnham made a long and persuasive statement. He mentioned the background of the Commission, told of its European trip to examine precedents for the Mall development, and recalled the painstaking manner in which it considered the exact width that would be most appropriate for the effect desired. He described how the Commission had arranged for lines of flagpoles to be erected on the Mall at various widths and how its members had finally decided on a three-hundred-foot width of turf as the minimum. Then he explained the Commission's investigations of the number of rows of trees that would be desirable and how far apart they should be planted and why they concluded that there should be four rows on each side fifty feet apart. Burnham was always a powerful speaker, and his clear and forceful statement at this meeting was one of his most convincing.[38]

McKim was called on and added this statement: "We have studied this enterprise very carefully and given our time and thought to it. We are firmly of the opinion that a greater rather than a less width is desirable, and that not by a single inch should it be narrowed." [39]

Other witnesses offered their opinions in support of the position maintained by Burnham and McKim. Members of the committee were shown the original drawings of the Commission and asked to compare them with new sketches indicating the effect that would be created by narrowing the Mall.[40] Gallinger and his colleagues found themselves unable to resist the weight of these arguments advanced by such a battery of experts; after a brief discussion they decided to reverse their former opinion and support the Senate resolution calling for the eight-hundred-foot mall.

Word of this action came to President Roosevelt. Probably he welcomed an excuse to support the Commission and to repudiate his earlier approval of the reduced width which had been urged upon him without consultation with those who had prepared the plan. On the same day as the committee hearing Roosevelt wrote the following to Secretary of Agriculture Wilson: "I am having great trouble about that 800-foot mall. The best architects and artists and most cultivated people I know feel that it is an outrage to encroach on the 800 feet. I very earnestly wish that under my administration we could refrain from such encroachment." [41]

The battle should have been at an end, but presidential reinforcement was to be required once again. Probably with Secretary Wilson's approval, the engineer in charge of construction for the agricultural building located the basement excavation a hundred feet to the east and established its ground level some eight feet higher than had been recommended by the Commission. Brown tells that he and McKim spent several hours at the site and that McKim was most disturbed over the fact that the base of the building would be higher than the base of the Washington Monument. Of this feature McKim commented: "One of the most important elements in the Mall plan is the continuous up grade from the Grant Statue to the Washington Monument; any grade leading first up and then down would have the effect of shortening the vista and of cutting off portions of the Monument." [42]

Wilson refused to make any change, arguing that some $10,000

[37] Brown, *Memories*, p. 276.
[38] The full text appears in Moore, *Burnham*, I, pp. 221–26.
[39] *ibid.*, pp. 226–27.
[40] Brown, *Memories*, p. 276.

[41] Letter from Roosevelt to Wilson, March 12, 1904, in Elting E. Morison (ed.), *The Letters of Theodore Roosevelt*, Cambridge, 1951, IV, p. 750. Roosevelt a few months later took credit for single-handedly saving the Mall. In a letter to Nicholas Murray Butler complaining about an article in the May 28, 1904, issue of *Collier's Weekly* attacking the President's policies on artistic matters, Roosevelt stated: ". . . this year I have forced the erection of the new buildings of the Agricultural Department in accordance with the plan known as the McMillan plan, preserving the . . . mall from the capitol to the Monument. Congress did not do this. I did it. . . ." Letter from Roosevelt to Butler, June 3, 1904 in Morison, *Letters*, IV, p. 814.
[42] As quoted in Brown, *Memories*, p. 278.

Figure 74. View of the Mall from the Washington Monument: 1906

"The President took Mr. McKim to task at once at the audacity of architects who wait 30 and 60 days, until plans have been completed, and then come in and attempt to make a change. Well, that was not a very good beginning, and I am afraid that our brother McKim thought the jig was up. But it so suited the Secretary of Agriculture that when there appeared a suggestion from an engineer that possibly not $10,000 or $5,000 would be sacrificed, but an economy might be introduced in another way, the Secretary, at the suggestion or the invitation of the President, said that he thought possibly it might be worked out that way, but the President insisted that if we did, we did not intend to waive the criticism that we had to make against the profession of architects by reason of their delay. And so we separated." [43]

McKim accompanied Taft to his office in the War Department. There, as Taft records it, "McKim and I walked up the steps of the War Department. I said, "Mr. McKim, I congratulate you on your victory." He turned and looked at me a moment, and said, "Was it a victory? Another such and I am dead." [44]

But it was a victory and a great one, for it established at what is the most critical time for any plan the principle that the one for Washington was to be respected and followed. It was this principle—so long disregarded in the development of Washington—that Roosevelt came to accept as his own, and after Roosevelt, Taft.

Further, as the photograph reproduced in Figure 74 shows, the new building line for the Mall became firmly fixed with the construction of the Department of Agriculture building, which appears on the right-hand side of the photograph. The two wings of this structure were eventually joined by a central administrative unit completed in the 1930's. At that time the old building to the north, located on the line of the Smithsonian and uncomfortably

already had been spent and that the deviations from the Commission's plan were extremely minor. McKim went to Taft, whose sympathetic attitude had already been made evident, and presented his case. Taft, in turn, took the matter up with Roosevelt, who agreed that the Commission plan should be supported once again, although he expressed dismay that the protest had not been filed before so much work had already been completed. Taft suggested a meeting to discuss the issue, and the President agreed. What then occurred is narrated by Taft as he recalled the incident a few years later when he had become president:

[43] William Howard Taft, "Address in honor of Mr. Charles Follen McKim," American Institute of Architects, *Charles Follen McKim Memorial Meeting*, Washington, 1910, p. 6. Taft's remarks were made on December 15, 1909, at a meeting called by the American Institute of Architects to memorialize McKim, whose death occurred on September 14, 1909.

[44] *ibid.*

close to the center line of the Mall, was finally removed. On the north side of the Mall and somewhat to the east can be seen the new National Museum building for the Smithsonian, a structure located in conformity to the Park Commission plan and which first defined the building line on that side of the Mall, which has been consistently followed to the present time.

It was remarkably fortunate for the future development of the city that Roosevelt the reformer became President at the beginning of these formative years of the Commission's plan. Roosevelt might have wavered at times and he might have been persuaded by such men as Secretary Wilson to approve deviations from the plan, but at heart he championed the efforts of those who supported the Commission. In persuading the President to stand behind their efforts, the watchdogs and lobbyists for a better Washington represented by the American Institute of Architects found themselves helped, paradoxically enough, by their old enemy, Speaker Joseph Cannon. Cannon and Roosevelt represented the two poles of the Republican party. There is every reason to believe that the reforming Roosevelt must have taken delight in open opposition to the conservative Cannon on matters affecting Washington, although he forced himself to minimize such conflicts on national political and economic issues for the sake of party unity.

The architects made every effort to win Roosevelt to their side. In this campaign McKim and Brown, among others, played important roles. McKim had come to know the President well when he was put in charge of remodelling the White House in 1902.[45] Brown, as Secretary of the American Institute of Architects, was frequently consulted on matters affecting Washington or those in which the Institute could be expected to have an interest. At the annual dinner of the Institute in January 1905 the President was invited to address the gathering along with such other dignitaries as Senator Elihu Root, Dr. Nicholas Murray Butler, Justice John Harlan, and, remarkably enough, Speaker Cannon. It was on this occasion that President Roosevelt uttered the words that came to be used by the supporters of the Washington plan whenever in later years it appeared to be endangered by

a proposed project not in conformity with it. In the course of his remarks, the President stated:

"The only way in which we can hope to have worthy artistic work done for the Nation, State or municipality is by having such a growth of popular sentiment as will render it incumbent upon successive administrations, or successive legislative bodies, to carry out steadily a plan chosen for them, worked out for them by such a body of men as that gathered here this evening.

"What I have said does not mean that we shall go, here in Washington for instance, into immediate and extravagant expenditures on public buildings. All that it means is that whenever hereafter a public building is provided for and erected, it should be erected in accordance with a carefully thought-out plan adopted long before, and that it should be not only beautiful in itself, but fitting in its relations to the whole scheme of the public buildings, the parks and the drives of the District." [46]

Perhaps the architects felt that Cannon's acceptance of a place at the speakers' table foretold some lessening of his hitherto unalterable opposition to their efforts. His speech, it is true, was mellow and, for him, conciliatory. He granted that beauty might even be considered when government buildings were contemplated. Rather wistfully, in talking about the need for economy in building, he conceded: "I may preach; but when you come and criticise and talk about 'sky line,' somehow or other you get the people with you." [47]

Cannon's opposition to the Commission's plan and all of its details remained, however, as stubborn as ever. But for the moment the architects could contemplate progress on the plan with considerable satisfaction. The Hall of Records project had been dropped, the controversy over the Agricultural Building had been resolved favorably, and construction of the Union Station was proceeding on the site favored by the Commission and following plans designed by Burnham. This massive structure, a few feet longer

<hr>

[45] See Chapter 16, "Charles McKim Restores the White House," in Moore, *McKim*, pp. 204–22.

[46] Theodore Roosevelt, "Art and the Republic," in Charles Moore (comp.) *The Promise of American Architecture,* Washington, 1905, pp. 17–18.
[47] Joseph G. Cannon, "Architecture and Appropriations," in Moore, *Promise of American Architecture,* p. 64.

Figure 75. View of Union Station: 1906

than the Capitol itself, is shown in Figure 75, an impressive addition to the Washington urban scene.

In addition, Congress had recently approved new office buildings for the Senate and the House of Representatives to be located near the Capitol exactly as the Park Commission had recommended. Moreover, Roosevelt, following a suggestion made to him in a memorandum by McKim, had appointed a Consultative Board in the spring of 1904 to advise him on questions affecting the location of buildings that might arise during that summer. The National Museum, which had been assigned a site on the north side of the Mall, was the principle item of concern.[48] As members of this group Roosevelt appointed the members of the Park Commission and Bernard R. Green, Superintendent of the Library of Congress. While this board was established by executive action and

was only temporary, it seemed to presage the creation of a permanent official board or commission to which all matters affecting the design and location of buildings and monuments could be referred to study and recommendations. This idea, of course, was one to which the architects were deeply committed.

Cannon's opposition to the Park Commission plans and to a permanent body to oversee the artistic development of the capital city remained strong and unremitting. He championed Secretary of Agriculture Wilson in his attempt to build on a portion of the Mall.[49] He fought unsuccessfully the location of the Grant Memorial, which the Park Commission had recommended for a site directly in front of the Capitol at the east end of the Mall.

[48] Moore, *Burnham*, I, pp. 228–29.

[49] According to Brown, Cannon wanted the building located in the very center of the Mall between the Washington Monument and the Capitol! Brown, *Memories*, p. 99.

151

Cannon and others of his persuasion battled this proposal on the grounds that it would necessitate the removal of the old Botanical Gardens and would cause the elimination of a number of large trees. This engendered a fierce controversy because at the time the Park Commission began its work Congress had authorized a memorial to Grant and had arranged for a commission to choose a site and select a sculptor. The committee announced a competition on April 10, 1901, as a means to choose the designer and designated a site located immediately south of the White House.[50] Burnham, McKim, Saint-Gaudens, and the sculptor Daniel French were eventually appointed as the jury to select the winner. When they did so and reported to Congress, they also recommended the change in location to conform to the plan of 1902. On this issue, once again, the artists, backed by their political allies in executive positions, emerged victorious.

It was a victory, however, which cost them a useful ally when the Grant statue and its flanking figures on a long and massive base began to take form. This site, according to the Park Commission's plan, was to be a great and formal square; McKim thought it would be comparable to the Place de la Concorde in Paris. According to the instructions to the Grant Memorial Commission they could locate the memorial on any unoccupied public ground. Unfortunately, the site shown on the plan contained many fine trees, at least one of which had been planted as a peace memorial. In addition, the greenhouse of the Botanical Gardens was located a few hundred feet to the east directly between the Grant Memorial site and the Washington Monument. An unsightly fence, part of the gardens, partially screened the spot chosen for the Grant statue.

The Washington *Evening Star,* which but a few years before had so warmly supported the Park Commission plan, now turned on the designers in hot fury. Calling the site of the Grant Memorial an "under-hand evasion" and a "disreputable trick" in violation of the intent of Congress, the *Star,* on January 14, 1908, continued:

"The placing of the monument upon this utterly unfit site in a swamp was in furtherance of the scheme to get possession of

[50] *Statue or Memorial of General Grant,* Washington, 1902.

Figure 76. Cartoon of McKim and Fellow Architects Replanning the Mall: 1908

the Botanic Garden, destroy all its trees and convert it into a bare asphalted street styled 'Union Square.' Their contention that only two or three trees would need to be disturbed . . . is an illustration of the false pretenses that have characterized every step of their progress. They knew perfectly well that a proper setting for the monument in this obscure position would require the demolition of not only all the fine old trees in the garden, but also of the government greenhouses. . . . They knew also that the possession of the Botanic Garden was only the entering wedge for their plan for the destruction of all the noble shade trees in the People's Park from the Capitol to the river to make way for a sixteen-hundred-feet wide track of desolation as bare and as hot as the Desert of Sahara." [51]

[51] The Washington *Evening Star,* January 14, 1908.

The *Star* singled out McKim for particularly biting criticism. He was pictured in a cartoon reproduced in Figure 76 as a disciple of Le Nôtre who arbitrarily wished to replace all signs of naturalistic planting with the rigid geometric plans of the renaissance. The proposed reflecting basin between the Washington Monument and the suggested memorial to Lincoln was compared to "the stinking old Washington canal that was the plague spot of the city for so many years." The *Star* stated its belief that the development of the many fountains proposed by the Park Commission would cause a water shortage in the District, and there was similar low-level criticism of many other features of the plan.

This blistering newspaper attack had not been the first voice of criticism. Ten weeks earlier the Washington Chapter of the American Institute of Architects, alarmed by the mounting protests over the removal of trees which threatened the entire Mall concept, adopted a resolution upholding the site selected for the Grant statue. This document correctly pointed out that because there had been no guiding plan for the central part of the city the formal treatment of the Mall envisaged by L'Enfant had been endangered through indiscriminate location of buildings and haphazard landscape treatment. Then, in endorsing the Park Commission's action in reestablishing and extending the original plan for central Washington, the Institute members resolved:

"That this chapter considers the vista treatment of the Mall, as contemplated by . . . [the commission] . . . a return to first principles, and by far the most logical, effective and monumental treatment yet suggested, and that a strict adherence to their plans will give to the American people the possibilities for the most beautiful capital in the world.

"We are confident that the necessity for the adoption of a comprehensive plan will be generally recognized, and would call attention to the fact that when adopted, the first step towards its fulfillment shall be the planting of trees in their allotted places. . . ." [52]

Cannon must have taken considerable pleasure in the *Star's* attack, which he may well have been instrumental in stimulating. Certainly he enjoyed seeing the architects on the defensive. But he must have writhed in frustration when he learned that on the eve of Roosevelt's departure from the White House, January 19, 1909, the President issued an executive order creating a Council of Fine Arts. This order required submission of all public building plans to the Council, the advice of which was to be followed unless the President directed otherwise. Twenty-one architects, four painters, four sculptors, and one landscape architect were named to membership, including Burnham, McKim, and Olmsted. This had come about after The American Institute of Architects and the Public Art League had failed in their attempts to gain congressional approval for a similar proposal, largely owing to Cannon's opposition. [53]

Shortly after Taft became President he revoked this order in the belief that such a body could not properly be created except by legislative action. Cannon's elation, however, proved to be only momentary. Again legislation was introduced in Congress to provide for a permanent body to study and advise on the location and design of buildings and monuments. Once again, the battle was joined.

The House debate on the measure took place on February 9, 1910. Representative Samuel McCall of Massachusetts led the fight for the bill. The opponents bitterly recalled all the events of the past ten years as proof that an appointed art commission would disregard the mandates of Congress and ignore practical considerations in favor of artistic theories. Representative James Mann of Illinois, who the following year would become the minority leader of the House, spoke of the Agricultural building controversy, saying:

"What I am trying to find out is whether we are legalizing such a commission which might perpetrate such an enormous crime as was perpetrated in the construction of the Agricultural building,

---

[52] The full text of the resolution appears in "The Grant Monument Site, Washington, D.C.," *The Architectural Record,* XXIII, No. 1 (January 1908), pp. 73–74.

[53] Brown tells the story of Roosevelt's action and includes the text of the letters between the American Institute of Architects and the President in his *Memories,* pp. 364–79.

in our day or hereafter. A future place will never be hot enough to properly singe a man for the present Agricultural Department constructed as it is." [54]

He explained that he was referring to the level of the building, which put part of the first story underground. This, of course, had been done at the insistence of McKim to preserve the slope of the Mall and its bordering buildings upwards to the Washington Monument. Representative James A. Tawney of Minnesota assailed the type of persons whom he felt certain would be appointed to such a commission as ". . . a class of men that do not know anything about law, and respect it less when it interferes with what they believe to be the artistic line. . . ." [55]

McCall and his backers patiently explained that the powers of the commission would be only advisory, that Congress would ultimately have to pass on appropriations for such projects as the commission would review, and that it was necessary for some professional body to examine all such proposals if Washington was not to develop in chaotic fashion.

Debate in the Senate, as usual, was rather more restrained. Ably, Senator Root steered the bill through. There were conflicts between the Senate and the House versions, but these were finally resolved by a conference committee. As finally approved by the President on May 17, 1910, the act provided for a Commission of Fine Arts composed of seven "well-qualified judges of the fine arts" appointed by the President for terms of four years. The powers and duties were specified as follows:

". . . to advise upon the location of statues, fountains, and monuments in the public squares, streets, and parks in the District of Columbia, and upon the selection of . . . artists for the execution of same. It shall be the duty of the officers charged by law to determine such questions in each case to call for such advice. The foregoing provisions of this act shall not apply to the Capitol Building of the United States and the building of the Library of Congress. The commission shall also advise generally upon questions of art when required to do so by the President, or by any committee of either House of Congress." [56]

The act made no provision for the Commission of Fine Arts to review proposals for buildings or the landscape treatment of parks or building approaches. Doubtless the proponents of the act felt that limiting the commission's jurisdiction to "statues, fountains, and monuments" would aid in its passage. But the last sentence in the passage quoted above provided a basis for President Taft to widen the powers of the commission. On October 10, 1910, Taft issued the following executive order: "Plans for no public building to be erected in the District of Columbia for the General Government shall be hereafter finally approved by the officer duly authorized until after such officer shall have submitted the plans to the Commission of Fine arts. . . ."

Subsequent executive orders by President Taft on February 2, 1912, President Wilson on November 28, 1913, and President Harding on July 28, 1921, widened the jurisdiction of the commission to include review of all federal buildings affecting the appearance of the city, the proposed improvement of any of the public grounds in the city, and the design of medals, insignia, and coins.[57]

Taft appointed Burnham as chairman, and Olmsted, Moore, Thomas Hastings, Daniel French, Francis Millet, and Cass Gilbert as members of the first commission. Thus at the beginning the Commission of Fine Arts included those who had been originally concerned and most deeply involved in the plan for central Washington. Now with official status and with strong presidential backing, this group prepared for the most important of its early efforts. This involved, of course, the location, character, and detailed design of the Lincoln Memorial, which had been proposed by the Park Commission as an essential feature of the great composition of the Washington Mall. Once this project had been firmly established, there appeared little likelihood that the plan could ever be subverted.

[54] Congressional Record. Proceedings and Debates of the 61st Congress, 2nd Session, House of Representatives. Washington, 1910, XLV, p. 1659.
[55] *ibid.*, p. 1661.

[56] Public Law 181, 61st Congress, 2nd Session, May 17, 1910. For a more complete account of the debates on the Commission of Fine Arts see Moore, *Burnham*, II, pp. 123–29.
[57] The text of these orders as well as Taft's order of October 10, 1910, may be found in U.S. Commission of Fine Arts, *Eleventh Report,* January 1, 1926–June 30, 1929, Washington, 1930, pp. 1–2.

CHAPTER 7

Building the Nation's Civic Center

Elihu Root, that staunch supporter of the Park Commission plan, recalled many years afterwards some of the events of the great struggle to provide a suitable memorial to Abraham Lincoln. As he told his biographer, "The fight grew very hot. Cannon came down to my office and said, 'There is a fight on about the location of the Lincoln Memorial and you keep out of it; it's none of your damned business. So long as I live I'll never let a memorial to Abraham Lincoln be erected in that God damned swamp.' " [1]

Cannon, a representative from Illinois with personal recollections of the Civil War president, doubtless felt that his voice should be given special weight in deciding on the nature and location of a Lincoln memorial. There can be little doubt also that he had firmly resolved to defeat any attempt to carry out the Park Commission's proposals at any cost and by any methods. For him it was to be the final struggle against the Commission from his seat of power as Speaker of the House.

Efforts to establish a memorial for commemorating President Lincoln began almost with his death. Congress by an act approved in March 1867 authorized the incorporation of the Lincoln Monument Association, although no federal appropriation was made. The association solicited funds, but eventually it lapsed into inactivity. Over thirty years later one of the corporate members of that organization, now a senator from Illinois, introduced legislation providing for a commission to plan and design a suitable monument.

The committee to which Senator Shelby M. Cullom's bill of 1901 was referred failed to approve the measure, but the following year it passed both houses, and President Roosevelt approved the act in June 1902. Not until nearly two years later did the commission hold its first meeting. At that time the group authorized one of its members, Representative James McCleary of Minnesota, to visit Europe to collect information on similar projects abroad and to submit a report not later than December 1, 1905. This gave McCleary over a year and a half; he took three times that long, finally reporting on January 16, 1909. [2]

McCleary, however, did reveal the substance of his recommendations in an article published in September 1908. His ideas were, to say the least, arresting. He began rather solemnly by considering and then rejecting for various reasons memorials in the form of a shaft, an equestrian statue, a triumphal arch, a university, an art gallery, and a bridge. It was while riding on the Appian Way, he relates, that he began to consider seriously a previous suggestion that he had received. Thus it was that McCleary developed the notion of a monumental highway from Washington to Gettysburg as the most appropriate memorial to the great President. Here is his description of this seventy-two-mile long, two-hundred-foot wide roadway:

"Down the middle of the road let there be a greensward forty or fifty feet wide, a well kept lawn looking like a beautiful green

[1] Statement by Elihu Root, as quoted in Philip C. Jessup, *Elihu Root*, New York, 1938, I, pp. 279–80.

[2] U.S. Lincoln Memorial Commission, *The Lincoln Memorial Washington*, Washington, 1927, pp. 15–17.

carpet of velvet. To lend variety to this central line of beauty, here and there flower gardens and other decorative features could be introduced. At intervals could be erected fountains and other monumental embellishments that might be appropriate.

"On each side of this central line of beauty let there be a smooth roadway forty or fifty feet wide. . . .

"Outside of these driveways could be double-tracked electric railways, occupying a width of twenty feet each and separated from the driveways by hedges. . . .

"Bordering 'The Lincoln Road' on each side there should be a row or rows of stately trees, the rows broken at points where could be obtained fine views of mountain or valley or river." [3]

McCleary suggested that trolley franchise charges and special licenses or tolls for private carriages and automobiles would pay the capital cost of the project. Embellishment of sections along the roadway could, he proposed, be assigned to states and patriotic societies. After describing this scheme in some detail and painting the inspiring picture of hundreds of thousands of Americans visiting Gettysburg via this splendid highway and returning to the capital ennobled in spirit and with the flame of their patriotism rekindled, McCleary asks: "If it were possible to consult Abraham Lincoln himself as to the character of memorial that would be most pleasing to him, can any one doubt what his answer would be?" [4]

One group that certainly entertained no doubts about the merits of this proposal were the road construction interests, the lobbyists of the oil companies, and the manufacturers of automobiles. The owners of land in the vicinity of the route and particularly in Gettysburg itself were also, naturally enough, wildly enthusiastic about the McCleary plan. In addition, opponents of the Park Commission proposal rallied behind this scheme as a concrete alternative to the Potomac Park location set forth in the plan of 1902.

Other sites also had their adherents. Representative Samuel McCall, in May 1908, introduced legislation calling for a memorial to Lincoln as an "enlargement of the Capital Grounds." Several additional locations were considered when this bill was referred to committee. One possibility that was explored was to use the plaza on which the new railroad station faced. Several members of Burnham's firm were attracted to this concept as a measure which would add further luster to that already monumental building. The Pennsylvania Railroad naturally favored the idea, and many members of Congress also looked with approval on a memorial to Lincoln near the Capitol and the House and Senate Office Buildings.

At McCall's request Burnham's office prepared several sketches for a number of sites near the Capitol, including the railroad station plaza. Burnham, who was in Europe, cabled his comments to McCall, who cited them on the floor of the House as support for the railroad plaza site.[5] Actually, Burnham's message was equivocal and could be interpreted in several ways. This apparent abandonment of the Park Commission plan by its own chairman deeply disturbed Glenn Brown and Charles McKim, and they immediately cabled Burnham asking for clarification. Burnham replied with a strong statement supporting the original recommendation for the memorial on the Potomac Park site.[6]

There were still other suggestions. One was the U.S. Soldiers' Home some two miles directly north of the Capitol at the end of North Capitol Street. Meridian Hill, about a mile and a half north of the White House at Sixteenth and W Streets, also had its supporters. These and other deviations from the Park Commission plan were strongly attacked by the articulate group that had consistently fought for and achieved adherence to the grand scheme of 1902. Root recalls how he dealt with the Gettysburg highway proposal: "I learned that there was real estate speculation going on on the route of the proposed highway. I got up a public meeting and went over and charged that this speculation existed, and they scuttled under their beds." [7]

Brown continued his tireless efforts on behalf of the plan of

[3] James T. McCleary, "What Shall the Lincoln Memorial Be?" *The American Review of Reviews,* XXXVIII, No. 3 (September 1908), p. 340.
[4] *ibid.,* p. 341.

[5] A portion of McCall's speech and the text of Burnham's cablegram may be found in Charles Moore, *Daniel Burnham,* Boston, 1921, II, pp. 121–22.
[6] Glenn Brown, *Memories,* Washington, 1931, pp. 284, 347.
[7] As quoted in Jessup, *Root,* I, p. 280.

1902. He alerted the provincial chapters of the American Institute of Architects and the American Federation of Arts, and their members soon began a campaign of support directed at senators and congressmen.[8] On the occasion of his election to the National Institute of Arts and Letters, Brown addressed this distinguished body in New York, describing the proposals then before Congress and vigorously advocating the Potomac Park location. Following his speech the Institute unanimously approved a resolution calling on Congress to follow the Park Commission proposal.[9] Brown presented much the same statement on December 13, 1910, before the Washington Chamber of Commerce, which promptly published his talk in an illustrated pamphlet designed for mass distribution.[10]

It was not until early in 1911 that both houses of Congress could agree on a course of action. On February 9 President Taft signed into law an act providing for the Lincoln Memorial Commission with power to fix a location and to plan and design a suitable monument. The act named as commission members the President, Senators Shelby M. Cullom of Illinois, George P. Wetmore of Rhode Island, and Hernando D. Money of Mississippi, and Representatives Champ Clark, Samuel McCall, and Joseph Cannon. Congress reserved the right to pass on the design, but not on the location of the memorial. The act authorized the commission, through the Secretary of War, to enter into contracts of not more than two million dollars for the construction of the memorial, and it appropriated fifty thousand dollars for expenses in procuring plans and designs.

At the first meeting of the commission on March 4 President Taft was selected as chairman. The newly created Commission on Fine Arts was requested to submit a report on the desirability of several sites: Two sites at or near the railroad station plaza, sites on the Capitol grounds, the Potomac Park location, and "also any other location which they may deem suitable." The Fine Arts Commission was also asked to recommend the "best method of

selecting the artists, sculptors, and architects to make the proper designs and to execute them." [11]

The Fine Arts Commission submitted its report on July 17. It surely did not astonish anyone that this commission, after considering alternative locations, firmly and convincingly recommended the site in Potomac Park. This is not to suggest that the members did not honestly examine other possibilities, for their report discusses the problems and potentials of each of the locations they were directed to consider. However, for Burnham, Olmsted, and Moore, who sat on the Fine Arts Commission, such an investigation could have had no other result. They had, of course, ten years earlier been over much of the same ground, and although one or two possibilities had opened up since that time, no site could command as much importance as the one they had originally recommended. Their new report expanded on the reasons why the site had been selected by them in their previous deliberations. The Commission of Fine Arts was unanimous in its recommendations. It also suggested that a single architect be selected to prepare designs, although it also mentioned that a competition would be possible.[12]

In summing up their arguments for the Potomac Park location, the members of the Fine Arts Commission quoted the opinion of John Hay as it had been recalled by McKim shortly before he died:

"As I understand it, the place of honor is on the main axis of the plan. Lincoln, of all Americans next to Washington, deserves this place of honor. He was of the immortals. You must not approach too close to immortals. His monument should stand alone, remote from the common habitations of man, apart from the business and turmoil of the city—isolated, distinguished, and serene. Of all the sites, this one near the Potomac is most suited to the purpose." [13]

Although the Commission on Fine Arts unanimously recom-

[8] Brown, *Memories,* pp. 285–86.
[9] *ibid.,* pp. 293–94.
[10] Glenn Brown, *The Development of Washington With Special Reference to the Lincoln Memorial,* Washington, 1911.

[11] Resolution of the Lincoln Memorial Commission, March 4, 1911, *Report of the Lincoln Memorial Commission,* Washington, 1913, pp. 8–9.
[12] U.S. Commission of Fine Arts, *Report of the Commission of Fine Arts on the Site and the Selection of a Designer for the Lincoln Memorial,* July 17, 1911, Appendix A, Washington, 1911, pp. 19–23.
[13] *ibid.,* p. 22. This observation was reported by McKim to Cass Gilbert, who so recorded it. Moore, *Burnham,* II, pp. 133–34n. 2.

mended the site on the Mall axis, the Lincoln Memorial Commission members could not immediately agree. Representative Cannon remained adamant in his opposition to the location in "that God damned swamp," and advocated a site at the Soldiers' Home and later at Arlington. Apparently his strategy here was to gain support for a site in Virginia from the southern members of the Memorial Commission, including Representative Champ Clark of Missouri, who had succeeded Cannon as Speaker in 1911 when the Democrats gained control of the House of Representatives. It was suggested to Clark, however, that it would hardly be appropriate to erect a memorial to Lincoln in one of the states of the Confederacy. At a meeting of the Memorial Commission, Clark forcefully stated his objections, and the Arlington site was dropped from consideration.[14]

Many meetings took place, each faction maneuvering for advantage. On August 8, 1911, the Memorial Commission decided to invite architect Henry Bacon, who had been recommended by the Fine Arts Commission, to meet with them. Two days later Bacon was asked to prepare designs for a memorial on the Potomac Park site so that the Memorial Commission could judge the suitability of that location. The supporters of the Park Commission plan seemed to have won a victory. However, Cannon and his followers insisted that similar studies be made for the Soldiers' Home and Meridian Hill sites, and on August 22 architect John Russell Pope was engaged to prepare sketches of memorials on these sites. On December 9 and December 18 the Memorial Commission examined and discussed these three plans.[15]

Finally, on February 3, 1912, the Memorial Commission decided in favor of the Potomac Park site. The official records of the commission do not record how individual members voted, stating only that it was decided by "a majority vote," but certainly Cannon must have opposed this action.[16]

Before reaching its final decision on the exact design of the memorial, the commission requested Pope to submit sketches showing how his designs for memorials at the Soldiers' Home and Meridian Hill sites might be adapted to the chosen location. Bacon also was asked to restudy his first scheme and to make any modifications he cared to incorporate. The Memorial Commission requested the Commission of Fine Arts to study these final sketches and submit its recommendations. With these new materials before it, the Memorial Commission, on April 16, 1912, chose Henry Bacon as the architect for the memorial and directed him to prepare a final revised plan for their ultimate approval, which took place on December 4, 1912.[17]

The design which Bacon prepared and the commission submitted to the Congress for legislative action closely resembled the one prepared by McKim a decade earlier. Standing in the center of a circular drive near the Potomac River, the monument was to be located on a raised terrace which had the same elevation as the base of the Washington Monument. The design called for a rectangular hall, the walls of which would be surrounded by a colonnade of Doric columns. A statue of Lincoln inside the memorial hall was to be complimented by wall tablets containing the text of the Gettysburg Address and the second inaugural address. Between the Lincoln Memorial and the Washington Monument Bacon's design included a long reflecting pool. And, although not part of the Memorial Commission's concern, Bacon's plan also showed a proposed bridge leading to Arlington from the circle around the memorial exactly as suggested by the Park Commission in its report of 1902.

Congressional approval followed on January 29, 1913, although apparently not entirely without some off-stage rumblings of discontent. Construction began a year later and proceeded for many years. The First World War and difficulties with the foundations of the terrace delayed its completion. The dedication did not take place until May 30, 1922, and even at that late date much of the landscaping treatment remained unfinished. But, as Root had put it years before, another peg had been driven to mark the progress of the far-reaching plan of the Senate Park

---

[14] *ibid.,* II, pp. 135–36.
[15] *Report of the Lincoln Memorial Commission,* pp. 9–10. The reports of Pope and Bacon submitted with their drawings and models may be found on pp. 25–31, along with several of Bacon's drawings. Pope's two designs appear in "The Proposed Lincoln National Memorial," *Harper's Weekly,* LVI, No. 2874 (January 20, 1912), p. 21.
[16] *Report of the Lincoln Memorial Commission,* p. 10.

[17] U.S. Lincoln Memorial Commission, *Lincoln Memorial,* pp. 20–21.

Commission that had been submitted two decades before. With the approval of the Lincoln Memorial site, the axis of the Mall had been secured forever and the realization of the other recommendations of 1902 seemed assured. The Memorial, reflecting pool, and Arlington Bridge as they appeared in 1933 are shown in Figure 77, a view marred then and even now by the "temporary" World War I buildings on the north side of the pool.

There is an interesting footnote to the story of the political fights that took place over the memorial and its location. Shortly after Cannon had returned to the House of Representatives in 1915 after he failed to be reelected in 1913, Glenn Brown encountered him on a Washington trolley. After congratulating him on his return to Congress, Brown asked Cannon if he had not changed his mind about the memorial to Lincoln which was then taking shape. Cannon, mellowed by advancing years and perhaps touched by his old enemy's courtesy, replied: "I have been in many fights, some I have lost—many I have won—it may have been better if I had lost more. I am pleased I lost the one against the Lincoln Memorial." [18]

During the long years occupied by the controversy over the Lincoln Memorial, a number of other building projects had been put under way. Three of these occupied an area south of the Corcoran Art Gallery on 17th Street facing the grounds of the White House. Here the Park Commission had recommended that buildings of a semi-public nature should be constructed, and this is what occurred. This portion of the central composition may be seen in the upper right-hand part of the photograph reproduced in Figure 78, which also reveals the unfinished condition of the Mall and its clutter of World War I temporary structures as it existed in 1933.

Two of these buildings were completed in 1910. The southernmost, standing at the northwest corner of the intersection of 17th Street and Constitution Avenue, is the Pan-American Union. Plans for this structure were conceived in 1903 and became a reality when Andrew Carnegie donated most of the necessary funds. Albert Kelsey and Paul Cret were selected as the designers after a jury viewed many sketches submitted in competition. In later

[18] Quoted in Brown, *Memories,* p. 102.

years an annex has been built to the west facing Constitution Avenue, one of several buildings providing an architectural frame for this monumental avenue to the west of the White House Axis. Other early buildings along the western end of Constitution Avenue, for which the Park Commission strangely enough made no recommendations, include the National Academy of Sciences, designed by Bertram Goodhue and completed in 1924, and the American Institute of Pharmacy, designed by John Russell Pope and finished in 1933. The former provides a terminus for the short diagonal boulevard leading from the Lincoln Memorial and named in honor of its designer, Henry Bacon.

Immediately north of the Pan-American Union building is the Memorial Continental Hall of the National Society of the Daughters of the American Revolution. The structure, designed by Edward P. Casey, was started in 1904 and completed six years later. Later additions to this structure include an administration building completed in 1923 and the huge Constitution Hall to the west, designed by John Russell Pope.

Between Continental Hall and the Corcoran Gallery stands the building of the American National Red Cross. Designed by the firm of Trowbridge and Livingston, this building was started in 1913 and finished in 1917. Two later buildings of the organization occupying the same block were completed in 1929. Thus, before the end of the First World War this portion of the Mall System as proposed by the Park Commission stood completed as planned. In architectural style all the buildings are neo-classic in inspiration and of a scale appropriate to the great expanse of the White House grounds on which they face.

Three other buildings were built during this era in accordance with the Park Commission plan or in harmony with its general intent. One of these was the Treasury Annex, the final plans for which, prepared by Cass Gilbert, received Fine Arts Commission approval in 1918. This building is located across Pennsylvania Avenue to the north of the main Treasury Building and occupies a site recommended by the Park Commission as one of those surrounding Lafayette Square, which were to house buildings for administrative departments.

A few years earlier, in 1914, the Bureau of Engraving and

Figure 77. Aerial Photograph of the Washington Monument and Lincoln Memorial, Looking Northwest: 1933

Figure 78. Aerial Photograph of the Mall and Adjacent Area, Looking West: 1933

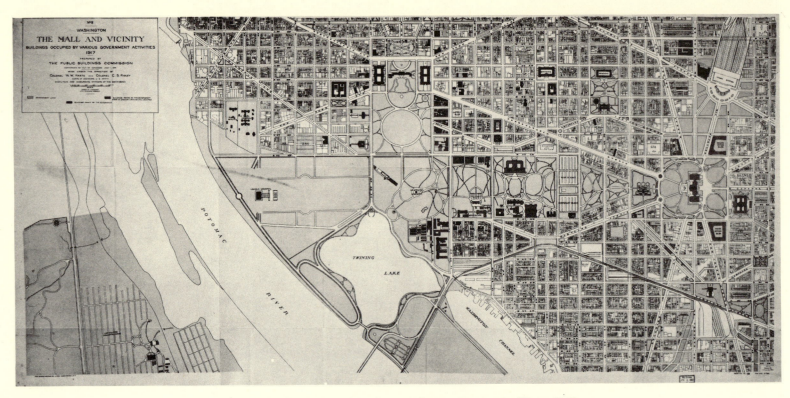

Figure 79. Plan of Central Washington Showing Existing Buildings: 1917

Printing moved to its new building, which had been started in 1907. This structure in Roman Doric style faces 15th Street southwest and looks westward to the Tidal Basin. Although the Park Commission plan had not shown any building in this location, the site chosen for this structure seemed suitable at the time, and the building, with its long line of columns on the west façade and its monumental scale, serves to reinforce and define the axis of the White House south of the Mall to what is now the location of the Jefferson Memorial.[19]

[19] The designs of the building were reviewed by the Commission of Fine Arts, and a number of changes were suggested. Correspondence between the commission and the Department of the Treasury on this matter appears in U.S. Commission of Fine Arts, *Report* for the year ending June 30, 1912, Washington, 1912, pp. 34–37.

Between the Agricultural Building, which had given rise to such violent controversy, and the Smithsonian Institution, a new museum building was located in 1915. This was the Freer Gallery of Art to house the magnificent collection which Charles Lang Freer had offered to the government in 1904 on condition that a suitable building be provided for its storage and display. A site was authorized to conform to the building line established along the south side of the Mall. The gallery, designed by Charles A. Platt in the manner of a Florentine Renaissance palace, opened to the public in 1923.

These additions to the development of Washington appear on the plans reproduced in Figures 79 and 80 showing conditions in the central portion of the city in 1917 and as proposed for

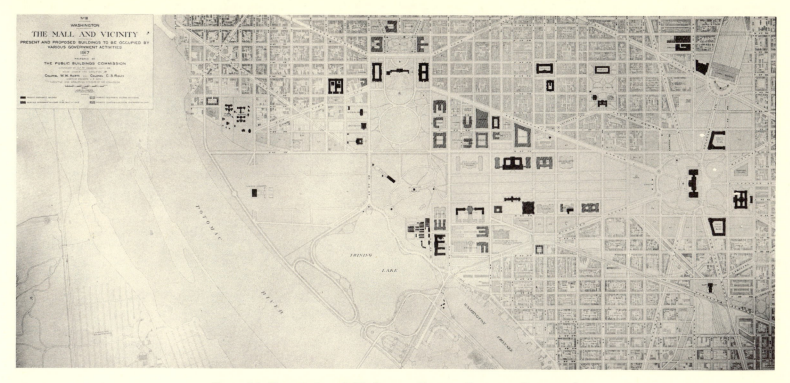

Figure 80. Plan of Central Washington Showing Existing and Proposed Buildings: 1917

eventual development by the Public Buildings Commission following the plans of the Park Commission.

In addition to these building projects, Congress authorized an important step on June 25, 1910, to improve the area between the Capitol and the railroad station. Although this action was not strictly speaking in furtherance of the Park Commission plan, it was closely related to it and obviously in direct harmony with its underlying spirit. Through the efforts of Senator George Wetmore of Rhode Island, whose earlier support of the Park Commission will be recalled, Congress authorized the acquisition of 12 city blocks in the area now bounded by the station, North Capitol Street, Louisiana Avenue, Constitution Avenue and 1st Street, northeast.

Burnham's imposing railroad station had been completed by 1907. Shortly thereafter the city Post Office immediately adjacent to the northwest was finished, itself a monumental building also designed by Burnham and intended to complement the station. In front of the station some work had been started on what was to become the impressive semicircular plaza dominated by the Columbus Memorial. But at that time the area between the station and the Capitol grounds was rough and unsightly, partially built on, and scarcely providing the monumental entrance to the city that Burnham and his colleagues envisaged.

Wetmore's legislation set in motion activities that eventually culminated in the renewal of this strategically located land, although it was to take many years for the completion of the project.

Legal difficulties prevented the immediate acquisition of all building sites in these twelve blocks, and many of them remained at the time of the American involvement in the First World War. Because of its location and nearly vacant condition, this area became the site of temporary government barracks and hotels for wartime civilian government employees, as the view of the area in 1920 shown in Figure 81 reveals. Eventually in the early 1930's work began again on this project following plans prepared by Bennett, Parsons, and Frost under the direction of David Lynn, architect of the Capitol.[20] The present fountain and reflecting pool directly north of the Capitol amidst an expanse of lawn was the result, an improvement shown on Inauguration Day, 1933, in the photograph reproduced in Figure 82.

Wartime exigencies caused incursions on the Mall as well. Incredibly, some of these "temporary" structures of the First World War still remain, as did for many years some less sturdy temporary buildings erected during the Second War. Particularly damaging to the appearance of the Mall are those near the Lincoln Memorial, fronting on Constitution Avenue and stretching southward almost to the banks of the long reflecting pool between the Memorial and the Washington Monument. While in 1921 the Commission of Fine Arts could write the following critical but hopeful passage, its optimism proved ill-founded, and a later generation still finds these "temporary" buildings hindering a full appreciation of the great composition of Washington's Mall:

"These temporary buildings are so factorylike in design and they so invade, encroach upon and disfigure Potomac Park that the American people will not suffer them permanently to overawe and dwarf one of their greatest memorials. Sooner or later the Lincoln Memorial will drive the intrusive structures to destruction. They represent to-day one of the hideous consequences of the Great War." [21]

And yet the commission could sum up the work of twenty years of progress toward fulfilling the Park Commission plan with considerable satisfaction:

"In comparing the projects . . . the District of Columbia as presented in the report of the Senate Park Commission with the actual accomplishment during two decades one must be struck with the largeness of the actual accomplishment. . . . Even the most optimistic of its authors could not have anticipated the actual strides toward accomplishment that 20 years would bring about. It is a tribute to the inherent worth of the plan that, while so little has been done contrary to it, so much has been achieved in accordance with it." [22]

Graphic evidence of the accuracy of this evaluation appears in Figure 83, which the Commission of Fine Arts presented in its report of 1921. Federal buildings in central Washington located since 1901 are shown in black, while those proposed are indicated in outline. Only the building for the Department of the Interior, located on the block bounded by 18th and 19th and E and F Streets, fails to conform to the specific or general recommendations of the Park Commission plan. This map also indicates the substantial areas of land acquired for governmental purposes in accordance with the Park Commission proposals. In 1921 the far-reaching scheme that had been devised in 1902 was far from complete, but the directions taken had been correct, and there seemed little likelihood that serious departures from the Mall concept would be tolerated by even the most insensitive.

During the 1920's a number of new projects were authorized which resulted in the realization of additional aspects of the plan. One of the most important was the Arlington Memorial Bridge leading from the circle around the Lincoln Memorial to Arlington National Cemetery. Congress in 1922 created the Arlington Memorial Bridge Commission. That commission reported two years later, recommending a project of five important elements. One, of course, was the bridge itself, which was to be aligned between the Lincoln Memorial and the Lee Mansion in Arlington, thus not only providing a important traffic artery but contributing

[20] A rendered view by the architects, showing their proposed design in 1929, is reproduced in *The American Architect,* cxxxv, No. 2569 (May 20, 1929), p. 651.
[21] U.S. Commission of Fine Arts, *Ninth Report,* Washington, 1921, pp. 25–26.

[22] *ibid.,* p. 37.

Figure 81. Aerial Photograph of the Capitol Area and Railroad Station, Looking Northeast: 1920

Figure 82. Aerial Photograph of the Area Between Union Station and the Capitol: 1933

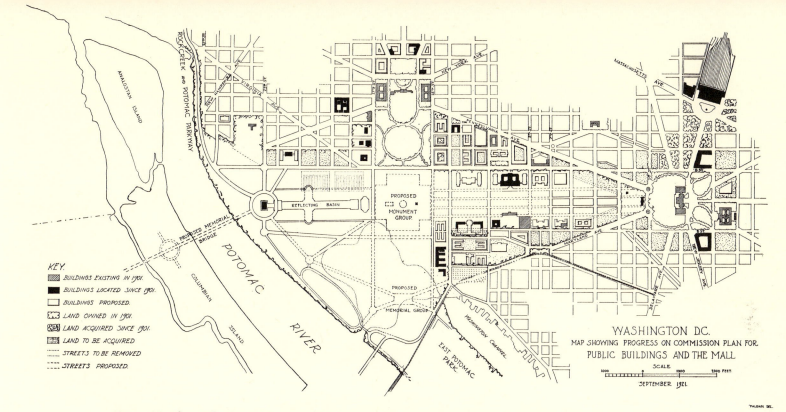

KEY.
//// BUILDINGS EXISTING IN 1901.
████ BUILDINGS LOCATED SINCE 1901.
☐   BUILDINGS PROPOSED.
▨   LAND OWNED IN 1901.
▨   LAND ACQUIRED SINCE 1901.
▨   LAND TO BE ACQUIRED
····· STREETS TO BE REMOVED
- - - STREETS PROPOSED.

WASHINGTON D.C.
MAP SHOWING PROGRESS ON COMMISSION PLAN FOR
PUBLIC BUILDINGS AND THE MALL

SCALE
1000   0   1000   2000 FEET

SEPTEMBER 1921.

Figure 83. Plan of the Central Portion of Washington Showing Proposals by the U.S. Commission of Fine Arts: 1921

to the appearance of the city by focusing attention on two of its most impressive structures. The second and third elements consisted of a bridge plaza and a Water Gate between the bridge and the parkway proposed to lead to Rock Creek Park following the banks of the Potomac and Rock Creek itself. A fourth feature of the plan consisted of proposed improvements to Columbia Island, which was located in the District of Columbia but which lay close to the Virginia shore of the Potomac. The final element of the plan called for the creation of a ceremonial entrance to Arlington National Cemetery.

Congress authorized development of the bridge and some of its appurtenances in 1925, and construction began the following year on plans prepared, appropriately enough, by the firm of McKim, Mead, and White. The Water Gate was completed in 1931 and the bridge in 1932. Both are fitting elements in the plan of Washington, following almost exactly the recommendations of the Park Commission for the treatment of the river crossing and the embellishment of the banks of the Potomac, as can be seen in

Figure 84. Indeed, the rendering by Carlton T. Chapman of McKim's design prepared in 1902 for the Lincoln Memorial, the Water Gate, the Arlington Bridge, and the river parkway to Rock Creek Park might easily be mistaken for a modern depiction of the projects as actually carried out.[23]

The third decade after the Park Commission plan also saw definitive steps taken toward the replanning of the great triangle between Pennsylvania Avenue, 15th Street, and Constitution Avenue. This area had been singled out by almost every person or body considering the problems of Washington's development as one which should be acquired for public purposes. Several attempts had been made to acquire land and to erect buildings in this location for governmental departments. In 1910 Congress had approved plans for three departments—Justice, Commerce and Labor, and State—on sites between 14th and 15th Streets and

[23] The original color rendering has disappeared. A color reproduction may be found in Moore, *Burnham*, I, opposite p. 162. Figure 72 is a copy of the rendering.

Figure 84. Aerial Photograph of the Lincoln Memorial and the Arlington Bridge: 1933

Figure 85. View of Proposed Buildings Facing the East Side of the White House Grounds Designed in 1910 by Don Barber, Arnold Brunner, and York & Sawyer

Pennsylvania and Constitution Avenues. Land was acquired for this purpose, preliminary designs were prepared for the buildings, the Commission of Fine Arts was asked to review them, but actual construction was deferred.[24] The design then proposed for buildings to accommodate three of the executive departments is shown in Figure 85.

In 1916 Congress created a Public Buildings Commission to investigate thoroughly the many pressing problems of housing an expanding bureaucracy and to recommend adequate solutions. The voluminous report that body submitted at the end of the following year included a recommendation that all of the land in the triangle formed by Pennsylvania Avenue and Constitution Avenue be acquired.[25]

Hastily erected temporary buildings put up during the war solved some of the immediate problems of space, but it was obvious to all that a major federal building effort lay ahead. President Coolidge, in a message to Congress in December 1925,

requested substantial appropriations for the next year to begin a major program of public buildings. Congress responded with a public buildings bill that authorized $50,000,000 for buildings in the District of Columbia. Congress placed responsibility for administering the program in the hands of the Secretary of the Treasury, who was assisted by a board of architectural consultants as well as the Commission of Fine Arts and the Public Buildings Commission.

A great many plans or suggestions for the treatment of the triangle were prepared. A drawing from the report of the Public Buildings Commission in 1926 showed not only the triangle as proposed by that body but sites for other badly needed structures, including a new building for the U.S. Supreme Court flanking the Library of Congress and facing the Capitol.[26] As revised in 1931, this plan is reproduced in Figure 86. The board of architectural consultants to the Treasury, headed by Edward H. Bennett (who had been associated with Burnham in the preparation of the famous plan for Chicago in 1909), produced a number of pre-

[24] Reproductions of views of the proposed buildings appear in U.S. Commission of Fine Arts, *Report,* Washington, 1921, following p. 32.

[25] U.S. Public Buildings Commission, *Public Buildings in the District of Columbia,* Washington, 1918.

[26] U.S. Public Buildings Commission, *Annual Report,* 1926, Washington, 1927.

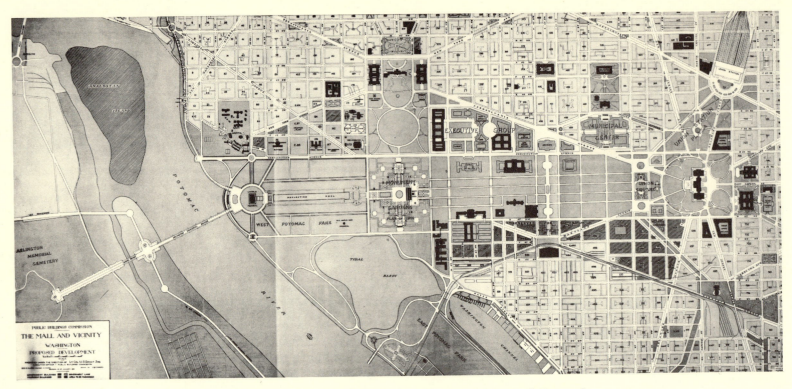

Figure 86. Plan of Central Washington Showing Existing and Proposed Buildings: 1931

liminary sketches. These were reviewed by the Fine Arts Commission, and that agency submitted its comments on them to Secretary of the Treasury Andrew Mellon.[27]

On January 13, 1928, Congress passed a new act authorizing the acquisition of all private lands in the triangle area at a cost not to exceed $25,000,000. With the assurance that the entire triangle could be planned as a unit, as the Fine Arts Commission urged, the board of architectural consultants prepared a comprehensive scheme for the area. The results of their studies, presented in models, drawings, and plans, were revealed to participants of the annual convention of the American Institute of Architects in Washington on April 25 and 26, 1929. There Secretary Mellon, President Hoover, Senator Reed Smoot, Chairman of the Public

Buildings Commission, and architect-planner Edward Bennett described and analyzed the proposals.[28]

Actual development closely followed this plan, although individual buildings took somewhat different form, and a proposed large central court between the Commerce and Post Office Departments became an automobile parking lot. The buildings are all of neo-classic design, some being fairly restrained, although John Russell Pope's National Archives building is rather more elaborately imposing. Uniform cornice and belt lines along Constitution and Pennsylvania Avenues serve to tie individual buildings together and relate them to one another. The great mass of the Commerce Building facing the White House grounds on 15th Street

[27] For the text of these comments dated April 5, 1927, see U.S. Commission of Fine Arts, *Eleventh Report,* Washington, 1930.

[28] The addresses at this meeting, together with reproductions of many of the illustrations and models, are collected in *Development of the United States Capital,* Washington, 1930.

*Figure 87. Aerial Photograph of Washington Looking Northwest to the
Federal Triangle from a Point Above the Capitol: 1937*

Figure 88. Aerial Photograph of Central Washington Looking Southeast: 1938

forms an effective frame for that large and important open space. This complex of buildings as it appeared in 1937 can be seen in Figure 87, which also shows the beginning of construction on the National Gallery of Art, a notable addition to the north side of the Mall between 4th and 7th Streets.

Under the Public Buildings Act that produced the Federal Triangle, other buildings were constructed that implemented the Park Commission plan. The Supreme Court was provided with its own quarters for the first time in an ornate structure facing the east front of the Capitol. The two wings of the Agricultural Department structure were finally joined by an administration building. The fourth side of the Senate Office Building was completed in 1933. A new House Office Building immediately west of the old one built in 1908 was finished in 1933 and joined the now growing group of structures ringing the Capitol as the Park Commission had proposed.

In 1934 the old Botanic Garden greenhouses were eliminated from the head of the Mall west of the Capitol, their functions being removed to a new enclosure at the southwest corner of the Capitol grounds between 1st and 2nd Streets southwest. At about the same time the original building of the Department of Agriculture, which had been constructed in 1868 near the center of the Mall, was finally taken down. Thus the Mall as planned by the Park Commission was now free of buildings, with the exception of the Smithsonian Institution, and the planting of the parallel rows of elms began to give form to this great open space. All of these improvements can be seen in the air view of the central portion of the city in 1938 which appears in Figure 88.

This enormous spurt of building activity along with related improvements and changes in landscape treatment of the new structures and the Mall itself did much to change the appearance of central Washington in a few short years. It was not at all inaccurate for the Commission of Fine Arts to entitle a major section of its Report of 1934 "The Central Composition Reaching Completion." Yet two important features of the Park Commission plan had not been undertaken—the formal treatment of the Washington Monument terrace and gardens, and the development of a building or group of buildings to terminate the southern end of the White House cross-axis. A brief discussion of these two elements of the plan seems appropriate.

Sentiment for a memorial to Thomas Jefferson began to gather in the early 1930's. Congressional support for such a memorial was strengthened, of course, by the election victories of the Democratic party. A number of sites were suggested, but the one which appeared most favored was the location at the end of the White House cross-axis at its intersection with Maryland Avenue. It will be recalled that the Park Commission showed this site as a great memorial center but did not specify its exact purpose.

In 1935 the National Capital Park and Planning Commission, which had been created in 1926 to prepare and revise plans for the improvement of the capital city, appointed a committee to study and report on the various sites suggested for a memorial to Jefferson. William T. Partridge, whose association with Washington began with his work for McKim on the Park Commission plan, and Gilmore D. Clarke, a landscape architect and member of the Commission of Fine Arts, received appointments for this purpose. They consulted with members of the Jefferson Memorial Commission, especially Dr. Fiske Kimball, an art historian, author of a critical study of Jefferson as an architect, and Director of the Pennsylvania Museum of Art in Philadelphia. They all agreed that a location on the southern bank of the Tidal Basin, if properly treated, would be ideal.[29]

The Jefferson Memorial Commission then engaged John Russell Pope as its architectural adviser. Charles Moore, then nearing the end of his long tenure as member, since 1910, and chairman, since 1915, of the Fine Arts Commission, was asked to attend the meetings of the Memorial Commission along with the chairman of the National Capital Park and Planning Commission. In February 1937 the Memorial Commission revealed its proposed design as prepared by Pope—a building resembling the Pantheon in Rome and quite similar to that shown by McKim in his drawings of the proposed group of buildings for the site as depicted in the Senate Park Commission plan. Then followed a remarkably bitter and,

[29] U.S. Commission of Fine Arts, *Report to the Senate and the House of Representatives Concerning the Thomas Jefferson Memorial,* Washington, 1939, p. 1.

in retrospect, unnecessary conflict. That controversy should arise concerning an important memorial merely carried on a long Washington tradition; the peculiar feature of this one arose from the fact that the Commission of Fine Arts, the guardian of the plan of 1902 all these years, seemingly opposed the development of one of its important features.

Opposition of the Fine Arts Commission became clear when the Jefferson Memorial Commission submitted Pope's design for review and approval. It was promptly rejected. Moore and Clarke stated a number of reasons for this action. The most fundamental seemed to be that a building containing a portrait statue of Jefferson closely duplicated the concept of the Lincoln Memorial, that the Pantheon-type building suggested was too imitative, and that a more open memorial would be desirable to permit views from the White House south to the Potomac. The Fine Arts Commission members were also upset that there had been no competition for the design of the memorial and that they had not been formally consulted on its details until final plans had been prepared.[30] Another factor may have been the low regard Clarke, who was soon to become chairman of the Commission of Fine Arts, held for Kimball.[31]

A second submission of a revised and somewhat smaller Pantheon building reached the Commission of Fine Arts on February 3, 1938, when Kimball appeared to argue for its approval. This, too, failed to win acceptance, whereupon on the same day two different designs were laid before a joint meeting of the Fine Arts and Park and Planning Commissions. The second of these incorporated two semicircular colonnades enclosing a statue of Jefferson. This design had been prepared by the firm of Eggers and Higgins, who had succeeded John Russell Pope after his death in the summer of 1937. This scheme, however, closely resembled an early study by Pope for a memorial to Theodore Roosevelt on approximately the same location. The new design was for a building substantially smaller than the one originally proposed by Pope. Although the Jefferson Memorial Commission finally bowed to the wishes of the Fine Arts Commission and adopted this scheme for its memorial, it was unable to gain Mrs. Pope's assent to the use of the design on a much reduced scale and somewhat modified in appearance. Finally, after another try to obtain Fine Arts Commission approval of the Pantheon design, the Jefferson Memorial Commission, on March 30, 1938, announced that it intended to construct the memorial on this plan.

When the matter came to Congress for decision there was an unusually large and diverse group of opponents. The Commission of Fine Arts argued rather ineffectively against constructing the memorial until a study could be made of the entire south side of the Tidal Basin and also employed the aesthetic arguments it had already advanced. There were some members of Congress, naturally, who favored no monument at all on the grounds of economy. And, outside the halls of Congress, architects and art critics of modern persuasion maintained that both pantheon and open colonnade stemmed from a bygone era and that their classical architectural details represented mere appled archaeology.[32] One or two senators were bothered by the very close similarity between the pantheon dome and the central portion of the National Gallery of Art, also designed by Pope, then being erected on the north side of the Mall between 4th and 7th Streets. When on June 15, 1938, the Senate put its approval on a House measure to provide the initial appropriation for construction, the controversy was almost at an end. An appeal to the President from Chairman Clarke proved fruitless.

Thus it was that the Jefferson Memorial, shown in Figure 89,

[30] See the extract from the minutes of the joint meeting of the Commission of Fine Arts and the National Capital Park and Planning Commission on March 20, 1937, extract from the minutes of the meeting of the Commission of Fine Arts on March 20, 1937, and a letter from Moore to Representative John J. Boylan, Chairman of the Jefferson Memorial Commission, April 8, 1937, in U.S. Commission of Fine Arts, *Report to the Senate and the House,* pp. 9–13.

[31] In a draft of the commission's report to the Senate and House of February 1939, which Clarke prepared, Kimball is referred to as "opinionated, pompous and dogmatic." Typewritten memorandum, "The Thomas Jefferson Memorial Controversy," Fine Arts Library, Cornell University. The memorandum is almost identical to the printed version, lacking only Exhibit P, which deals with the subject of public toilets in the Jefferson Memorial.

[32] For an indictment of the memorial as first designed signed by a number of distinguished critics, architects, and planners, see the letter to the editor in *The New Republic,* LXXXX, No. 1166 (April 7, 1937), pp. 265–66.

Figure 89. Aerial Photograph of the Jefferson Memorial and Tidal Basin: 1954

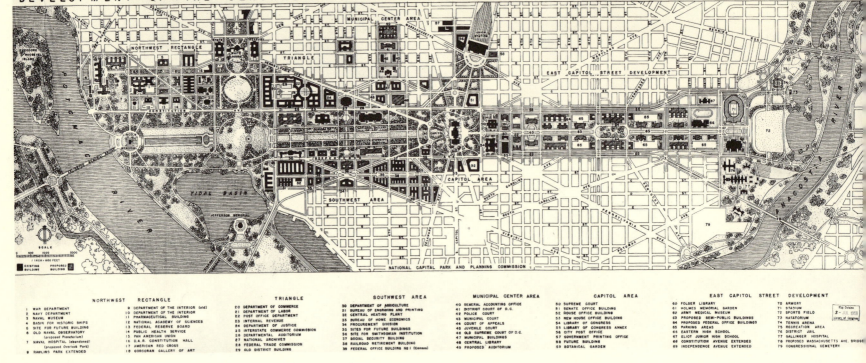

Figure 90. Plan for Central Washington and the East Mall: 1941

took its place among the many buildings located on sites suggested by the Park Commission at the turn of the century. With its completion and dedication most of the old arguments were forgotten, and even those who intellectually scorn its design as empty classicism are emotionally moved by the monumental scale of the gleaming structure and its lovely surroundings.

The memorial to Jefferson as built departed from the Park Commission plans in one important way. In 1902 the Commission felt that the Tidal Basin could be filled, or at least changed in form, so that a formal land approach could be made to the memorial or building located on this site. The landscape treatment, if one is to judge from the drawings and perspective views of that time, was to be similar to the Mall. The unification of this southern part of the cross-axis with the rest of the great central composition was to be accomplished by the Washington Monument terrace and

gardens. Here is the one element of the Park Commission plans which has defied solution to the present day and which, until completed in some satisfactory manner, interferes with the appreciation and understanding of the entire design of the Mall system.

The periodic reports of the Commission of Fine Arts frequently called attention to the need to consider eventual planning of the Washington Monument grounds. In 1928 a bill was introduced in Congress that would have authorized $5,000,000 to carry out the McKim design for the terrace and gardens.[33] The Director of Public Building and Public Parks, Ulysses S. Grant, III, suggested that engineering and related studies should be carried out to determine if the plan were feasible. By May 1930 an advisory committee was organized. This group examined the Monument, studied old construction drawings, and had a number of test borings made

[33] House Joint Resolution 128, January 5, 1928.

to determine sub-soil conditions and the depth to bedrock. They concluded that unless the Monument could be underpinned to bedrock or dismantled and reassembled on a new foundation extending to bedrock, the plan of 1902 could not be carried out because of the excessive cut that would be necessary to create the sunken gardens on the west side. They recommended that the plan be abandoned, since the expense of underpinning (which they regarded as hazardous in any event) would cost an estimated $600,000. Dismantling and rebuilding the Monument was estimated at $1,000,-000. The group considered at that time two other much less elaborate plans—one by architect William A. Delano, which was essentially a formal scheme, and one by Frederick Law Olmsted and Henry Hubbard, which was relatively simple and informal.[34] Delano's scheme was also judged difficult or impossible from an engineering standpoint, while Olmsted's was given cautious approval if extreme care were exercised in disturbing the ground in the vicinity of the Monument. However, in November, 1932 the National Capital Park and Planning Commission and the Commission of Fine Arts recommended that no work at all should be undertaken until a more satisfactory plan could be found. In its years of scrutinizing carefully the development of the plan of Washington, the Fine Arts Commission had learned to take the long view. As it commented in one of its reports at this time,

"The Commission of Fine Arts are convinced that the treatment to be accorded to the Washington Monument grounds is of the essence, and, therefore, cannot be compromised. When it is objected that the stability of the Monument might be seriously affected by shifting the dirt load, the Commission have replied that if the Monument is not absolutely proof against such a trivial contingency the American people would want its stability established beyond doubt or question. Then and only then can a proper setting be provided. It is not necessary now to proceed with this portion of the plan. It is better to wait a quarter of a century rather than resort to any compromise plan. Public taste is of slow growth. When the Mall shall be completed, Union Square finished, Colum-

bia Island laid out, the Rock Creek Parkway extended, public taste will call imperatively for the treatment of the Washington Monument grounds as the gem for which the other parts are but a setting. Time is not the essence of this problem.

"Such has been the reason of this Commission in rejecting . . . tentative plans which seemed so small, so inadequate, as to appear but futile." [35]

Three decades have elapsed since these words were written, yet the Monument grounds remain today in almost the same condition. Extensive treatment of this portion of the Mall is badly needed. The cross-axis of the White House and Jefferson Memorial requires strengthening, something which can only be accomplished by formal landscape development of the area west of the Washington Monument. Some day this last unrealized major feature of the plan of 1902 will be achieved, although not necessarily in the exact form prescribed by the Senate Park Commission.

By the end of the 1930's, following the rapid growth of federal responsibilities, Washington planners turned their attention to possibilities for further building expansion to meet the future space needs for the national establishment. The National Capital Park and Planning Commission took the lead. In 1941 the commission unveiled a plan, based on earlier studies, for development from the Capitol to the Anacostia River prepared by its consultant, Gilmore D. Clarke. This proposal, shown in Figure 90, suggested a complex of public and semi-public buildings flanking East Capitol Street, with a major focal point at Lincoln Square, one of the public reservations established by L'Enfant. Beyond, on the west bank of the Anacostia, was to be a stadium and major recreation area, a proposal which has since been carried out although in slightly different form. While the other features of this plan have not been implemented, some version of this scheme may well be considered in the future and might prove a worthy extension to the great plan of 1902.

Meanwhile new development still follows the Park Commission plan. Space does not permit tracing the origins of these projects

---

[34] The Delano and Olmsted plans are illustrated in the report dated January 5, 1933, by the Director of Public Buildings and Public Parks, *Improvement of the Washington Monument Grounds,* Washington, 1934.

[35] U.S. Commission of Fine Arts, *Twelfth Report,* Washington, 1936, p. 15.

Figure 91. Aerial Photograph of Central Washington Looking Southeast: 1958

in detail, but some of the more important may be noted briefly. These changes appear in Figure 91, a view of central Washington in 1958, and in Figure 92, a vertical aerial photograph taken in 1963.

In the Capitol area a new Senate Office Building now faces the older office building across 1st Street at Constitution Avenue. A third office building for the House of Representatives, the monstrous Rayburn Building, now has been completed south of Independence Avenue. The projected James Madison Memorial building of the Library of Congress will soon occupy the now empty site at 1st Street and Independence Avenue. Together with the Library of Congress, which existed prior to 1901, and the U.S. Supreme Court Building, these structures of the Capitol division of the Mall system closely follow the recommendations put forward by the Senate Park Commission.

The Mall, too, has taken form as planned. On the north the National Gallery of Art and the recently completed Museum of History and Technology flank the older Museum of Natural History, one of the first buildings sited according to the plan of 1902. On the south side of the Mall a new Air Museum will join the other structures of the Smithsonian, and its modern design will provide an effective contrast to the neo-classicism of the National Gallery of Art, which it will face to the north. South of Independence Avenue a number of recent federal office buildings have joined the new building for the Department of Agriculture, which was completed in the 1930's immediately to the south of the Department's building on the Mall over which there was so much controversy in Theodore Roosevelt's day. Located to the east are the sites for the Forrestal Building and the Hirshhorn Gallery, which will fill the last gaps along the south side of Independence Avenue facing the Mall. Although the Park Commission plan showed only two buildings south of the Mall, this recent development is in harmony with the intent of the plan, and, although many of the buildings lack real architectural distinction, the ensemble which they compose is an effective treatment of this portion of the city.

South of this is the vast Southwest Urban Renewal area, now rapidly nearing completion. This complex of residential, commercial, and office structures replaces an extensive district of blight and slums which was not only a civic but a national disgrace.

The district surrounding the White House has not developed entirely as recommended by the Park Commission. Most of the federal departments are now located in the triangle south of Pennsylvania Avenue and east of 15th Street or in a corresponding area to the west of the White House grounds, where more recent buildings have been located indiscriminately, unguided by an over-all plan. A monumental grouping of major departmental buildings around Lafayette Square, as advocated by the Park Commission to correspond with the similar complex on Capitol Hill, has been only partly realized. Reluctance to interfere with some of the historic domestic buildings fronting the square has resulted in a modern plan for the treatment of this area. Office buildings will be built in the rear of these older structures, and an attempt will be made to integrate the old and the new. It remains to be seen if this plan will be effective either aesthetically or functionally. It makes impossible the creation of a unified and imposing frame for Lafayette Square, while at the same time radically altering the appearance of the old buildings fronting on Madison Place and Jackson Place, the two streets forming the east and west boundaries of the square. The individual buildings will be saved, but their domestic scale will be imperiled by the towering blocks to their rear which will dwarf them.[36]

To the west the Lincoln Memorial and the Arlington Memorial Bridge appear almost exactly as envisaged by Charles McKim nearly seventy years ago. From the Lincoln Memorial northward extends the Rock Creek and Potomac Parkway, following the alignment proposed by Olmsted as an important link between the two major open spaces of the city. Nearby will be the John F. Kennedy Center on a site overlooking the Potomac.

And at last Pennsylvania Avenue has received the attention it has so badly needed. In 1964 the President's Council on Pennsylvania Avenue, appointed by President Kennedy, submitted its report of improvements recommended for this vital artery.[37] The

[36] A description and illustrations of this proposal now being carried out appear in Bernard L. Boutin, "Lafayette Square—The Final Word," *A.I.A. Journal,* XXXIX, No. 1 (January 1963), pp. 55–56.

[37] U.S. President's Council on Pennsylvania Avenue, *Pennsylvania Avenue,* Washington, 1964. The council consisted of a distinguished group of

Figure 92. Vertical Aerial Photograph of Washington: 1963

Figure 93. Plan for Pennsylvania Avenue and Vicinity, Proposed by the President's Council on Pennsylvania Avenue: 1964

Pennsylvania Avenue plan, reproduced in Figure 93, proposes the treatment of this strategically located boulevard as a monumental, ceremonial, and formal connection between Capitol Hill and the White House. To accomplish these goals wholesale redevelopment will be needed for much of the area north of the avenue, and some modifications and extensions will be required for the existing complex of federal buildings along its southern edge.

architects, planners, landscape architects, and administrators: Nathaniel A. Owings, Frederick Gutheim, Douglas Haskell, Frederick L. Holborn, Dan Kiley, Daniel P. Moynihan, Chloethiel Smith, Paul Thiry, Ralph Walker, and William Walton. Minoru Yamasaki resigned as a member after the first year.

The plan recommends the creation of several new urban open spaces. One of these shown in Figure 94 will be opposite the National Archives, with its northern axis extending to the National Portrait Gallery, the imposing structure terminating 8th Street once occupied by the Civil Service Commission and originally erected as the Patent Office. Immediately south of the Archives Building, between Constitution Avenue and the Mall and adjacent to the National Gallery of Art, a formal outdoor sculpture court extends this new cross-axis.

Market Square, the name suggested for the new plaza because of its proximity to the old public market, would serve as one entrance to an extensive system of pedestrian courts and con-

181

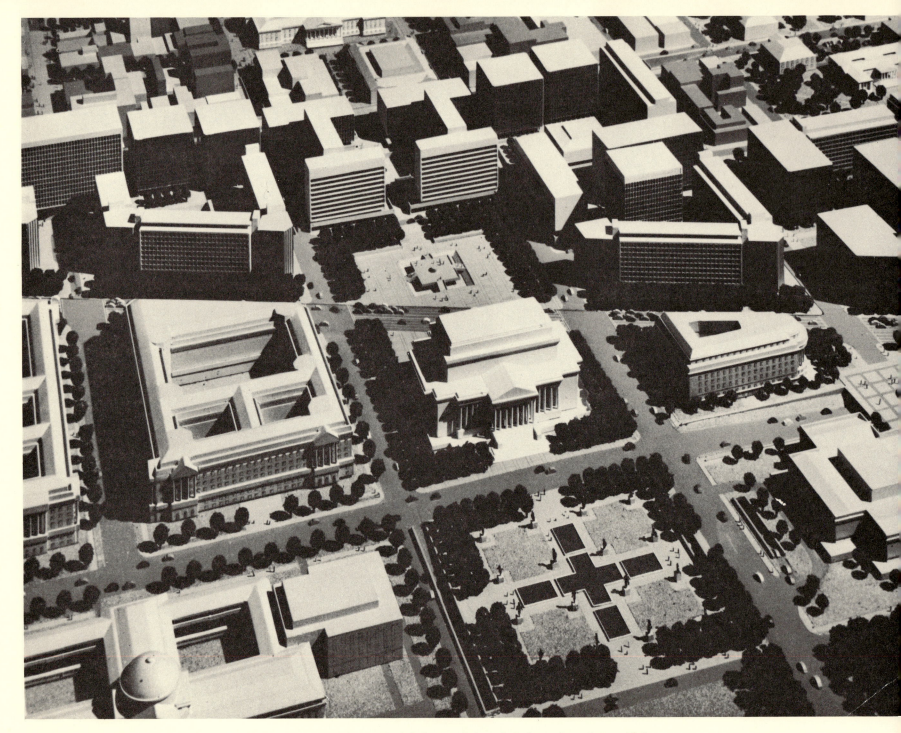

*Figure 94. View of Model Showing Proposed Archives Cross-Axis in Plan
for Pennsylvania Avenue: 1964*

courses providing unobstructed movement by foot on a platform level above underground parking facilities and depressed vehicular arteries. From this square to a point near the present terminus of Pennsylvania Avenue at the Treasury and extending two blocks toward the Capitol, new buildings would line the avenue's northern side. While many of these would be devoted to governmental use, others would be occupied by offices, hotels, and retail activities. Figure 95 shows the avenue and adjacent area as viewed from the Capitol.

South of the avenue in the existing Federal Triangle, additions would be made to complete the Grand Plaza originally planned between the Post Office Department building and the Department of Commerce. Existing parking, now cluttering this space, would be placed underground, and the plaza would be replanned as a second great urban square. The old city post office would be demolished, but its fine tower would be retained and used as an observation platform.

A third civic plaza, which can be seen in Figure 96, is proposed north of the Department of Commerce building as a National Square, the site for major ceremonies and public gatherings and as a formal entrance to the grounds of the White House. Near the center of the square, which would be only slightly smaller than the Place de la Concorde in Paris, a large but low fountain would serve as the terminal feature for the avenue. On its north side would stand a raised, heavily shaded terrace or belvidere. The great portico of the Treasury would extend well south of the square's northern boundary and would thus form part of its western side. A massive gateway south of the Treasury would mark the entrance to the White House grounds. Immediately inside, a raised terrace on the south and a similar although smaller one on the north would define a forecourt or ceremonial entry to the presidential precinct. Figure 97 shows how this enormous civic plaza might appear.

The plan suggests many changes in the vehicular circulation system to simplify traffic movement on Pennsylvania Avenue and in its adjoining area and to enhance the monumental character of this historic boulevard. An underpass for Constitution Avenue would eliminate what is now an awkward and dangerous inter-section. A much larger underpass under both of these avenues and the Mall for the northern expressway entering the area between 2nd and 3rd Streets would also be needed. Other Mall underpasses, in addition to that existing for 12th Street, are called for at 9th and 14th Streets. The latter street would also be carried under the National Square. E Street would also run underneath the pedestrian platform westward from 6th Street and then in a tunnel below the National Square and the White House Grounds.

Along Pennsylvania Avenue double and triple rows of clipped trees are planned to emphasize its visual continuity. A new building line along the northern side would permit a much wider sidewalk. Extra curbs, 5 and 10 feet back from the edge of the roadway, would provide a grandstand effect for better visibility during parades. The buildings on the northern side would also be constructed with arcades for shade in the hot Washington summers and as protection against rain and snow, an echo of the L'Enfant proposal years earlier for East Capitol Street. Pavement for the avenue would consist of brick over concrete to give a distinctive texture and color to its broad expanse.

Finally, complementing these exciting plans for the city's most important thoroughfare are even more recent proposals prepared for the National Park Service by Skidmore, Owings, and Merrill for the Mall, that great expanse of lawn, trees, drives, museums, and memorials forming the green heart of the city. The Mall plan, made public on December 14, 1965, retains most of the basic features of the 1902 design but includes many additional suggestions and refinements. Figure 98 shows the proposed redesign of the Mall and the area around the Tidal Basin as well as the principal details of the closely related Pennsylvania Avenue scheme.

At the Capitol end the Mall begins beyond the reflecting pool which is here shown in a form somewhat changed from that appearing in the Pennsylvania Avenue plan. The Grant Memorial would extend into this six-acre expanse of water which would mark the boundary between the Capitol grounds and the Mall. Canal Street to the south and Louisiana Avenue to the north would be connected by a gently curving boulevard forming the western edge of the pool. The Central Leg Freeway, running north and south, would be placed under the pool and the new boulevard, one of

Figure 95. View of Model Showing Proposed Improvements for Pennsylvania Avenue: 1964

Figure 96. View of Model Showing Proposed National Square and Improvements for Pennsylvania Avenue: 1964

*Figure 97. View of Proposed National Square Looking from Pennsylvania
Avenue to the White House Grounds: 1964*

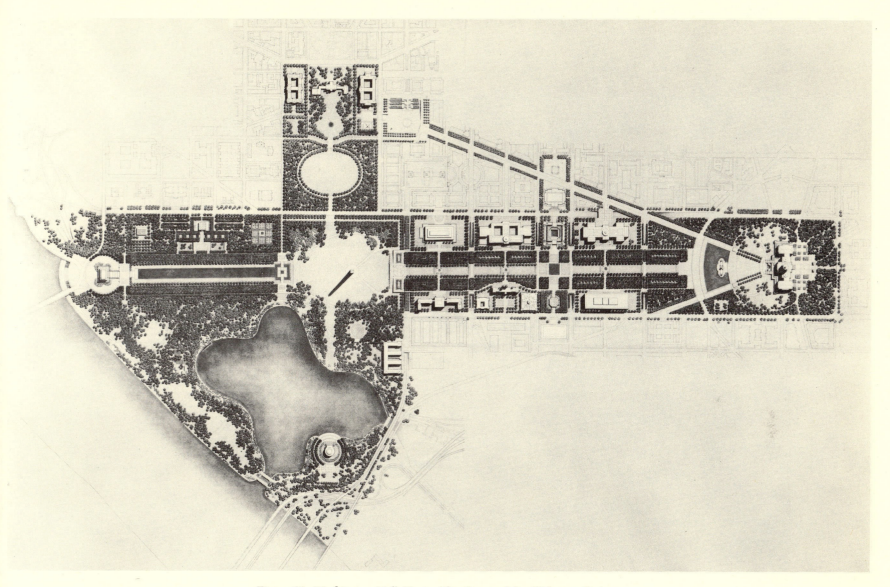

*Figure 98. Washington Mall Master Plan Proposed by Skidmore, Owings,
and Merrill for the National Park Service: 1965*

Figure 99. View of Model Showing Proposed Treatment of Capital Grounds and Mall: 1965

*Figure 100. View of Model Showing Proposals for the Western Section of
the Mall: 1965*

Figure 101. View of Model Showing Proposals for the Washington Monument and the White House Axis: 1965

several traffic arteries planned to underpass the Mall and thus free it completely for its entire length from vehicular surface traffic.

The proposed treatment of this portion of the Mall can be seen in Figure 99, a photograph of the model showing the details of the plan. This reveals the suggested landscape treatment of the Mall between the Capitol reflecting pool and the Washington Monument. The rows of trees on either side would be doubled to provide deeply shaded walkways along a graveled surface similar to the gardens of the Tuilleries in Paris. Down the center of the composition would extend a narrowed stretch of lawn, broken at intervals by hard-surfaced courts, pools, and fountains. Pavillions, kiosks, and bandstands would be located within the tree-lined portion of the Mall to provide refreshment and recreation facilities and to create a lively atmosphere.

For the western end of the Mall the plan calls for a slight lengthening of the reflecting pool of the Lincoln Memorial to terminate at an island lookout platform on the axis of 17th Street. The traffic circle around the Lincoln Memorial would be eliminated, providing direct pedestrian access between the Memorial and the Mall. This section of the plan appears in Figure 100 which also shows suggested changes in the Tidal Basin area. The Kutz Memorial Bridge, which now crosses the northern tip of the Basin, would be eliminated along with its approach roadways which now separate the Tidal Basin from the Mall. Traffic would be accommodated by a highway tunnel extending from 14th Street under the Tidal Basin and emerging beyond the Lincoln Memorial. The area between the Tidal Basin and the Potomac would be extensively replanned to include a Japanese tea garden, a children's zoo, and additional park facilities.

The changes proposed for the White House-Jefferson Memorial cross-axis and the Washington Monument grounds can be seen in Figure 101. To the east of the Monument near the present crossing of 14th Street the Mall slopes downward and then rises again to the base of the great obelisk. At the eastern side of this change in elevation the plan calls for the creation of a formal terrace terminating this portion of the Mall and providing a dramatic point from which to view the Washington Monument. Below the terrace would be a visitor's center easily accessible from the Monument with 14th Street carried under the Mall by a vehicular tunnel.

The designers suggest an informal treatment for the Monument hill, with only additional planting and slight regrading of the terrain. While this fails to provide the needed strengthening of the potentially important cross-axis from the White House to the Jefferson Memorial, it at least does nothing to prejudice the eventual development of this portion of the Mall system in a more forceful and harmonious manner at some future time.

Here, then, is a renewed attack on visual blight in the nation's capital—a fresh approach to the replanning and refurbishing of the core of central Washington. The scope and scale of these recommendations are truly magnificent, and these contemporary plans stand as worthy successors to the Senate Park Commission plan of 1902 and L'Enfant's original generous vision of a monumental capital for a mighty nation.

Thus, as one looks back over more than half a century, the enormous influence of the Senate Park Commission plan of 1902 can be appreciated. Not everything recommended by that small group of designers has been realized, but almost everything carried out has been in accord with the Commission's proposals. And as their plan was itself shaped and directed by L'Enfant's grand design, so contemporary planners of the city have been guided and directed by the work of Burnham, McKim, Olmsted, and Saint-Gaudens.

No other American city can demonstrate the same faithfulness in following the proposals of a comprehensive area plan for so many years and in so many details. The remarkable results of this continuity of planning are familiar to most Americans, since the nation's capital has continued to attract citizens of all ages in informal pilgrimages of ever-increasing numbers. Washington seldom fails to impress these visitors and those from foreign lands as well. But rarely do they—or, for that matter, residents of the city—ask themselves how it was that this all came about. It is with this subject of how the plan of 1902 proved so influential in guiding urban development in Washington and its effect on American city planning elsewhere that the concluding chapter will deal.

CHAPTER 8

The Washington Plan: Influence and Example

The influence exerted on American city planning by the Senate Park Commission plan for Washington and its gradual implementation was enormous. The wide and overwhelmingly favorable publicity given to the plan helped to make its chief features known throughout the country. Burnham, McKim, Olmsted, and Moore, in countless conversations and public addresses aided in providing understanding of the plan and its objectives. It was little wonder that civic leaders in other communities soon began to think of duplicating the Washington effort in attempts to beautify their own cities. The seed of discontent with the ugliness of American cities had already been sown at the Chicago World's Fair of 1893. This seemed the time to cultivate the idea of the city beautiful throughout urban America, with the apparently vigorous growth of Washington as an example of what might be achieved by skillful planning and hard work.

This emphasis on civic beauty coincided with a more general reform movement in the nation's cities. Studies of inefficiency, graft, and corruption in urban government had already led to attempts at remedial action. Proposals for reorganization of administrative structure, introduction of the merit system for municipal employees, and the prosecution of dishonest city officials had caught the public fancy. To this movement for "good" government was added the drive for the city beautiful. The city of Paris as re-

planned by Baron Haussmann under Napoleon III during the third quarter of the nineteenth century was frequently cited as an example of what might be achieved if the principles of the Washington plan were applied.[1]

In 1902, soon after the completion of the Senate Park Commission plan, a group of civic leaders in San Francisco requested Burnham to prepare just such a plan for that city. Burnham began work in the fall of 1904, under the sponsorship of the Association for the Improvement and Adornment of San Francisco and with the cooperation of the Outdoor Art League and the California chapter of the American Institute of Architects.[2] During this period Burnham was also commissioned by the Secretary of War to replan Manila and to produce a plan for the summer capital of the Philippines at Baguio.

While these were plans for entire cities, emphasis was placed on the design of the city center, its approaches, and the grouping of public buildings in great monumental compositions. More restricted in its objectives and closely resembling the effort at Wash-

[1] See, for example, the plan of Paris as replanned by Haussmann in Daniel H. Burnham and Edward H. Bennett, *Plan of Chicago Prepared under the Direction of the Commercial Club during the Years MCMVI, MCMVII, and MCMVIII,* Chicago, 1909, p. 16.

[2] For reproductions of 4 of the drawings from the San Francisco plan see my *The Making of Urban America,* Princeton, 1965, pp. 515–18.

ington was the so-called Group Plan at Cleveland, begun in the summer of 1902 by a commission of experts composed of Arnold Brunner, John Carrère, and Burnham as chairman. Their report the following year provided the basic plan for the Cleveland Civic Center.

Burnham's most notable contribution to city planning was his great plan of Chicago, completed in 1909 in association with Edward H. Bennett, who had also assisted him in San Francisco. Here, too, much of the emphasis was on a monumental civic center, together with proposals for beautification of the lake front and the banks of the Chicago River. Burnham also proposed, as he had in his plans for San Francisco and Manila, sweeping boulevards radiating outwards from major points of interest and connected with a system of parks and playgrounds.[3]

During the years before the First World War other cities and other planners joined in similar proposals. St. Louis, Dallas, Newark, Detroit, Madison, Pittsburgh, Grand Rapids, Minneapolis, Buffalo, Columbus, Los Angeles, and Oakland were among those in which such would-be Haussmanns as Burnham, John Nolen, Charles Mulford Robinson, Bennett, Arnold Brunner, George Kessler, and other pioneer American city planners set about their tasks. A great civic renaissance seemed to be under way.

These early plans were commissioned by private groups of business, professional, and industrial leaders. Not until 1907, with the establishment by charter amendment of an official planning commission in Hartford, did the planning movement gain official recognition. Two years later Chicago established by executive action its Mayor's City Plan Commission. Other cities soon followed the lead of Hartford and Chicago, and within a decade there were several dozen cities with official commissions charged with the preparation of plans for urban improvements.

In the content of their plans, in their reliance on elaborate published reports, in their employment of experts, and above all in their use of baroque planning devices for civic squares, monumental grouping of buildings, and imposing boulevards, the plan-

ning programs of these cities closely resembled what had been produced at Washington in 1902. One major and important difference existed. At Washington virtually all of the proposals embodied in the Park Commission plan ultimately attained acceptance and were carried out. In the other cities of America the record of success, as measured by completion of proposed improvements, remained at best spotty and unimpressive.

Doubtless in each city special reasons made realization of planned change difficult or impossible. Yet it is also true that most, perhaps all, of these circumstances also threatened at one time or other to block or hamper the carrying out of the plan of Washington.

Certainly no other plan for a major American city achieved such success as the one for Washington. At our own time in history, when city planning activities have never been more widespread and when more public funds are being spent in efforts to guide new growth and renew existing neighborhoods than ever before, it is both instructive and imperative that we consider the reasons which led to the implementation of the plan for Washington.

Such an inquiry is, of course, one of the justifications of historical research. What does the history of Washington's planning have to teach us today? Was the success of the Washington plan merely fortuitous and not likely to be duplicated elsewhere? Or, can we learn lessons from this great experience that might be applied in other cities, under different circumstances, and in our own time? The answers to such questions are not easy, and the conclusions that can be drawn must be regarded as tentative. History is not science, and every city is unique. Yet it is important that we make the effort at a time in our nation's development when the urban way of life has become almost ubiquitous and when the shaping of the urban environment to meet the needs of the future has become a national responsibility.

Some of the reasons for the plan's success stem from the unique position of Washington as the nation's capital. These will have limited utility in other cities, although the planners of the fifty state capitals might well find some helpful suggestions with possible application to their special types of communities. Other factors

[3] A brief description and 4 of the drawings from the Chicago plan appear in *ibid.*, pp. 519–24.

responsible for the carrying out of the plan for Washington have wider application and can be examined with profit by planners and civic leaders everywhere.

What, then, were the reasons for the plan's success?

First, and most obvious, there *was* a plan—a specific proposal for the future. The Park Commission did not limit itself to mere statements of objectives, of goals, of principles, or of land development standards. It went beyond this in providing a concrete image of the city of the future in plans, models, and perspective drawings. For the planners of that day this was unremarkable. Planning involved and required plans. In our own era this seemingly self-evident proposition has been questioned. The idea of a plan expressed in graphic form has somehow come to be regarded as faintly old fashioned. Instead, the doctrine has been advanced that cities should aim primarily at setting general development objectives, formulating somewhat more specific principles, and perhaps adopting a set of standards that would apply to specific uses as they are developed. Individual development proposals would then be considered in the light of these objectives, principles, and standards and approved or disapproved, or stimulated or discouraged.

Whatever may be said for this approach to planning, it is safe to conclude that it will never result in the creation of great and noble civic compositions of the type achieved in central Washington. Goals and objectives, even principles and development standards, are altogether too susceptible to diverse interpretations through long periods of time to serve alone as guides for the future. A unifying plan—not necessarily as detailed as that for Washington in 1902—seems essential.

Second, the plan was bold and inspiring. Only later did Burnham coin his since much-repeated and often derided admonition, "Make no little plans, they have no power to stir men's souls," but this philosophy plainly pervaded the minds of those who prepared the proposals for the future of the nation's capital. It was a big plan, big in the resources it would require, big in spirit, and big in the demands it made on those responsible for carrying it out. The inspirational quality of this vision of the future proved to be enormously important. Almost overnight the plan captured the imagination of those who were exposed to it and built up a powerful body of opinion favorably disposed to the implementation of the proposals.

Here, again, modern urban planning fails by comparison. The emphasis has shifted over the years from plans that stressed the bold, the big, and the beautiful to those which hailed efficiency and economy as the chief goals. Utility in planning certainly must not be scorned, but beauty and monumentality should be given at least equal emphasis. The great cities of the world are not those which are merely efficient but those which over the years have risen above utilitarianism to achieve architectural nobility in one or more of their parts.

Third, the plan was simple in its broad outlines, and its essentials were easily grasped. The text of the official report and the drawings and models displayed at the exhibition and widely reproduced in national magazines clearly conveyed the recommendations of the Park Commission. The Commission, of course, inherited the simplicity and clarity of the central composition created by L'Enfant, and it naturally found it easy to communicate its proposals for reinforcing this earlier plan to persons familiar with the disposition of existing buildings. But the Commisson's own proposals were direct and uncomplicated, characteristics of most great examples of civic design in history.

Many modern American plans set a high standard of graphic communication, although few equal the verbal skill established by Moore and Olmsted. However, it is not so much the ability to communicate that counts as the quality of the message that is to be sent. Here one usually looks in vain for the unifying idea, the central concept lucidly expressed in plan and text around which the reader or the observer can organize the many details and qualifications that almost inevitably accompany such presentations. Admittedly modern city plans may deal with the entire city and with many more aspects of the city than its physical pattern and its three-dimensional elements, yet often one yearns for an initial straightforward statement, either verbal or graphic, that would instantly provide the key to an understanding of the focus of the plan.

Fourth, the plan of 1902 made use of existing features and

conditions in framing its long view of the distant future. Here good fortune walked with the planners. L'Enfant's uncanny and prophetic vision of the eventual space needs for the capital city provided a point of departure. And, despite many deviations from that early plan, the land areas essential for its ultimate realization still lay almost untouched. Perhaps the Commission deserves no credit whatsoever for choosing what now seems the path of inevitability in accepting this basic physical framework on which to hang their architectural embellishments. Yet they had the sense to realize their good fortune and to capitalize on it.

The city plans that followed that of Washington in the first decades of the century largely disregarded this consideration. Virtually all of these cities were gridiron towns, lacking the great diagonal boulevards, the equivalent of the Mall, and the many generous sites for major buildings found in Washington. Instead of accepting these limitations, the planners often advocated wildly unrealistic construction of new diagonal arteries cutting across the established pattern of streets and buildings. Burnham's plan for San Francisco in 1905 stands as the earliest and best example of this disregard for realities. Even the destruction of a large part of the city by earthquake and fire did not provide an opportunity for carrying out a proposal requiring such a radical revision of the basic pattern of the city.[4]

Fifth, the plan of Washington harmonized with the prevailing taste in architecture and civic design. The Chicago World's Fair of 1893 influenced a whole generation of Americans and conditioned it to expect and even demand monumental buildings that followed Greek and Roman models. That buildings so designed had been contemplated by L'Enfant when he prepared the original plan for the city was another piece of fortune to which the Park

[4] Fairmount Parkway (now Benjamin Franklin Parkway) in Philadelphia is one of the few exceptions to this generalization. Begun in the early years of this century, this great diagonal boulevard slashes through the east-west Philadelphia gridiron street system to run northwesterly from a point near the city hall to the southern end of Fairmount Park. The plan by Jacques Gréber provides a welcome relief to the monotony of the grid. Although other similar diagonal boulevards were proposed to balance this composition, only this project was carried out. For a reproduction of the various plans considered for this improvement see Fairmount Park Art Association, *The Fairmount Parkway,* Philadelphia, 1919.

Commission fell heir. While today we may regard as an aesthetic tragedy this imitation of architectural forms of another age, such a view is largely irrelevant in considering the reasons why the Washington plan succeeded so well.

Sixth, at a time when America was emerging as an important world power, the Commission plan seemed to symbolize this new status of the country in the community of nations. Moreover, the plan for the capital city came at just that moment when thoughtful persons were beginning to question the materialism of our society and the almost unquestioning faith in industrial accomplishments alone as the mark of a great nation. Quite likely this attraction of the plan for Washington remained an unconscious one, but it almost certainly was a real consideration in the minds of some of the influential supporters of the plan. The reform movement in America, which had largely been concerned with corruption in local government, exploitation of the laboring classes by big business, improvement in housing conditions in the large cities, and other social causes, quickly embraced the concept of the city beautiful as an American goal. The plan for Washington was, of course, the first and most complete statement of this new objective.

Seventh, the calibre of the decision-makers responsible for the plan of Washington and for its implementation was of the very highest. Burnham, McKim, Olmsted, and Saint-Gaudens probably represented the most skilled and knowledgeable technical team that could have been assembled for such a task. Charles Moore possessed a mind of great keenness, and his political skill had been thoroughly developed. Senator McMillan added his prestige and influence and his sense of practical idealism.

But beyond the group responsible for the plan's preparation were the political figures who held the power for implementing or subverting the plan. Then as now Washington attracted politicians and statesmen of great ability and imagination. Such men as President Theodore Roosevelt, Elihu Root, and John Hay, who were among the earliest supporters of the plan, possessed first-class intellects and were blessed as well with vision and imagination. Their successors, who from time to time were called on to reach important decisions in the development of the city, were, with a few exceptions, men of equal quality. Even the quality of the opposition, as personified in Speaker Joseph Cannon, was notable. Whatever one may think of the abilities of individual senators and congressmen, they are unquestionably men whose quality far exceeds that of the average city councilman. The government of the city of Washington is far from democratic, since its citizens have little voice in its affairs, but the intellectual resources that can be brought to bear on the problems of that community should be the envy of the other cities of the country.

Eighth, and related to the foregoing, those charged with decisions affecting the city's development were not responsible to a local constituency. No votes of a local city council, no public referenda were necessary for approval of the separate projects which have shaped the central part of the city. Nor were the decision-makers faced with the need to justify their actions when running for local office. Moreover, improvements in Washington could be authorized by those responsible for its destiny without regard for local reaction to an increased tax burden. Congress, in voting approval for projects in the city, has far fewer fiscal constraints than a city council in a typical municipality. The taxes necessary to raise funds for federal projects are imposed on the entire country. Even a vast public works program in the District of Columbia has but a minute impact on the federal income tax burden of its citizens, or, for that matter, on the average citizen elsewhere in the nation. Presidents, senators, and congressmen alike have thus been free to reach decisions affecting the physical development of Washington on their merits alone. As much as any other reason, this situation has been responsible for the success in implementing the plan of 1902.

Ninth, the position of the political decision-makers in Washington was immensely strengthened because of the extensive holdings of publicly owned land in the area under consideration. Although it would be necessary ultimately to acquire additional building sites in the Triangle area and smaller tracts immediately west of the Capitol grounds, the national government already controlled virtually all of the land needed to carry out the plan. This was another valuable legacy stemming from the generous vision of L'Enfant and the founders of the city. We have only lately come to realize the advantages of permanent or temporary public land ownership as a powerful instrument to implement planned improvements. In this respect, at least, the Washington experience furnishes additional encouragement for continuing and expanding our current programs of urban renewal through which municipal initiative can be most effectively utilized.

Tenth, because the Washington plan called for public investment almost exclusively, only one set of decision-makers was involved—the political and executive leaders of the national government. Once this group could be convinced of the wisdom and desirability of the plan, little else remained. It was, of course, not this simple, since the members of the governmental elite changed from time to time and shifts occurred in the positions of power. The advocates of the plan needed to maintain a constant program of information and education about its merits, but their task was enormously simplified because they could concentrate their efforts on a relatively few individuals whose place in the power structure was both visible and well defined. In other cities, where large numbers of private interests are directly concerned and whose mutual and timely agreement is necessary for implementing plans of this magnitude, the difficulties become vastly multiplied.

Eleventh, throughout the formative years of the development of the Mall and its surrounding area following the plan of 1902, a dedicated group of individuals and organizations acted as legislative guardians and watchdogs and as an influential and informed lobby to ensure the plan's eventual implementation. The members of the Park Commission themselves served this function. So also did the American Institute of Architects, which has continued to the present time to demonstrate special interest and concern with the development of the city in which its headquarters is located. Other individuals and organizations played this role from time to time as well.

But major credit must go to Charles Moore for providing a kind of continuity of conscience for more than four decades after the plan's preparation. First as a legislative assistant, then as a private citizen, next as a member of the Commission of Fine Arts, and finally as the Commission's chairman from 1915 to 1937, Moore dedicated his considerable talents and influence to the realization of the great scheme for central Washington which he had helped to conceive. Moore's name and the part he played in shaping the national capital are known by only a handful of persons. His only monument is a portrait hanging in the office of the Commission of Fine Arts. His contribution to the city, and thus to the nation, was truly remarkable and perhaps one day will be adequately recognized.

One has only to read the annual reports of the Commission of Fine Arts through the long years of Moore's chairmanship to appreciate his effectiveness as a champion of planning in general and the plan of the Park Commission in particular. His sense of the necessity for continuity and tradition in urban development was superb; never did he lose an opportunity to recall the historical basis for the plan of 1902 or to invoke the sacred names of Washington and Jefferson as those who had approved L'Enfant's original plan which was given fresh meaning and fuller detail by the Park Commission plan.

It was, perhaps, unfortunate that Moore doggedly opposed modern architectural design. He, like McKim and Burnham, felt that only Roman and Greek models were suitable for the monumental buildings of the capital city. He was, of course, not himself a designer, and did not appreciate that living architecture could not be nourished on the stale forms from past epochs. His taste became that of the Commission, and it is only in recent years that this influence has been partially overcome. Yet with full recognition of this aesthetic limitation one can only conclude that his persistence and determination provided the rallying point for all of those who cherished the idea of a capital city that would rival the great cities of the past in monumentality and grandeur. More important, his political abilities and persuasive talents provided the essential bridge between the almost utopian ideas of the planners and the practical world of legislative approval and appropriations.[5]

Finally, the creation of the Commission of Fine Arts as a federal organization charged with the duty of overseeing the aesthetic aspects of Washington's growth and development furnished an official base for the efforts of Burnham, Moore, and their successors in advising on governmental policies and projects affecting the city. Official recognition that the appearance of the city was an important consideration in community development provided increased political leverage that could be applied when needed. The effectiveness of this organization when compared to the comparatively modest appropriations for its operations demonstrates that vast sums are not always necessary to achieve adequate results.[6]

The lessons of Washington and its planned development can thus be read with mixed reactions. The history of its development gives heart to those who believe that long-range plans can be made and, despite strong and skillful political opposition, be ultimately carried out. The story of Washington also indicates that appeals to beauty and monumentality are not always disregarded in a country that has lately seemed to make economic advantage and functional efficiency its main goals.

Yet there is a pessimistic conclusion that also carries great weight. The special circumstances of the Washington situation cannot be duplicated in any other American city. The freedom of the decision-makers from recriminations by a local constituency and the existence of a nation-wide tax base from which funds for improvements in the federally controlled portions of central Washington could be obtained suggest that, where these two circumstances do not exist, plans of the type and scale that were implemented in the capital city will not be easy to duplicate elsewhere. This raises the broad and perplexing question of how great civic design can be obtained at all in a democratic society. The lesson of history is not reassuring.

Since the time of the Greeks most of the noble achievements of urban design have been created in societies dominated by kings, emperors, popes, or merchant princes. They were not the result of mass support by the people. The three *places* of Nancy; the great central composition of St. Petersburg; the Piazza del Popolo, the Campidoglio, and the Piazza di San Pietro of Rome; the Place

[5] Moore's background and his contribution to the plan of Washington are reviewed in H. Paul Caemmerer, "Charles Moore and the Plan of Washington," Columbia Historical Society, *Records,* XLVI–XLVII (1944–45), Washington, 1947, pp. 237–58.

[6] The act of May 17, 1910, creating the Commission of Fine Arts authorized an annual appropriation of $10,000. In only three years during the period 1910–39 did expenditures meet or exceed this amount. In 14 of those years expenditures were under $8,000. U.S. Commission of Fine Arts, *Thirteenth Report,* January 1, 1935, to December 31, 1939, Washington, 1940, p. 135.

de la Concorde, its related Tuileries Gardens and the Avenue des Champs d'Elysées in Paris; the Piazza di San Marco in Venice; the great residential squares of London and the superb Regent Street development in the same city, to name but a few, fall in this category.

To some extent the improvements in Washington from the turn of the century resemble these achievements of other eras and other countries. One can argue, of course, that ultimately the public officials who voted for and supported these improvements were accountable for their actions at the polls. But it seems doubtful if in any congressional or presidential election a single candidate failed or succeeded because of his vote or action to recommend or support a single public building in the District of Columbia. In their immunity from public reaction where it counts—at the polling places—the federal officials responsible for the development of Washington more closely resemble Napoleon III and his advisers than the mayors, planners, city managers, and city councilmen of the nation's cities who must shape their own city patterns in an atmosphere where the public demands economy and is suspicious of attempts to create beauty.

This argument cannot be pressed too far, of course. One can point, for example, to Chicago, St. Louis, and, more recently, Philadelphia, where the electorate has, with only occasional lapses, supported extensive civic improvements. This is the great challenge of democracy in our cities: Whether they can be made beautiful as well as passably functional, inspiring communities in which the citizens can take pride and be uplifted by their nobility and magnificence and not just great machines supplying lodging and employment. History would seem to indicate that this will be a trying challenge and one in which the results are not at all inevitable.

Perhaps Washington is both the testing ground and the symbol of change in our approach to city development. Possibly, however, the lessons of Washington mean that as a price for beauty we must make governmental and institutional readjustments in other urban areas so that decision-making can be lifted somewhat above the narrow political conflicts that now prevent action of the type possible in our capital city. Or, perhaps it means that we must wait until the level of intelligence and taste in general has reached the level exhibited, with only few notable lapses, by the national lawmakers and executive officials who have guided the destiny of the capital.

Modern history supplies several analogues to Washington: New Delhi, Brazilia, Ottawa, Canberra, Chandigarh, Ankara, and Islamabad, the new and planned capitals of India, Brazil, Canada, Australia, the Punjab, Turkey, and Pakistan. Here too, other countries have produced new capital cities intended to exhibit a scale of luxury, monumentality, and civic grandeur unmatched elsewhere in those lands. Nowhere have the results been as satisfactory as Washington, and much of the credit must be attributed to the planners at the turn of this century who recaptured the vision of L'Enfant and inspired the entire nation to a realization of the greatness which the capital city might achieve.

The work is still incomplete. Pennsylvania Avenue has as yet not become the great boulevard envisaged by L'Enfant, nor is the Mall the magnificent formal open space intended by the original designer or his followers in 1902. The future, however, appears bright. Presidents John F. Kennedy and Lyndon B. Johnson have been vigorous in their initiation and support of programs to enhance the visual quality of the national capital. Mrs. Johnson's advocacy of beautification efforts have proved particularly important and promise to bring about long-needed improvements in the appearance of Washington's public spaces.

The recent proposals for the replanning of Pennsylvania Avenue and for the refurbishing of the Mall are also hopeful signs, but these plans must be supported by other studies now in progress for the central business district, the freeway network, the subway system, and the long-range plan for the District of Columbia in 1985. Needed as well is a new and comprehensive design plan for the entire city which would provide a firm basis for decisions on projects affecting the urban environment.

If all these plans can be coordinated and the details of their execution entrusted to gifted designers of sensitivity and imagination, the heart of the city of Washington—the civic center of the nation—can in this century at last achieve the generous vision of its founders and its planners.

Notes on the Illustrations

This list contains bibliographic information about the illustrations reproduced in this work. The following symbols indicate the source of these materials:

A	Author's collection
ACIC	Aeronautical Chart Information Center
CPA	Temporary Commission on Pennsylvania Avenue
CU-FA	Fine Arts Library, Cornell University
CU-O	Olin Library, Cornell University
FAC	Fine Arts Commission
LC-M	Map Division, Library of Congress
LC-MS	Manuscript Division, Library of Congress
LC-N	Newspaper Division, Library of Congress
LC-P	Prints and Photographs Division, Library of Congress
NA	National Archives
NY-S	Stokes Collection, New York Public Library
SOM	Skidmore, Owings, and Merrill
US-CGS	United States Coast and Geodetic Survey

Illustrations

1. *A Map of the Most Inhabited Part of Virginia Containing the Whole Province of Maryland.* . . . Portion of map of Virginia and Maryland in 1755, drawn by Joshua Fry and Peter Jefferson, engraved and published by Thomas Jeffreys. London: 1755.   LC-M

2. Untitled manuscript marginal sketch by Thomas Jefferson in 1790 showing suggested land division in a city block, from a manuscript note dated November 29, 1790, entitled "Proceedings to be had Under the Residence Act." Papers of Thomas Jefferson.   LC-MS

3. Untitled manuscript marginal sketch by Thomas Jefferson in 1790 of a plan for a capital city on the site of Carrollsburg, District of Columbia, from a manuscript note dated November 29, 1790, entitled "Proceedings to be had Under the Residence Act." Papers of Thomas Jefferson.   LC-MS

4. *Plan de Versailles.* Plan of the town, château, and gardens of Versailles, France, drawn by Abbé Delagrive. Paris: 1746.   A

5. *Partie du Plan Général de Paris.* Plan of Paris showng proposed squares and monuments to Louis XV, drawn by Pierre Patte in 1765, from Patte, *Monumens Érigés en France à la Gloire de Louis XV*. Paris: n.p., 1765.   CU-O

6. *Sketch of Washington in Embryo.* Map showing the division of land on the site of the national capital in 1791, drawn by E. F. M. Faehtz and F. W. Pratt, based on research by Dr. Joseph M. Toner. Washington: 1874.   LC-M

7. Untitled, undated manuscript plan by Thomas Jefferson for the United States Capital on the site of Washington, D.C., probably drawn in March 1791. Papers of Thomas Jefferson. LC-MS

8. Untitled, undated manuscript plan for Washington, D.C., drawn by Pierre Charles L'Enfant in August 1791, with later manuscript additions.   LC-M

9. *Plan of the City Intended for the Permanent Seat of the Government of the United States.* Copy by the United States Coast and Geodetic Survey in 1887 of the manuscript plan for Washington, D.C., drawn by Pierre Charles L'Enfant, 1791. A

10. *Plan of the City of Washington in the Territory of Columbia.* . . . drawn by Andrew Ellicott, engraved by Thackara & Vallance. Philadelphia: 1792. Restrike in 1962 from the original plate. A

11. *Plan of the City of Washington in the Territory of Columbia.* . . . Portion of plan drawn by Andrew Ellicott, engraved by Thackara & Vallance. Philadelphia: 1792. From a reproduction in 1964 published by Historic Urban Plans, Ithaca, N.Y. A

12. *North Front of the President's House.* View of the north front of the White House in 1820, from an insert on *A Correct Map of the City of Washington, Capital of the United States of America,* engraved by W. I. Stone, published by Peter Force. Washington: 1820. LC-P

13. *Georgetown and Federal City, or City of Washington.* View of Georgetown and Washington, looking southeast in 1801. Drawn by G. Beck, engraved by T. Cartwright. London: 1801. LC-P

14. *Washington.* View from the Capitol to the White House along Pennsylvania Avenue in 1834, drawn by J. R. Smith, engraved by J. B. Neagle, from Conrad Malte-Brun, *A System of Universal Geography,* II. Boston: 1834. LC-P

15. *Plan of the Washington Canal, No. 1.* Manuscript plan of the proposed Tiber Canal and locks drawn by Benjamin Henry Latrobe, February 5, 1804. LC-M

16. *View of the Capitol at Washington.* View of the west front of the Capitol, ca. 1837, drawn by W. H. Bartlett, engraved by C. J. Bentley, published by George Virtue, from W. H. Bartlett, *The History of the United States of North America,* III. New York: 1856. A

17. *Washington City 1821.* Painting by Madame Hyde de Neuville, wife of the French Minister, of the north front of the White House, center; the State and Treasury buildings, left; and the War and Navy buildings, right. NY-S

18. *Plan of the West End of the Public Appropriation in the City of Washington, Called the Mall, as Proposed to be Arranged for the Site of the University.* Manuscript plan for a national university on the Mall drawn by Benjamin Latrobe, January 1816. LC-M

19. *City Hall.* View of City Hall published by E. Sachse. Baltimore: ca. 1866. LC-P

20. *City of Washington From Beyond the Navy Yard.* View of Washington, D.C., in 1834 from the south bank of the Anacostia River, drawn by W. J. Bennett from a painting by George Cooke, published by Lewis P. Clover. New York: 1834. LC-P

21. *View of the City of Washington, the Metropolis of the United States of America. Taken from Arlington House, the Residence of George Washington P. Custis, Esq.* View from the west bank of the Potomac in 1838, published by P. Anderson, printed by T. Moore. Boston: 1838. LC-P

22. *View of Washington.* View in 1852 from the Capitol northwest to the White House, drawn and published by E. Sachse. Baltimore: 1852. LC-P

23. *The Washington National Monument.* View of the Robert Mills design of 1836 for the Washington Monument drawn by H. Warren, engraved by J. C. Armytage, published by George Virtue, from W. H. Bartlett, *The History of the United States of North America,* III. New York: 1856. A

24. *The President's House, From the River.* View of the White House from the Potomac River, ca. 1827, drawn by W. H. Bartlett, engraved by W. Radclyffe, published by George Virtue, from W. H. Bartlett, *The History of the United States of North America,* II. New York: 1856. A

25. *U.S. Treasury.* View of Treasury Building, ca. 1867, published by E. Sachse & Co. LC-P

26. *Patent Office.* View of the Patent Office, ca. 1860, published by E. Sachse & Co. LC-P

27. *General Post-Office.* View of Post Office, ca. 1869, drawn by Aug. Kollner. LC-P

28. *Topographical Map of the District of Columbia.* Portion of map of the District of Columbia, drawn by A. Boschke, published by D. McClelland, Blanchard, and Mohun. Washington: 1861. LC-M

29. *Plan Showing Proposed Method of Laying Out the Public Grounds at Washington.* Unsigned manuscript copy in 1867 of Andrew Jackson Downing's plan for the Mall of 1851, prepared to accompany the annual report of Brig. Gen. N. Michler, in charge of Public Buildings, Grounds, and Works, October 1, 1867.   FAC

30. *Washington City, D.C.* View of Washington looking east from the White House Grounds to the Capitol in 1869, drawn by Theo. R. Davis, from *Harper's Weekly,* March 13, 1869.   A

31. *View of Washington City.* View of Washington in 1871 from the Capitol northwest to the White House, published by E. Sachse & Co. Baltimore: 1871.   LC-P

32. *Plan of the City of Washington.* Portion of plan of Washington drawn by William Forsyth. Washington: 1870.   LC-M

33. *Exhibit Chart Showing Streets & Avenues of the Cities of Washington and Georgetown Improved Under the Board of Public Works, D.C.* Plan of Washington showing sewers constructed in 1872 and 1873, printed by J. G. Geoney. Washington: 1873.   LC-M

34. Untitled, unsigned, and undated view from the southwest of the State, War, and Navy Department building, ca. 1888. LC-P

35. *Department of Agriculture, Washington, D.C.* View of the Department of Agriculture building and grounds, ca. 1870, drawn by Van Ingen. Synder.   LC-P

36. *Our National Capitol, Viewed From the South.* View of Washington, looking north to the Mall, the Capitol, and the White House in 1882, drawn by Theo. R. Davis, from *Harper's Weekly,* May 20, 1882.   A

37. *Scene at the Pennsylvania Avenue Entrance to the Capitol Grounds at Washington on the Daily Adjournment of Congress.* View of railroad tracks at foot of Capitol Hill in 1866, drawn by F. Dielman, from *Harper's Weekly* April 28, 1866. LC-P

38. *The Altograph of Washington City, or, Strangers' Guide.* Pictorial map of Washington published by James T. Du Bois, printed by Norris Peters Co. Washington: 1892.   LC-M

39. *The City of Washington.* Portion of view from the south of Washington in 1892, published by Currier & Ives. New York: 1892.   LC-P

40. *Plan of Proposed Pennsylvania Avenue, Union and National Avenues.* Plan for central Washington in 1890 by Franklin W. Smith, from Franklin W. Smith, *Design and Prospectus for the National Gallery of History & Art.* Washington: 1891. CU-O

41. *Plan in Fulfillment of Condemnations Hereinbefore Proposed.* Plan for central Washington in 1900 by Franklin W. Smith, from Franklin W. Smith, *National Galleries of History and Art. The Aggrandizement of Washington.* Washington: 1900. CU-FA

42. *Map of the City of Washington Showing United States Reservations.* Plan of Washington showing public reservations in 1900, prepared under the direction of Colonel Theo. A. Bingham, drawn by F. D. Owen and F. F. Gillen, from U.S. War Department, Report of Chief of Engineers, Part 8. Washington: 1900.   LC-M

43. *The Historic Mall Designed by L'Enfant and Approved by Washington. Study for its Realization and Embellishment in Connection with Potomac Park and Memorial Bridge.* First study of a plan by Theodore Bingham for central Washington in 1900, drawn by Fred D. Owen, from Annual Report of Theo. A. Bingham, Officer in Charge of Public Buildings and Grounds, June 30, 1901.   CU-O

44. *The Historic Mall Designed by L'Enfant and Approved by Washington. Study for its Realization and Embellishment in Connection with Potomac Park and Memorial Bridge.* Second Study of a plan by Theodore Bingham for central Washington in 1900, drawn by Fred D. Owen, from Annual Report of Theo. A. Bingham, Officer in Charge of Public Buildings and Grounds, June 30, 1901.   LC-M

45. *Study of the Embellishment and Use of Potomac Park.* Plan by Theo. A. Bingham for East Potomac Park in 1900, drawn by Fred D. Owen, from Annual Report of Theo. A. Bingham,

Officer in Charge of Public Buildings and Grounds, June 30, 1901.   CU-O

46. *Working Plan for that Section of the District of Columbia Situated South of Pennsslyvania Avenue and North of B Street Southwest Washington, D.C.* Plan for central Washington in 1900 by Samuel Parsons, Jr., from William V. Cox (comp.), *Celebration of the One Hundredth Anniversary of the Establishment of Government in the District of Columbia,* Washington, 1901.   A

47. Photograph of model showing Theodore Bingham's proposals in 1900 for remodeling the White House. View of north front. LC-P

48. *Scheme for Grouping Government Buildings Landscape and Statuary on the Mall and Pennsylvania Ave. Washington, D.C.* Plan for central Washington in 1900 by Glenn Brown, from Glenn Brown (comp.), *Papers Relating to the Improvement of the City of Washington, District of Columbia. Washington:* 1901.   CU-FA

49. *Study for Grouping of Buildings, City of Washington, D.C.* Plan for central Washington in 1900 by Cass Gilbert, from Glenn Brown (comp.), *Papers Relating to the Improvement of the City of Washington, District of Columbia. Washington:* 1901.   CU-FA

50. *Study for the Grouping of Public Buildings in the City of Washington, D.C.* Plan for central Washington in 1900 by Paul J. Pelz, from Glenn Brown (comp.), *Papers Relating to the Improvement of the City of Washington, District of Columbia.* Washington: 1901.   CU-FA

51. *Sketch Plan of Proposed Boulevard.* Plan for central Washington in 1900 by Edgar V. Seeler, from Glenn Brown (comp.), *Papers Relating to the Improvement of the City of Washington, District of Columbia.* Washington: 1901.   CU-FA

52. *Suggestion for Grouping Government Buildings Upon the Mall.* View of proposals for central Washington in 1900 by George O. Totten, Jr., from Glenn Brown (comp.), *Papers Relating to the Improvement of the City of Washington, District of Columbia.* Washington: 1901.   CU-FA

53. View of Portion of model showing existing conditions in central Washington prepared by George Curtis in 1902 for the Senate Park Commission.   FAC

54. View of preparations for the 1902 exhibit in the Corcoran Gallery of the plans by the Senate Park Commission for Washington.   FAC

55. View of Model showing proposed development, prepared by George Curtis in 1902 for the Senate Park Commission.   NA

56. *Bird's Eye View of General Plan, from Point Taken 4,000 Feet Above Arlington.* View drawn by F. L. V. Hoppin for the Senate Park Commission in 1902 showing the proposals for Washington.   FAC

57. *General Plan of the Mall System.* Unsigned plan showing proposals for central Washington prepared in 1902 by the Senate Park Commission.   FAC

58. *Washington, D.C. Diagram of a Portion of City Showing Proposed Sites for Future Public Buildings.* Plan for central Washington from Senate Park Commission, *The Improvement of the Park System of the District of Columbia.* Washington, 1902.   A

59. View of model of central Washington showing existing conditions, prepared by George Curtis in 1902 for the Senate Park Commission.   FAC

60. View of model of central Washington showing proposed development, prepared by George Curtis in 1902 for the Senate Park Commission.   FAC

61. View of portion of model of central Washington showing existing conditions, prepared by George Curtis in 1902 for the Senate Park Commission.   FAC

62. *View of Capital as Seen from Mall (Third Street).* View drawn by Robert Blum for the Senate Park Commission in 1902 showing the proposals for central Washington.   FAC

63. *View Showing the Proposed Treatment of Union Square at the Head of the Mall.* View drawn by C. Graham for the Senate Park Commission in 1902 showing the proposals for central Washington.   FAC

64. *View in Mall at Sixth Street.* View drawn by Jules Guerin for

the Senate Park Commission in 1902 showing the proposals for central Washington.   FAC

65. *General View of the Monument Garden and Mall, Looking Toward the Capitol.* View drawn by C. Graham for the Senate Park Commission in 1902 showing the proposals for central Washington.   FAC

66. *View in the Monument Garden, Main Axis, Showing Proposed Treatment of Approaches and Terraces, Forming a Setting for the Washington Monument. Looking East.* View drawn by Jules Guerin for the Senate Park Commission in 1902 showing the proposals for central Washington.   FAC

67. *Plan Showing Proposed Treatment of the Monument Garden.* Plan drawn by George de Gersdorff for the Senate Park Commission in 1902 showing the proposals for central Washington. FAC

68. *View from Terrace, Base of Monument, Looking Toward White House.* View drawn by Jules Guerin for the Senate Park Commission in 1902 showing proposals for central Washington.   FAC

69. *View of the Monument and Terraces from the White House.* View drawn by Jules Guerin for the Senate Park Commission in 1902 showing the proposals for central Washington.   FAC

70. *View of the Washington Common and Public Playgrounds, Showing Proposed Memorial Building, Baths, Theater, Gymnasium, and Athletic Buildings.* View drawn by Jules Guerin for the Senate Park Commission in 1902 showing proposals for central Washington.   FAC

71. *View Showing Proposed Development of Site for Lincoln Memorial, Seen from Canal.* View drawn by Robert Blum for the Senate Park Commission in 1902 showing the proposals for central Washington.   NA

72. *Proposed Development of Lincoln Memorial Site, Seen from Riverside Drive.* View drawn by Carlton T. Chapman for the Senate Park Commission in 1902 showing the proposals for central Washington.   FAC

73. *Viewing the Exhibit in the Hemicycle.* Drawing of President Theodore Roosevelt, Senator McMillan, and Secretaries Long and Wilson viewing the exhibition of the Senate Park Com-

mission in the Corcoran Gallery, on January 15, 1902, from the Washington *Post.* January 16, 1902.   LC-N

74. Photograph of the Mall and adjacent area, from the Washington Monument looking east, ca 1906. Photograph by Detroit Publishing Co.   LC-P

75. *Union Station, Washington, D.C., 1906.* View of railway station, published by Penn Engraving Co. Philadelphia, 1906. LC-P

76. *Group of Le Notre-McKim Tree-Butchers and Nature-Butchers.* Cartoon drawn by Berryman depicting architects replanning the Mall from the Washington *Evening Star,* January 14, 1908.   LC-N

77. Aerial photograph of the Washington Monument and Lincoln Memorial, looking northwest in 1933.   ACIC

78. Aerial photograph of the Mall and adjacent area, looking west in 1933.   ACIC

79. *Washington: The Mall and Vicinity, Buildings Occupied by Various Government Activities, 1917.* Plan of central Washington showing existing buildings in 1917, drawn by K. Hilding Beij, for the U.S. Public Buildings Commission. LC-M

80. *Washington, The Mall and Vicinity, Present and Proposed Buildings to be Occupied by Various Government Activities, 1917.* Plan of central Washington showing existing and proposed buildings in 1917, drawn by C. P. Punchard, for the U.S. Public Buildings Commission.   FAC

81. Aerial photograph of the Capitol area and railroad station, looking northeast in 1920. Wittemann Collection photograph No. 10181.   LC-P

82. Aerial photograph in 1933 of the area between Union Station and the Capitol, looking southwest.   ACIC

83. *Washington, D.C. Map Showing Progress on Commission Plan for Public Buildings and the Mall.* Plan of the central portion of Washington, drawn by F. W. Jones in 1921, from U.S. Commission of Fine Arts, *The Plan of the National Capitol.* From the Ninth Report of the Commission. Washington, 1923.   A

84. Aerial photograph of the Lincoln Memorial and the Arlington Bridge in 1933.   ACIC

85. *Perspective of Composition of Departments of Justice, of State, and of Commerce and Labor in the Competition of 1910.* View of proposed buildings facing the east side of the White House grounds designed in 1910 by Don Barber, Arnold Brunner and York & Sawyer, from U.S. Public Buildings Commission, *Public Buildings in the District of Columbia, Washington, 1918.*   FAC

86. *The Mall and Vicinity, Washington, Proposed Development.* Plan of central Washington, in 1931 showing existing and proposed buildings, drawn by J. Q. Cannon, for the U.S. Public Buildings Commission.   LC-M

87. Aerial photograph of Washington in 1937 looking northwest to the Federal Triangle from a point above the Capitol. ACIC

88. Aerial photograph of central Washington looking southeast in 1938.   ACIC

89. Aerial photograph of the Jefferson Memorial and Tidal Basin in 1954.   ACIC

90. *Development of the Central Area West and East of the Capitol—Washington, D.C., 1941.* Plan for central Washington and the east Mall in 1941 by the National Capitol Park and Planning Commission.   LC-M

91. Aerial photograph of central Washington in 1958 looking southeast.   US-CGS

92. Vertical aerial photograph of Washington, April 12, 1963, U.S. Geological Survey photograph 7-21, GS-VAQW.   US-CGS

93. *Illustrative site plan, Pennsylvania Avenue Proposal, The President's Council for Pennsylvania Avenue, 1964.* Plan for Pennsylvania Avenue and vicinity, proposed in 1964, from U.S. President's Council on Pennsylvania Avenue, *Pennsylvania Avenue,* Washington, 1964.   A

94. *Archives Cross-Axis, Model View from South.* View of model showing Archives cross-axis proposed in 1964, from U.S. President's Council on Pennsylvania Avenue, *Pennsylvania Avenue, Washington,* 1964.   CPA

95. Untitled view of model showing improvements proposed in 1964 for Pennsylvania Avenue and vicinity, prepared by the U.S. President's Council on Pennsylvania Avenue.   CPA

96. *Model View of Proposed New Pennsylvania Avenue from White House to Capitol.* View of model showing improvements proposed in 1964 for Pennsylvania Avenue and vicinity, from U.S. President's Council on Pennsylvania Avenue, *Pennsylvania Avenue,* Washington, 1964.   CPA

97. *Artist's Sketch of Pennsylvania Avenue's Western Termination in a Great New "National Square."* View of National Square proposed in 1964, drawn by Nicholas Solovioff, from U.S. President's Council on Pennsylvania Avenue, *Pennsylvania Avenue,* Washington, 1964.   CPA

98. Untitled plan for the improvement of the Washington Mall proposed in 1965 by Skidmore, Owings, and Merrill for the National Park Service.   SOM

99. View of model showing proposed treatment of the Capitol grounds and Mall by Skidmore, Owings, and Merrill in 1965. SOM

100. View of model showing proposals for the western section of the Mall by Skidmore, Owings, and Merrill in 1965.   SOM

101. View of model showing proposals for the Washington Monument and the White House axis by Skidmore, Owings, and Merrill in 1965.   SOM

Acknowledgments

Many persons and oragnizations have generously extended help and encouragement to me during the course of my research and in the preparation of the manuscript. It is with deepest appreciation that I acknowledge this assistance. They should not, of course, be held responsible for errors of fact or judgment.

Burnham Kelly, Dean of the College of Architecture at Cornell University, made available funds for travel and for the collection of graphic materials at an early stage in the study. As Vice Chairman of the Commission of Fine Arts, his knowledge of Washington is extensive, and his suggestions on a number of points were of substantial help.

During the period of research and writing Professor Stephen Jacobs of Cornell read and commented on the manuscript, and guided me on many occasions to source material that might otherwise have been overlooked. He also gave me the benefit of his interpretations on several matters of judgement which were both informed and stimulating.

In 1965 the American Institute of Architects generously granted me fellowship funds to permit the completion of the book uninterrupted by other duties. The Institute, as I hope this book makes clear, has had a long association with the city of Washington and its improvement, and I am honored to have received the support of such a distinguished organization.

I also wish to acknowledge my debt to the John Simon Guggenheim Foundation, whose fellowship grant in 1958 for the completion of an earlier book made possible my first exploration of materials relating to the national capital. Additional financial aid was extended by the Cornell University Faculty Research Grants Committee for travel and photoduplication expenses.

Research in a number of libraries, offices, and societies was facilitated by the efficient assistance of staff members of the Columbia Historical Society, the Commission of Fine Arts, the American Institute of Architects, the New York Historical Society, the Library of the Graduate School of Design of Harvard University, the National Capital Planning Commission, the Temporary Commission on Pennsylvania Avenue, the U.S. Geological Survey, the New York Public Library, the National Park Service, the Aeronautical Chart Information Center, the National Archives, and the District of Columbia Library.

I am especially grateful for help over the years by the several members of the Reference Department of Olin Library and the Librarian and staff of the Fine Arts Library of Cornell University. The skilled and informed aid given by Richard Stephenson of the Map Division and Milton Kaplan of the Division of Prints and Photographs in the Library of Congress, and L. R. Wilson, former Secretary of the Commission of Fine Arts is also deeply appreciated.

I wish to thank James Merriam Moore for permission to include several quotations from Charles Moore's two works, *Daniel H. Burnham* and *The Life and Times of Charles Follen McKim*, and the Dodd, Mead & Co. for permission to quote from Philip Jessup's *Elihu Root*.

Portions of the manuscript were typed by Eileen Kohles, Jacquelyn Haskins, and Michele Lokken. Their accurate work was of great assistance.

To Gail Filion who edited the manuscript and to Marshall Henrichs who designed the book go my thanks for tasks skillfully accomplished. Their highly competent work has made this volume more readable and more attractive than I had hoped.

Finally, to my wife, Constance Peck Reps, to whom this book is dedicated, I extend my thanks for her continued encouragement of scholarly activities and her willingness to arrange family affairs to accommodate the erratic schedule of an author in the pursuit of an idea.

Bibliography

American Institute of Architects, *An Appeal to the Enlightened Sentiment of the People of the United States for the Safeguarding of the Future Development of the Capital of the Nation*. Washington: American Institute of Architects, 1916.

——, *Charles Follen McKim Memorial Meeting*. Washington: Gibson Brothers, 1910.

——, *Letter File*, 1900.

——, *Washington In Transition*, A.I.A. *Journal*, XXXIX, No. 1 (January 1963), Entire issue.

——, Washington-Metropolitan Chapter, *Of Plans and People*. Washington: n.p., 1950.

Baily, Francis, *Journal of a Tour in Unsettled Parts of North America in 1796 and 1797*. London: Baily Brothers, 1856.

Baldwin, Elbert F., "Washington Fifty Years Hence," *The Outlook*, LXX, No. 14 (April 5, 1902), pp. 817–29.

Barnes, James, "The Site for the Lincoln Memorial," *Harper's Weekly*, LVII, No. 2928 (February 1, 1913), p. 9.

Bartholomew, Harland, "History of City Planning in Washington, D.C." Lecture presented at the course on City and Metropolitan Planning, Washington, D.C., September 24, 1958. Washington: n.p., 1958.

"Basin Battle," *Time*, XXIX, No. 16 (April 19, 1937), pp. 33–35.

Birkbeck, Morris, *Notes on a Journey in America from the Coast of Virginia to the Territory of Illinois*. London: J. Ridgeway (3rd ed.), 1818.

Bolles, Blair, *Tyrant From Illinois*. New York: W. W. Norton & Co., 1951.

Boutin, Bernard L., "Lafayette Square—The Final Word," A.I.A. *Journal*, XXXIX, No. 1 (January 1963), pp. 55–56.

Brown, Glenn, "A Suggestion for Grouping Government Buildings; Landscape, Monuments, and Statuary," *The Architectural Review*, VIII, No. 8 (August 1900), pp. 89–94.

——, *History of the United States Capital*. 2 vols, Senate document No. 60, 56th Congress, 1st Session. Washington: Government Printing Office, 1900.

——, *Memories*. Washington: W. F. Roberts Co., 1931.

—— (comp.), *Papers Relating to the Improvement of the City of Washington, District of Columbia*. Senate Document No. 94, 56th Congress, 2nd Session. Washington: Government Printing Office, 1901.

——, "Selection of Sites for Federal Buildings," *The Architectural Review*, III, No. 4 (August 1894), pp. 27–29.

——, *The Development of Washington with Special Reference to the Lincoln Memorial*. Washington: Chamber of Commerce of Washington, D.C., 1911.

Bryan, Wilhelmus Bogart, *A History of the National Capital*. 2 vols. New York: The Macmillan Co., 1914–1916.

—— (comp.), *Bibliography of the District of Columbia . . . to 1898*. Senate Document No. 61, 56th Congress, 1st Session. Washington: Government Printing Office, 1900.

Burnham, Daniel, "White City and Capital City," *The Century Magazine*, LXIII, No. 4 (February 1902), pp. 619–20.

Burnham, Daniel H., and Edward H. Bennett, *Plan of Chicago Prepared Under the Direction of the Commercial Club During the Years MCMVI, MCMVII, and MCMVIII*. Edited by Charles Moore. Chicago: The Commercial Club, 1909.

Busey, Samuel C., *Pictures of the City of Washington in the Past*. Washington: William Ballantyne & Sons, 1898.

Caemmerer, H. Paul, "Charles Moore and the Plan of Washington," Columbia Historical Society, *Records,* XLVI–XLVII (1944–1945), pp. 237–58. Washington: Columbia Historical Society, 1947.

———, *Historic Washington, Capital of the Nation.* Washington: Columbia Historical Society, 1948.

———, *The Life of Pierre Charles L'Enfant, Planner of the City Beautiful, The City of Washington.* Washington: National Republic Publishing Company, 1950.

———, *Washington: The National Capital.* Senate Document No. 332, 71st Congress, 3rd Session. Washington: Government Printing Office, 1932.

Clark, Allen C., "Origin of the Federal City," Columbia Historical Society, *Records,* XXXV–XXXVI (1935), pp. 1–97. Washington: Columbia Historical Society, 1935.

Clarke, Gilmore D., "The Thomas Jefferson Memorial Controversy," Typescript, 1938. Fine Arts Library, Cornell University.

Cox, William V. (comp.), *Celebrations of the One Hundredth Anniversary of the Establishment of the Seat of Government in the District of Columbia.* Washington: Government Printing Office, 1901.

Dahl, Curtis, "Mr. Smith's American Acropolis," *American Heritage,* VII, No. 4 (June 1956), pp. 39–43, 104–05.

Development of the United States Capital. Addresses delivered in the auditorium of the United States Chamber of Commerce Building, Washington, D.C., at meetings held to discuss the development of the national capital. April 25–26, 1929. House Document No. 35, 71st Congress, 1st Session. Washington: Government Printing Office, 1930.

Dickens, Charles, *American Notes.* London: Hazell, Watson & Viney, Ltd., n.d.

Downing, Andrew Jackson, *Explanatory Notes to Accompany the Plan for Improving the Public Grounds at Washington,* March 3, 1851. Manuscript in National Archives, Record Group No. 42, LR, Vol. 32, No. 1358½.

———, *Rural Essays.* New York: G. P. Putnam and Co., 1853.

Duncan, John M., *Travels Through Part of the United States and Canada in 1818 and 1819.* Glasgow: Hurst, Robinson & Company, 1823.

Ellis, John B., *The Sights and Secrets of the National Capital.* New York: United States Publishing Company, 1869.

Faehtz, E. F. M., and F. W. Pratt, *Washington in Embryo.* Washington: Gibson Brothers, 1874.

Fairmount Park Art Association, *The Fairmount Parkway.* Philadelphia: Fairmount Park Art Association, 1919.

Forbes-Lindsay, C. H., *Washington: The City and the Seat of Government.* Philadelphia: The John C. Winston Co., 1908.

Forty Years of Achievement Commemorating the Fortieth Anniversary of the Establishment of the National Commission of Fine Arts, 1910–1950. Senate Document No. 128, 81st Congress, 2nd Session. Washington: Government Printing Office, 1950.

Frary, I. T., *They Built the Capital.* Richmond: Garrett & Massie, 1940.

———, *Thomas Jefferson Architect and Builder.* Richmond: Garrett & Massie, 1931.

Granger, Alfred Hoyt, *Charles Follen McKim: A Study of his Life and Work.* Boston: Houghton Mifflin Company, 1933.

Green, Constance McLaughlin, *Washington: Village and Capital, 1800–1878.* Princeton: Princeton University Press, 1962.

———, *Washington: Capital City, 1879–1950.* Princeton: Princeton University Press, 1963.

Greenough, Horatio, *Form and Function: Remarks on Art, Design, and Architecture.* Edited by Harold A. Small, with an introduction by Erle Loran. Berkeley: University of California Press, 1957.

Gwinn, William Rea, *Uncle Joe Cannon, Archfoe of Insurgency: A History of the Rise and Fall of Cannonism.* New York: Bookman Associates, 1957.

Goff, Frederick, "Early Printing in Georgetown (Potomac), 1789–1800 and the Engraving of L'Enfant's Plan of Washington, 1792," Columbia Historical Society, *Records,* LI–LII (1955), pp. 103–19. Washington: Columbia Historical Society, 1955.

Hamlin, Talbot, *Benjamin Henry Latrobe.* New York: Oxford University Press, 1955.

Hegemann, Werner, and Elbert Peets, *The American Vitruvius: An Architects' Handbook of Civic Design.* New York: The Architectural Book Publishing Co., 1922.

Heyburn, W. B., "Improving the National Capital," *The Independent,* LXIV, No. 3083 (January 2, 1908), pp. 37–39.

House and Garden, LXXVIII, No. 1 (July 1940). Entire issue.

Howe, Franklin T., "The Board of Public Works," Columbia Historical Society *Records,* III, pp. 257–78. Washington: Columbia Historical Society, 1900.

Hutchins, Stilson, and Joseph W. Moore, *The National Capital, Past and Present*. Washington: The Post Publishing Co., 1886.

Improvement and Care of Public Buildings and Grounds in the District of Columbia—Washington Monument. Report of Col. John M. Wilson, U.S.A., Officer in Charge for the Fiscal Year Ending June 30, 1893. Appendix CCC, Report of the Secretary of War. House Ex. Document No. 1, Part 2, 53rd Congress, 2nd Session, Vol. II, Part 6, pp. 4313–4342. Washington: Government Printing Office, 1893.

Improvement and Care of Public Buildings and Grounds in the District of Columbia—Washington Monument. Report of Col. Theodore A. Bingham, United States Army, Officer in Charge, for the Fiscal Year Ending June 30, 1901. Annual Reports of the War Department for the Fiscal Year Ending June 30, 1901. Report of the Chief of Engineers, Part 5. Appendix DDD. House Document No. 2, 57th Congress, 1st Session. Washington: Government Printing Office, 1901, pp. 3689–3760.

"Improvement of Potomac Flats, Washington," *Scientific American,* LXV, No. 12 (September 19, 1891), pp. 180–81.

Jensen, Amy LaFollette, *The White House and its Thirty-Three Families*. New York: McGraw-Hill Book Company, New Enlarged Edition, 1962.

Jessup, Philip C., *Elihu Root,* 2 vols. New York: Dodd, Mead & Co., 1938.

"Journal of William Loughton Smith, 1790–1791," Massachusetts Historical Society, *Proceedings,* LI (1917–1918), pp. 20–88. Massachusetts Historical Society, 1918.

King, Nicholas, *The King Plats of the City of Washington in the District of Columbia, 1803*. Washington: N. Peters, 1888.

Kite, Elizabeth S., *L'Enfant and Washington, 1791–1792*. Baltimore: Johns Hopkins Press, 1929.

Lambeth, William Alexander and Warren Manning, *Thomas Jefferson as an Architect and a Designer of Landscapes*. Boston: Houghton Mifflin Co., 1913.

Latrobe, Benjamin Henry, *A Private Letter to the Individual Members of Congress on the Subject of the Public Buildings of the United States at Washington from B. Henry Latrobe, Surveyor of the Public Buildings*. Washington: Samuel H. Smith, 1806.

———, *The Journal of Latrobe*. New York: D. Appleton and Co., 1905.

Lear, Tobias, *Observations on the River Potomac, the Country Adjacent, and the City of Washington*. New York, Samuel Louden and Son, 1793. Reprinted, Baltimore: S. T. Chambers, 1940.

Mathews, Catherine Van Cortlands, *Andrew Ellicott: His Life and Letters*. New York: The Grafton Press, 1908.

Mayer, Frederick W., "The History of the McMillan Commission Plan of Washington." Unpublished seminar paper, Department of City and Regional Planning, Cornell University, Ithaca, New York, 1963.

McCleary, James T., "What Shall the Lincoln Memorial Be?" *The American Review of Reviews,* XXXVIII, No. 3 (September 1908), pp. 334–41.

McKim, Charles F., *Charles F. McKim Papers*. Manuscript Division, U.S. Library of Congress.

Mechlin, Leila, "New Public Buildings at Washington," *The Architectural Record,* XXIV, No. 3 (September 1908), pp. 180–206.

Mellon, Andrew W., "The Development of Washington," *The American Magazine of Art,* XX, No. 1 (January 1929), pp. 3–9.

———, "The New Washington," *American Magazine of Art,* XXII, No. 3 (March 1931), pp. 175–78.

"Memorial Dispute," *The Literary Digest,* CXXIII, No. 16 (April 17, 1937), pp. 6–7.

Michigan Legislature, *In Memory of Hon. James McMillan, Senator in the Congress of the United States from Michigan*. Proceedings of the Senate and the House of Representatives in Joint Convention, Wednesday, April 2, 1903. Sketch of Senator McMillan's Life by Charles Moore. Lansing: Published by Authority of the Legislature, 1903.

Moore, Charles, *Charles Moore Papers*. Manuscript Division, U.S. Library of Congress.

———, *Daniel H. Burnham*. 2 vols. Boston: Houghton Mifflin Co., 1921.

——— (comp.), *Park Improvement Papers*. Senate Document No. 94, 57th Congress, 2nd Session. Washington: Government Printing Office, 1903.

———, "The Improvement of Washington City," *The Century Magazine,* LXIII, No. 4 (February 1902), pp. 621–28, and No. 5 (March 1902), pp. 747–57.

———, *The Life and Times of Charles Follen McKim*. Boston: Houghton Mifflin Co., 1929.

——— (comp.), *The Promise of American Architecture*. Washington: American Institute of Architects, 1905.

————, *Washington, Past and Present.* New York: The Century Co., 1929.

Moore, Joseph West, *Picturesque Washington.* Providence: J. A. & R. A. Reid, 1887.

Moore, Thomas, *The Poetical Works of Thomas Moore.* New York: D. Appleton & Co., 1868.

Morgan, James Dudley, "Maj. Pierre Charles L'Enfant, the Unhonored and Unrewarded Engineer," Columbia Historical Society, *Records,* II (1899), pp. 116–57. Washington: Columbia Historical Society, 1899.

Morris, Edwin Bateman, "The City of Washington Today," *Architecture,* LXVIII, No. 4 (October 1933), pp. 189–212.

Morrison, Alfred J. (comp.), *The District in the XVIIIth Century . . . As Described by the Earliest Travellers.* Washington: Judd & Detweiler, 1909.

Morrison, William M., *Stranger's Guide to the City of Washington.* Washington: William M. Morrison, 1842.

National Capital Park and Planning Commission, *Plans and Studies: Washington and Vicinity,* Supplementary Technical Data to Accompany Annual Report, 1928. Washington: Government Printing Office, 1929.

Nicolay, Helen, *Our Capital on the Potomac.* New York: The Century Co., 1924.

Olmsted, Frederick Law, "Beautifying a City," *The Independent,* LIV, No. 2801 (August 7, 1902), pp. 1870–77.

Padover, Saul K. (ed.), *Thomas Jefferson and the National Capital.* Washington: Government Printing Office, 1946.

Parsons, Samuel, "Report of Mr. Samuel Parsons, Jr., Landscape Architect," *Plans for Treatment of that Portion of the District of Columbia South of Pennsylvania Avenue and North of B Street, SW., and for a Connection Between Potomac and Zoological Parks.* U.S. House of Representatives Miscellaneous Document No. 135, 56th Congress, 2nd Session. Washington: Government Printing Office, 1900.

Partridge, William T., "L'Enfant's Methods and Features of his Plan for the Federal City," National Capital Park and Planning Commission, *Reports and Plans, Washington Region.* Supplementary Technical Data to Accompany Annual Report. Washington: Government Printing Office, 1930, pp. 21–38.

Patte, Pierre, *Monumens Érigés en France à la Gloire de Louis XV . . .* Paris: n.p. 1765.

Patton, John S., *Jefferson, Cabell and the University of Virginia.* New York: The Neale Publishing Co., 1906.

Peets, Elbert, "Ancestry of the Washington Plan," Baltimore *Sunday Sun* Magazine Section, February 10, 1929, p. 31.

————, "Famous Town Planners: L'Enfant," *Town Planning Review,* XIII, No. 1 (July 1925), pp. 30–49.

————, "L'Enfant's Washington," *Town Planning Review,* XV, No. 3 (May 1933), pp. 155–64.

————, "New Plans for the Uncompleted Mall," Baltimore *Sunday Sun* Magazine Section, March 3, 1935, pp. 1–2.

————, "The Geneology of L'Enfant's Washington," *A.I.A. Journal,* XV, No. 4 (April 1927), pp. 115–19; No. 5 (May 1927), pp. 151–54; No. 6 (June 1927), pp. 187–91.

————, "The Lost Plazas of Washington," Baltimore *Sunday Sun* Magazine Section, April 24, 1932, pp. 4–5.

————, "The New Washington—A Sharp Complaint," Baltimore *Sunday Sun* Magazine Section, January 26, 1930, pp. 1–2.

Phillips, Philip Lee, *A Descriptive List of Maps and Views of Washington and District of Columbia, Including Mount Vernon.* Typescript, February, 1916, Division of Maps, U.S. Library of Congress.

————, *List of Maps and Views of Washington and District of Columbia in the Library of Congress.* Senate Document No. 154, 56th Congress, 1st Session. Washington: Government Printing Office, 1900.

————, *The Beginnings of Washington as Described in Books, Maps and Views.* Washington: Published for the Author, 1917.

Rand McNally & Co., *Pictorial Guide to the City of Washington.* Chicago: Rand, McNally & Co., 1901.

————, *Pictorial Guide to Washington.* Chicago: Rand, McNally & Co., 1908.

Reps, John W., *The Making of Urban America: A History of City Planning in the United States.* Princeton: Princeton University Press, 1965.

Richardson, Albert, *Garnered Sheaves from the Writings of Albert D. Richardson.* Hartford: Columbian Book Co., 1871.

Roberts, Chalmers M., *Washington, Past and Present: A Pictorial History of the Nation's Capital.* Washington: Public Affairs Press, 1949–50.

Roosevelt, Theodore, *Letters,* Selected and edited by Elting E. Morison. 8 vols. Cambridge: Harvard University Press, 1951–54.

Saint-Gaudens, Augustus, *Reminiscences.* Edited and amplified by

Homer Saint-Gaudens. 2 vols. New York: The Century Co., 1913.

Schuyler, Montgomery, "The Art of City Making," *The Architectural Record,* XII, No. 1 (May 1902), pp. 1–26.

———, "The Nation's New Capital," New York *Times,* Supplement, January 19, 1902, pp. 4–5.

———, "The New Washington," *Scribner's Magazine,* LI, No. 2 (February 1912), pp. 129–48.

Scisco, Louis Dow, "A Site for the 'Federal City': The Original Proprietors and Their Negotiations with Washington," Columbia Historical Society, *Records,* 1957–1959. Washington: Columbia Historical Society, 1961, pp. 123–47.

Smith, Franklin Webster, *Design & Prospectus for the National Gallery of History & Art.* Washington: Gibson Bros., 1891.

———, *National Galleries of History and Art. The Aggrandizement of Washington.* Senate Document No. 209, 56th Congress, 1st Session. Washington: Government Printing Office, 1900.

Statue or Memorial of General Grant. Senate Document No. 307, 57th Congress, 1st Session. Washington: Government Printing Office, 1902.

Sunderland, Byron, "Washington As I First Knew It, 1852–1855," Columbia Historical Society *Records,* V (1902), pp. 195–211. Washington: Columbia Historical Society, 1902.

Taft, William Howard and James Bryce, *Washington, The Nation's Capital.* Washington: The National Geographic Society, 1915.

Thatcher, Erastus, *Founding of Washington City.* Washington: The Law Reporter Co., 1891.

The American Architect, CXXXV, No. 2569 (May 20, 1929). Entire issue.

"The Beautifying of Washington," *Harper's Weekly,* XLVI, No. 2354 (February 1, 1902), pp. 144–46.

"The Grant Monument Site, Washington, D.C.," *The Architectural Record,* XXIII, No. 1 (January, 1908), pp. 73–74.

"The Improvement of Washington," *Scientific American,* LXXXVI, No. 7 (February 15, 1902), pp. 108–09.

"The Jefferson Memorial," *The Nation,* CXLIV, No. 16 (April 17, 1937), p. 448.

"The Jefferson Memorial," *The New Republic,* LXXXX, No. 1166 (April 7, 1937), pp. 265–66.

"The L'Enfant Memorials," Columbia Historical Society, *Records,* II (1899), pp. 72–110. Washington: Columbia Historical Society, 1899.

"The Need of a Permanent Federal Art Commission," *The Architectural Record,* XXII, No. 4 (November, 1907), pp. 323–24.

"The Proposed Lincoln National Memorial," *Harper's Weekly,* LVI, No. 2874 (January 20, 1912), p. 21.

"The Writings of George Washington Relating to the National Capital," Columbia Historical Society, *Records,* XVII (1914), pp. 3–232. Washington: Columbia Historical Society, 1914.

Tindall, William, "A Sketch of Alexander Robey Shepherd," Columbia Historical Society, *Records,* XIV (1911), pp. 49–66. Washington: Columbia Historical Society, 1911.

———, *Standard History of the City of Washington.* Knoxville: H. W. Crew & Co., 1914.

———, "The Origin of the Parking System of This City," Columbia Historical Society, *Records,* IV (1901), pp. 75–99. Washington: Columbia Historical Society, 1901.

Trollope, Frances, *Domestic Manners of the Americans.* London: Whittaker, Treacher, & Co. (4th ed.), 1832.

Twining, Thomas, *Travels in America 100 Years Ago.* New York: Harper and Brothers, 1894.

U.S. Arlington Memorial Bridge Commission, *Report of the Arlington Memorial Bridge Commission,* April 22, 1924. Senate Document No. 95, 68th Congress, 1st Session. Washington: Government Printing Office, 1924.

U.S. Commission for Enlarging of the Capitol Grounds, *Enlarging of the Capitol Grounds.* Final report of the Commission, June 21, 1940. Senate Document No. 251, 76th Congress, 3rd Session. Washington: Government Printing Office, 1943.

U.S. Commission of Fine Arts, *Annual Reports.* Washington: Government Printing Office, 1911–65.

———, *Report to the Senate and the House of Representatives Concerning the Thomas Jefferson Memorial.* Washington: The Commission of Fine Arts, 1939.

———, *The Central Composition of the National Capital and the Public Buildings Program.* From the 11th Report of the Commission of Fine Arts. Washington: Government Printing Office, 1930.

———, *The Plan of the National Capital,* from the 9th Report of the Commission of Fine Arts. Washington: Government Printing Office, 1923.

U.S. Director of Public Buildings and Public Parks, *Improvement of The Washington Monument Grounds.* House Document No. 528,

72nd Congress, 2nd Session. Washington: Government Printing Office, 1934.

U.S. Federal Writers' Project, Works Progress Administration, *Washington: City and Capital*. Washington: Government Printing Office, 1937.

U.S. House of Representatives, Committee for the District of Columbia, *Affairs in the District of Columbia*. House Document No. 72, 43rd Congress, 2nd Session. Washington: Government Printing Office, 1872.

U.S. Joint Select Committee of Congress Appointed to Inquire into the Affairs of the Government of the District of Columbia, *Report*, June 16, 1874. Senate Document No. 453, 43rd Congress, 1st Session, Parts I, II, and III. Washington: Government Printing Office, 1874.

U.S. Library of Congress, *District of Columbia Sesquicentennial of the Establishment of the Permanant Seat of the Government*. Washington: Government Printing Office, 1950.

U.S. Lincoln Memorial Commission, *Report*. Senate Document No. 965, 62nd Congress, 3rd Session. Washington: Government Printing Office, 1913.

U.S. Office of Public Buildings and Grounds, *Plans for Treatment of That Portion of the District of Columbia South of Pennsylvania Avenue and North of B Street, SW, and for a Connection Between Potomac and Zoological Parks*. House Document No. 135, 56th Congress, 2nd Session. Washington: Government Printing Office, 1900.

U.S. Office of Public Buildings and Public Parks, *The Lincoln Memorial, Washington*. Prepared under the direction of the Director of Public Buildings and Public Parks of the National Capital by Edward Concklin. Washington: Government Printing Office, 1927.

U.S. President's Council on Pennsylvania Avenue, *Pennsylvania Avenue*. Washington: Government Printing Office, 1964.

U.S. Public Buildings Commission, *Annual Report for the Calendar Year of 1926*. Senate Document No. 240, 69th Congress, 2nd Session. Washington: Government Printing Office, 1927.

————, *Public Buildings in the District of Columbia*. Senate Document No. 155, 65th Congress, 2nd Session. Washington: Government Printing Office, 1918.

U.S. Senate Committee on the District of Columbia, *City Planning*. Hearing on the subject of City Planning, June 1, 1909. Senate Document No. 422, 61st Congress, 2nd Session. Washington: Government Printing Office, 1910.

————, *Report of the Senate Committee on the District of Columbia on The Improvement of the Park System of the District of Columbia*. Senate Report No. 166, 57th Congress, 1st Session. Washington: Government Printing Office, 1902.

U.S. Thomas Jefferson Memorial Commission, *Report of the Thomas Jefferson Memorial Commission*, May 31, 1938. House Document. No. 699, 75th Congress, 3rd Session. Washington: Government Printing Office, 1938.

————, *Report*, August 18, 1937. House Document No. 367, 75th Congress, 1st Session. Washington: Government Printing Office, 1937.

Varnum, Joseph B., *The Seat of Government of the United States*. New York: Press of Hunt's Merchants' Magazine, 1848.

Washington, George, *President Washington's Diaries, 1791 to 1799*. Transcribed and compiled by Joseph A. Hoskins. Summerfield, N.C.: n.p., 1921.

Washington *Evening Star*, 1900–1908.

Washington *Post*, 1900–1965.

"Washington: The Development and Improvement of the Park-System," *American Architect and Building News*, LXXV, No. 1362 (February 1, 1902), pp. 33, 35–36; No. 1367 (March 8, 1902), pp. 75–77.

Whyte, James H., *The Uncivil War: Washington During the Reconstruction, 1865–1878*. New York: Twayne Publishers, 1958.

Withey, Henry F., and Elsie Rathburn Withey, *Biographical Dictionary of American Architects (Deceased)*. Los Angeles: New Age Publishing Co., 1956.

Wright, Carroll D., "The Embellishment of Washington," *The Independent*, LIV, No. 2815 (November 13, 1902), pp. 2683–87.

Young, James Sterling, *The Washington Community, 1800–1828*. New York: Columbia University Press, 1966.

Index

Madison, Wisc., 193

Mall, in Washington, D.C., proposed as "Grand Avenue" in L'Enfant plan, 21; shown on Ellicott plan, 25; site for national university in Latrobe plan, 36–37; a "cow pasture," 50; plan for by Downing, 50–53; station of Baltimore and Potomac railway on, 66; reclamation of Potomac tidal flats, 66–69; proposals for centennial avenue through, 73–74; act to provide design for, 74; plans for by Bingham, 76–78; Parsons appointed to prepare plan for, 78; report on by Parsons, 79–80; plan for by Glenn Brown, 83–84; plans for proposed at convention of architects, 84–92; proposals for by Cass Gilbert, 85; proposals for by Paul Pelz, 87; proposals for by Edgar Seeler, 88; proposals for by George Totten, 89; proposals for by Frederick Law Olmsted, Jr., 91; plan for by Park Commission, 117–19; Park Commission proposals for discussed, 136–37; attempts to narrow, 145–47; width of as planned justified by Burnham, 147; new building line on observed by Freer Gallery, 162; condition in 1934, 173; existing conditions, 179

Manila, P.I., plan by Burnham, 192

Mann, James, opposed creation of Fine Arts Commission, 153–54

"map of dotted lines," submitted to Washington by L'Enfant, 17–18

Market Square, proposed in plan for Pennsylvania Avenue, 181–83

Maryland, extended financial aid for capital, 26

Massachusetts Avenue, 22; railway line across avoided, 100

Meigs, M. C., designed Pension Office, 66

Mellon, Andrew, 170

memorials, sites for suggested by Park Commission, 116, 125–26. *See also* Lincoln Memorial, Jefferson Memorial, Grant Memorial

Meridian Hill, proposed as site for Lincoln Memorial, 156

Millet, Francis, appointed member of Fine Arts Commission, 154

Mills, Robert, designed Washington Monument, 44; designed Treasury building, 45; designed General Post Office, 45

Minneapolis, Minn., 193

models, prepared to illustrate plans of Park Commission, 101; delivered unfinished, 105; viewed by Roosevelt, 107

Money, Hernando D., member of Lincoln Memorial Commission, 157

Monroe, James, letter from Jefferson regarding capital, 2

monumental design, *see* formal design

Moore, Charles, assessment of Glenn Brown, 83n; clerk of Senate Committee on District of Columbia, 93; suggested members of Park Commission, 93; account of Park Commission's European tour, 96, 97, 98; difficulties in arranging payments for Park Commission work, 101–03; role in work of Park Commission, 104–05; guide at exhibition, 108; wrote article on Park Commission plan, 140; appointed member of Fine Arts Commission, 154; chairman of Fine Arts Commission, 173; opposed Pope's design for Jefferson Memorial, 174; special credit for implementation of Washington plan due, 196-97; opposed modern design in architecture, 197

Moore, Thomas, poetical description of Washington, 38

Morris, Robert, 26

Mount Auburn Cemetery, Cambridge, Mass., 50

Mount Vernon, Va., 2

Mullet, A. B., designed State, War, and Navy Department building, 61

"Murder Bay," described in 1867, 44

Museum of History and Technology, part of Mall complex, 179

Museum of Natural History, part of Mall complex, 179

National Academy of Sciences, 159

National Archives, designed by John Russell Pope, 170; new square proposed near, 181. *See also* Hall of Records

national capital, plans for by Continental Congress, 1; constitutional provisions for, 1–2; debates over location in Congress, 2; Residence Act of 1790, 2; land acquisition for site suggested by Jefferson, 4; proposed building regulations in, 4; suggested street and block dimensions for, 4; plan for town by Jefferson at mouth of Anacostia River,

4; proclamation by Washington designating site, 5; L'Enfant requested appointment as designer for, 9; negotiations for land purchase, 9–10; plan by Jefferson for Hamburg site, 10–13; agreement between Washington and landowners, 13; report by L'Enfant on public building sites in, 13–14; first draft of plan for, 15; plan shown to landowners, 15; first plan described by L'Enfant, 15–17; L'Enfant's proposed development policy for, 16; functional basis for proposed street system, 16; "plan of dotted lines" submitted to Washington, 17–18; proposed development policy, 18; final plan submitted by L'Enfant, 18; description of L'Enfant plan, 18–21; building regulations adopted for, 18n; L'Enfant's proposals for Mall, 21; origins of L'Enfant's design details, 21–22; flaws in L'Enfant's plan, 22; removal of L'Enfant as planner, 22; proposed public buildings shown on Ellicott plan, 22–25; proposals for moving. *See also* Washington, D.C.

National Capital Planning Commission, created, 173; recommendation on Washington Monument grounds, 177; study of East Capitol Street, 177

National Gallery of Art, 173; similarity of design to Jefferson Memorial, 174; part of Mall complex, 179

National Institute of Arts and Letters, 157

National Museum, 61, 150

National Park Service, 183

National Portrait Gallery, 20, 45

National Square, proposed in Pennsylvania Avenue plan, 183

national university, plan by Latrobe for Mall site, 36–37

National War College, 20

Naval Observatory, 45

Navy, Department of, 36

Navy Yard, 38

Newark, N.J., 193

New Delhi, India, 198

Newlands, Francis, 146, 147

newspapers, reaction to Park Commission plan, 108; support for plan, 140–42

New York City, City Hall, remodeled by L'Enfant, 9; first capitol of U.S., 9

New York *Times,* article on Park Commission plan, 142

reflecting pool, proposed near Capitol in plan for Mall, 183

Renwick, James, designed Smithsonian Institution, 42; prepared plan for proposed National Gallery in 1890, 70

Residence Act of 1790, role of Jefferson in passing, 2; supported by Hamilton, 2; approved by Washington, 2; provisions of, 2; discussions by Washington and Jefferson for implementation, 2; amended, 5

retrocession, Virginia portion of original District of Columbia, 42

Robinson, Charles Mulford, 193

Rock Creek Park, 76, 80; boulevard to proposed by Brown, 84; drive from Lincoln Memorial, 127; parkway, 167

Rome, Italy, visited by Park Commission, 96–97

Roosevelt, Theodore, first visitor to Park Commission exhibit, 107; drawing of examining Park Commission plan, 140; in controversy over location of Agriculture building, 146–49; address at meeting of American Institute of Architects, 150; support for Park Commission plan, 150; appointed Consultative Board, 151; issued executive order creating Council of Fine Arts, 153; memorial to designed by Pope, 174

Root, Elihu, Secretary of War, 80; suggested political strategy to McKim, 104; supported Park Commission plan in annual report, 104; support for Park Commission plan, 143; steered bill for Fine Arts Commission through Senate, 154; recalled comment by Cannon on Lincoln Memorial site, 155; attacked Gettysburg highway as Lincoln Memorial, 156

Saint-Gaudens, Augustus, appointed member of Park Commission, 95

St. Louis, Mo., 193

St. Paul's Chapel, New York City, window designed by L'Enfant, 9

St. Petersburg, Russia, 8

San Francisco, Cal., plan for by Burnham, 192

Schuyler, Montgomery, article on Park Commission plan, in New York *Times,* 142; in *Architectural Record,* 143

Seeler, Edgar V., proposals for central Washington, 88–89; advocated commission to re-

view development plans, 88–89; biographical note, 89n

Senate, approved funds for study of Washington, 92; Committee on District of Columbia, 144; District Committee in controversy over Agriculture building, 146–47; office building for, 151; fourth side of office building completed, 173; new office building constructed, 179

Senate Park Commission, appointed, 93; first meeting, 94; plans for European tour, 94–95; visit to Virginia towns and estates, 95; Saint-Gaudens appointed member, 95; European tour, 95–98; visit to Rome, 96–97; visit to Paris, 96, 97–98; visit to Venice, 97; visit to Vienna, 97; influence of French formal garden design on plans, 97–98; visit to London, 98; arrangements for detailed studies, 98–99; numerous meetings on Washington plan, 99; decisions on presentation of proposals, 100; arranged to have models built, 101; difficulties with expenses, 101–03; meeting with McMillan, 103; plans for developing political support, 103–04; publicity policy, 105; arrangements for exhibition, 105–07; report presented to Senate, 107; newspaper reaction to plan, 108; plan of 1902 summarized, 109–11; text of report quoted, 112–33; plan for Capitol area, 112–17; plan for Mall, 117–19; plan for Washington Monument grounds, 119–21; plan for Washington Common, 121–26; plan for Lincoln Memorial, 126–28; plan for memorial bridge, 128–29; plan for Analostan Island, 129; proposals for National Cemetery, 129–31; plan for White House and executive office, 131–32; plan for Pennsylvania Avenue, 132–33; influenced by L'Enfant plan, 133–34; discrepancy in recommendations for Lafayette Square, 134–35; analysis and criticism of plan, 134–38; lack of recommendations for north side of Pennsylvania Avenue, 135; omitted Smithsonian Institution in plan, 135; site recommended for Supreme Court criticized, 136; proposals for Mall discussed, 136–37; plans for Washington Monument grounds discussed, 137; plan criticized by Elbert Peets, 137n; general appraisal of plan, 137–38; initial public reaction to plan, 139; public relations policies, 140; plan of 1902 as guide to

location of public buildings, 144–45; plan of 1902 nearly complete, 191; influence of plan on American city planning, 192–93; reasons for success of plan, 193–97

Shaw, Leslie M., in controversy with Burnham over site for Hall of Records, 144–45

Shepherd, Alexander Robey, an American Haussmann, 56; appointed to Board of Public Works, 58; elected Vice-President of Board, 58; prepared plan for public works improvements, 58; appointed Governor of territory, 59; nominated as commissioner, 61; statue of, 61

Skidmore, Owings, and Merrill, design for Mall, 183–91

Smith, Franklin W., plans for improvements in Washington, 70–72

Smith, John Cotton, description of Washington, 29

Smithmeyer, John L., designed Library of Congress, 61

Smithson, James, 42

Smithsonian Institution, origins, 42; in 1871, 56; omitted in Park Commission plan, 135

social conditions, in "Murder Bay," 44

Soldiers' Home, proposed as site for Lincoln Memorial, 156

southwest urban renewal area, 179

State Department, 36; building for, 167

State, War, and Navy Department building, designed by A. B. Mullet, 61

Steuben, Baron von, L'Enfant drawings for his military manual, 8

streets, baroque designs as inspiration for L'Enfant plan, 21

Stuart, David, appointed commissioner under Residence Act, 5

Sullivan, Louis, 134

Supreme Court, site for mentioned by L'Enfant, 17–18; site for not shown on L'Enfant plan, 20; supposed intended location, 20; site for recommended by Park Commission, 115; Park Commission site criticized, 136; building for proposed, 169; building constructed, 173

Taft, William H., in controversy over location of Agriculture building, 146–49; account of meeting between Roosevelt and McKim, 149; revoked order creating Council of Fine Arts,

220